The Chain of Representation

How do formal institutions affect the extent to which democracies adopt policies that reflect the preferences of their citizens? Based on a chain of representation model in which electoral rules and policy-making powers link citizens, politicians, and policies, this book reveals the conditions under which citizen preferences and implemented policies diverge. Comparative quantitative analyses encompassing eighteen Latin American countries show that presidential democracies vary greatly in the degree to which they demonstrate responsiveness to their electorates. Often, individual presidents with strong legislative powers have prompted policy changes that are unrepresentative of voter preferences. Other times, their interactions with legislatures result in more representative policies. Grounded in clear theory and thorough empirics, this study shows how rules can introduce dissonance between voters and politicians, but also how they can potentially reduce it. This is an excellent resource for scholars and graduate students interested in comparative politics, institutional design, economic policy, and Latin American studies.

BRIAN F. CRISP is Professor of Political Science at Washington University in St. Louis. His work on electoral systems, legislative politics, interbranch relations, and policy choices has been published in *The American Journal of Political Science, The American Political Science Review,* and *The Journal of Politics.* He is also the Executive Editor of Legislative Studies Quarterly.

SANTIAGO OLIVELLA is Assistant Professor of Political Science at the University of North Carolina at Chapel Hill. His research focuses on developing quantitative tools to study issues in electoral and legislative politics. He has published articles in *Political Analysis,* the *American Journal of Political Science,* the *British Journal of Political Science,* the *Journal of Politics,* and *Electoral Studies.*

GUILLERMO ROSAS is Associate Professor of Political Science at Washington University in St. Louis. His research explores the economic consequences of political regimes and political elite behavior. He is the author of *Curbing Bailouts: Bank Crises and Democ   Accountability in Comparative Perspective* and coauthor of *La Systems* (Cambridge University Press, 2010).

The Chain of Representation

Preferences, Institutions, and Policy across Presidential Systems

BRIAN F. CRISP
Washington University in St. Louis

SANTIAGO OLIVELLA
University of North Carolina at Chapel Hill

GUILLERMO ROSAS
Washington University in St. Louis

CAMBRIDGE
UNIVERSITY PRESS

CAMBRIDGE
UNIVERSITY PRESS

University Printing House, Cambridge CB2 8BS, United Kingdom

One Liberty Plaza, 20th Floor, New York, NY 10006, USA

477 Williamstown Road, Port Melbourne, VIC 3207, Australia

314–321, 3rd Floor, Plot 3, Splendor Forum, Jasola District Centre, New Delhi – 110025, India

79 Anson Road, #06–04/06, Singapore 079906

Cambridge University Press is part of the University of Cambridge.

It furthers the University's mission by disseminating knowledge in the pursuit of education, learning, and research at the highest international levels of excellence.

www.cambridge.org
Information on this title: www.cambridge.org/9781108478014
DOI: 10.1017/9781108775564

© Cambridge University Press 2020

First published 2020

A catalogue record for this publication is available from the British Library.

ISBN 978-1-108-47801-4 Hardback
ISBN 978-1-108-74541-3 Paperback

Cambridge University Press has no responsibility for the persistence or accuracy of URLs for external or third-party internet websites referred to in this publication and does not guarantee that any content on such websites is, or will remain, accurate or appropriate.

Contents

List of Figures   *page* ix

List of Tables   xi

Acknowledgments   xiii

List of Abbreviations   xv

1   Studying the Chain of Representation   1
    1.1 *Summary of Our Findings*   3
    1.2 *A Chain of Representation*   6
    1.3 *Points and Distributions*   7
    1.4 *Locating Economic Preferences and Policies*   9
    1.5 *Institutional Linkages*   11
    1.6 *Structure of the Book*   14

2   Our Solutions to the Challenges of Studying the Chain
   of Representation   18
    2.1 *A Closer Look at the Chain of Representation* 19
    2.2 *Congruent with and Responsive to Whom?*   20
    2.3 *A Common Space for Preferences and Policies*   23
    2.4 *Institutional Linkages*   25
    2.5 *Some Connections Left Unmade (At Least for Now)* 27

PART I STAGES

3   Stage 1: Citizens' Preferences   33
    3.1 *Data Coverage for Citizens' Preferences*   34
    3.2 *Citizen Policy Moods in Latin America, 1996–2014* 42
    3.3 *How Does Our "Policy Mood" Compare with Other
        Indices?*   45
    3.4 *Chapter Summary*   51

4 Stage 2: Policy-Makers' Preferences   52
   4.1 *Data Coverage for Policy-Makers' Preferences*   53
        4.1.1 *Inferring the Issue Stances of Other Political Actors*   57
   4.2 *Policy-Maker Policy Moods in Latin America, 1993–2013*   62
        4.2.1 *Representatives*   65
        4.2.2 *Senators*   69
        4.2.3 *Presidents*   70
   4.3 *Legislative Party Positions*   72
   4.4 *Chapter Summary*   76

5 Stage 3: Public Policies Chosen   77
   5.1 *What Is Policy Orientation?*   78
   5.2 *Time Trends in Different Policy-Making Arenas*   80
   5.3 *Country-Specific Policy Orientations*   85
   5.4 *Chapter Summary*   90

6 Placing Preferences and Policies on a Common Scale   91
   6.1 *A Method to Obtain Policy Moods from Aggregate Data*   92
        6.1.1 *Adding Prior Information to the Model*   100
        6.1.2 *Pooling Information Partially across Groups and Countries* 101
   6.2 *A Principled Index of Pro-Market Public Policy*   107
   6.3 *Assessing Model Fit*   113
   6.4 *Chapter Summary*   115

PART II LINKAGES

7 Linkage 1: Electoral Systems   119
   7.1 *Congruence, Responsiveness, and the Strength
        of Electoral Systems*   120
   7.2 *Components of Electoral Systems and Their
        Effect on Strength*   124
        7.2.1 *District Magnitude*   124
        7.2.2 *Seat Allocation Formula*   125
        7.2.3 *Legal Thresholds*   126
        7.2.4 *Aggregating the Components of Electoral Systems into
               Families*   127
   7.3 *Combinations of Electoral System Components*   129
        7.3.1 *Lower or Only Houses*   129
        7.3.2 *Upper Houses*   131
        7.3.3 *Executives*   133
   7.4 *A Simulation-Based Taxonomy of Electoral Systems*   133
        7.4.1 *Simulating Elections*   135
        7.4.2 *Analyzing Results from Simulation Runs*   137
        7.4.3 *Results*   139
   7.5 *Electoral Incentives in Latin America's Separation
        of Powers Systems*   141
   7.6 *Chapter Summary*   143

8   Linkage 2: Policy-Making Processes (PMP)   147
    8.1   *The PMP in Separation of Powers Systems*   148
    8.2   *Policy-Making Powers: Legislators*   151
          8.2.1   *Lower or Only Houses*   153
          8.2.2   *Upper Houses*   156
    8.3   *Policy-Making Powers: Presidents*   156
          8.3.1   *Proactive Powers*   159
          8.3.2   *Reactive Powers*   161
          8.3.3   *Proactive and Reactive Powers Combined*   161
    8.4   *PMPs in Separation of Powers Systems*   164
    8.5   *Chapter Summary*   167

PART III   TESTING THE CHAIN OF REPRESENTATION

9   From Citizens to Policy-Makers   171
    9.1   *Constant or Evolving Moods*   172
    9.2   *What Is Congruence? What Is Responsiveness?*   174
          9.2.1   *Measuring Congruence*   174
          9.2.2   *A Simulation-Based Benchmark of Congruence Levels* 176
          9.2.3   *Measuring Responsiveness*   179
          9.2.4   *A Simulation-Based Benchmark of Responsiveness Levels*   180
    9.3   *Congruence and Responsiveness between Citizens
          and Policy-Makers*   181
          9.3.1   *Responsiveness as a Function of Electoral Institutions* 188
    9.4   *Chapter Summary*   192

10 From Policy-Makers to Policies   194
    10.1 *Congruence and Responsiveness between Policy-Makers and
          Policy*   196
          10.1.1 *Measuring Policy-Makers to Policy Congruence*   196
          10.1.2 *Measuring Policy-Makers to Policy Responsiveness*   202
          10.1.3 *Do PMPs Affect Congruence?*   203
    10.2 *Do PMPs Affect Responsiveness?*   207
    10.3 *Chapter Summary*   210

11 From Citizens to Policies   212
    11.1 *Citizen-to-Policy Congruence: Typical Levels and Their
          Relationship to the Chain's Institutional Linkages*   213
          11.1.1 *Does Citizen-to-Policy Congruence Vary by Institutional
          Design?*   216
    11.2 *Responsiveness of Policy to Changes in Citizen Moods*   222
          11.2.1 *Do Institutions Affect Responsiveness of Policy to
          Citizen Moods?*   223
    11.3 *Chapter Summary*   227

12 A Chain Is Only as Strong as Its Weakest Link   229
   12.1 *Stages in the Chain of Responsiveness: Moods*
      and Policy Orientations   231
   12.2 *Links in the Chain of Responsiveness: Electoral Systems and*
      PMPs   234
   12.3 *Congruence and Responsiveness: From Citizens to*
      Politicians to Policy   236
   12.4 *A Final Takeaway*   238

Appendix: Question Wording   241

Bibliography   245

Author Index   253

Subject Index   257

Figures

1.1	The chain of representation	*page* 2
3.1	Availability of citizen survey data across countries and years	35
3.2	Availability of stimuli in Argentina and the Dominican Republic	38
3.3	Policy moods of the median citizen in eighteen Latin American countries	43
3.4	Heterogeneity of citizen policy preferences in eighteen Latin American countries	44
3.5	"Policy mood" against voter-revealed rightism and A–M scores	47
4.1	Availability of legislator survey data across countries and years	54
4.2	Availability of stimuli in Brazil and Mexico	56
4.3	Discrepant seat shares in upper and lower houses	59
4.4	Estimated policy moods among policy-makers	63
4.5	Policy moods of policy-makers in eighteen Latin American countries	66
4.6	Average heterogeneity scores in Latin American lower and upper houses	68
4.7	Legislative policy moods and alternative measures of policy preferences	69
4.8	Presidential policy mood scores and presidential party expert scores	71
4.9	Policy moods of legislative and party-specific medians	74
5.1	Within-country distribution of observed values of reserve requirements	80
5.2	Average Latin American policy implementation in six different issue areas	83
5.3	Policy orientations of Latin American countries	86
6.1	The core IRT model	96
6.2	Posterior distribution of discrimination hyperparameters	105

6.3   Posterior distribution of item discrimination parameters   106
6.4   Posterior distribution of policy discrimination hyperparameters   111
7.1   Taxonomy of electoral systems   140
8.1   Policy-Making Processes   166
9.1   Simulated congruence, citizen to policy-makers   178
9.2   Observed congruence, citizen to policy-makers   179
9.3   Simulated responsiveness, citizen to policy-makers   180
9.4   Predicted median-to-median citizen-to-politician congruence by
      electoral system group   184
9.5   Predicted distribution-to-median congruence from citizens to
      politicians by electoral system group   185
9.6   Predicted distribution-to-distribution congruence by electoral
      system group   187
9.7   Predicted citizen heterogeneity by electoral system group   188
9.8   Predicted probability of responsiveness of policy-makers to
      citizen mood by electoral system strength   191
10.1 Winset illustration   197
10.2 Winset and distribution-to-policy congruence among
      policy-makers   200
10.3 Responsiveness of policy to policy-makers   203
10.4 Predicted winset and distribution-to-policy congruence, by PMP   206
10.5 Predicted responsiveness of policies to policy-maker mood
      changes, as a function of PMP   209
11.1 Observed and simulated congruence between policies and
      citizens   215
11.2 Estimated median citizen-to-policy congruence, by institutional
      arrangement   219
11.3 Estimated citizen distribution-to-policy congruence as function
      of electoral system strength, by PMP   221
11.4 Simulated and observed citizen-to-policy responsiveness   223
11.5 Predicted policy responsiveness to citizen mood changes as
      function of electoral system strength, by PMP   226

Tables

3.1   Aggregate information from mass surveys in Argentina;
twenty-four stimuli observed throughout 1996–2014 (part I)   *page* 40

3.2   Aggregate information from mass surveys in Argentina;
twenty-four stimuli observed throughout 1996–2014 (part II)   41

3.3   Pairwise-complete correlations among three different scales   49

5.1   Sources and time coverage of all indicators included in the
policy orientation scale   79

5.2   Ratio of between to total variance achieved by coding
continuous indicators into categorical indicators   82

5.3   Average Latin American policy implementation in six different
issue areas   89

6.1   Predictive success of the graded response component of the
model of policy moods and policy orientations   114

6.2   Confusion matrix for ordered outcomes   115

7.1   Electoral systems for lower houses   130

7.2   Electoral systems for upper houses   132

7.3   Electoral systems for presidents   134

7.4   Electoral system strength   142

7.5   The strength of electoral systems for selecting sets of
policy-makers   144

8.1   Legislators' policy-making powers   152

8.2   Lower chambers' policy-making powers   154

8.3   Upper chambers' policy-making powers   157

8.4   Presidents' policy-making powers   158

8.5   Presidents' proactive powers   160

8.6   Presidents' reactive powers   162

8.7   Legislative powers of presidents   163

9.1   Regression of citizen congruence on electoral system groups   183

9.2   Policy-maker responsiveness to citizens, by electoral system
      group   190
10.1 Regression of policy congruence on PMPs   205
10.2 Multilevel model of responsiveness of policy to PM mood change   208
11.1 Multilevel model of policy-to-citizen congruence   218
11.2 Mixed-effects model of citizen-to-policy responsiveness   224

Acknowledgments

In a book about the role played by institutions in shaping the quality of democratic representation, we start by acknowledging the constant support we received from our academic institutions. The departments of Political Science at Washington University in St. Louis (Wash U) and University of North Carolina (UNC) at Chapel Hill provided us with the time and resources we needed to see this project through. In particular, we are grateful to our departments for making it possible to host a short (but incredibly productive!) book conference during the spring of 2018. Mark Crescenzi, chair of the department at UNC, graciously agreed to host us in Chapel Hill after having suggested we organize a conference in the first place. Thank you!

We are also grateful to Andy Baker, Ernesto Calvo, Cecilia Martínez-Gallardo, Bing Powell, and Karen Remmer for attending that conference. Their careful reading of the manuscript's first draft, as well as their invaluable advice on how to improve it on a variety of fronts, helped us sharpen our arguments and empirical analyses. We are similarly indebted to the three anonymous reviewers selected by Cambridge University Press. The book benefited immensely from these focused readings. We would also like to thank the participants at the 2016 ALACIP conference in Chile (and Carol Mershon in particular), the 2016 APSA meeting in Philadelphia (and Francisco Cantú in particular), and the 2017 Latin American PolMeth meeting in Chile for their feedback.

Too often in the study of separation of powers or presidential systems the role of upper houses is not given sufficient attention in either theoretical or empirical terms. A theme throughout this book is that bicameralism matters. In part, our research was thus supported by a National Science Foundation grant (# SES-1227186) to study the effect of bicameral legislatures. The Weidenbaum Center at Wash U has similarly supported our work throughout the years.

The entire project would not have been possible without the invaluable trove of elite-level data collected by Manuel Alcántara and the rest of the Parliamentary Elites of Latin America team at University of Salamanca. We owe a similar debt of gratitude to the teams that collect and manage the citizen-level data curated by the Latin American Public Opinion Project at Vanderbilt University and the Latinobarómetro Corporation.

One of the most challenging issues we faced was the harmonization of these and other disparate data sources. This Herculean task was tackled primarily by an outstanding group of graduate students at Wash U, who truly are data-wrangling wizards. Mauricio Vela Barón, David Carlson, Taishi Muraoka, Elif Özdemir, and Yang Zhang, along with other members of the Democratic Institutions Research Team, worked long hours to help us build the empirical foundations of the book.

We should also acknowledge the fact that, had any one of us tried to undertake this project on our own, we would have failed. This book truly is the result of a team effort – a team that, more often than not, also included our encouraging spouses: Sue, Jill, and Tabea. We are grateful to you most of all.

Abbreviations

AB	AmericasBarometer
A–M	Aldrich–McKelvey
CART	Classification and Regression Tree
IADB	Inter-American Development Bank
IRT	item-response theory
LB	LatinBarometer
MC	member of congress
MNTV	multiple nontransferable vote
PELA	Parliamentary Elites of Latin America
PMP	policy-making process
PR	proportional representation
SMD	single-member district
SMDP	single-member district decided by plurality
SNTV	single nontransferable vote
TR	two-round
WB	World Bank
WDI	World Development Indicators

Studying the Chain of Representation

This book is about representation. More specifically, we explore how formal democratic institutions affect the extent to which democratic governments adopt policies that reflect the preferences of their citizens. Policies that govern the management of the economy are fundamental to every citizen's quality of life, which is why we strive to "locate" citizens, politicians, and policy on a single state-to-market continuum. As the terms suggest, at one end of the spectrum the state dominates governance of the economy, while at the other end of the spectrum management of the economy is left to market forces. We conceive of citizens' preferences, politicians' preferences, and policies as *stages* in a chain of representation, as we show in Figure 1.1. The stages are held together by *linkages* composed of formal democratic institutions (Powell Jr. 2000). Citizens (Stage 1) are linked to politicians (Stage 2) by the electoral rules (Linkage I) that are employed when the former choose the latter. Politicians (Stage 2) are linked to policies (Stage 3) by the powers politicians wield during the policy-making process (PMP) (Linkage II).

Our contribution is a focus on the *entirety* of this chain. Because electoral rules affect decisions by political elites to compete for public office and choices that voters make about whom to support, we avoid using aggregate electoral results to measure citizen preferences about economic governance. We require a measure of those preferences that predates elections, not one that is affected by them. Fortunately, we have access to surveys that help us describe citizens' moods regarding management of the economy and that do not rely on vote choices. At the other end of the chain, accepting what parties promise in manifestos as if those statements were actual policy ignores that elected representatives might find themselves stymied in their efforts to build a consensus behind a new policy status quo. We collect systematic information on policies that governments actually implement in order to avoid reliance on campaign promises or manifesto pronunciations as indicators of actual policy.

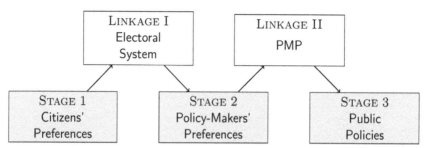

FIGURE I.I. The chain of representation. An idealized model of how representative democracy works by using electoral systems to translate citizen preferences into policy-makers, whose preferences are in turn processed through institutional policy-making powers to generate public policies.

We focus on separation of powers systems where the branches are characterized by separate origins and survival. While doing so, we do not simply treat a gain in presidential power as a loss in legislative power. Instead, we treat them as distinct phenomena with their own scales, allowing for the possibility, for example, that some constitutions leave both branches ill-equipped to readily change the policy status quo. In sum, we seek to understand whether the policies implemented in a given country actually reflect the preferences of its citizenry while accounting for the two sets of institutional linkages (elections and policy-making procedures) that separate, yet hold them together. We thus provide a fuller account of how formal democratic institutions help shape the extent to which policies reflect citizens' desires.

This contribution is only possible because of our ability to locate citizens, politicians, and policies in a common "space." Without placing all of these elements in a shared space, our chain would be broken down into parts lacking a common yardstick, making examination of the quality of representation across all three stages impossible. In other words, in terms of theoretical motivation, we strongly believe in the need to examine a single, uninterrupted chain of representation that ultimately spans from citizens' preferences to policies implemented. This means, for example, that, if we measure politicians' preferences in order to examine whether they are in line with citizens' preferences, we must then use the same measure of politicians' preferences when we examine whether implemented policies are in line with politicians' preferences. This theoretically motivated decision has significant implications for our empirical analyses. Undoubtedly, we could explore multiple measures of key concepts and a variety of modeling strategies to look at the relationships among these measures, thus obtaining clearer and stronger results at each stage of the analysis. Instead, given our commitment to the analysis of the complete chain of representation, we will very explicitly make a single set of measurement and modeling decisions and stick with them throughout the book.

Empirically, we examine eighteen cases from Latin America (spanning North America, Central America, South America, and the Caribbean). Our observations begin in the early 1990s and end in 2014. Taken together, we marshal a broad set of empirical observations to address our theoretical conjectures about how variations in the institutional designs of separation-of-powers systems impact the nature of representation.

In the rest of this chapter, we first provide a summary of our findings so that readers can proceed through our analysis knowing where we will ultimately end up. As a second step, we elaborate on how we understand the process of representative democracy. In other words, we give a fuller description of the chain of representation. We will then discuss how and why our focus in the book shifts from one-to-one representation, through many-to-one representation, to many-to-many representation. We are interested in the preferences of the median citizen and the median politician, but we are also interested in the distribution of preferences held by those around them. These all relate, more closely in some places than others, to the policy orientation that gets chosen. Our third step is to describe the sources we use to infer citizens' preferences, politicians' preferences, and policy. These are the stages in our chain. After that, we will describe our sources for capturing variation in electoral rules and PMPs, which are the linkages in our chain. The chapter concludes with an outline of the structure of the rest of the book, where all of the concepts touched upon briefly in this chapter get more detailed treatment.

1.1 SUMMARY OF OUR FINDINGS

Before going any further, we need to get more systematic about our terminology. We have referred to our primary focus as being on the "quality of representation," but more specifically we will use the term "representation" to cover two distinct concepts that we use carefully – "congruence" and "responsiveness." Congruence involves proximity between two sets of actors – citizens and politicians – or between a set of actors and a policy orientation. In our case, this means their closeness on a scale that spans from complete state control over the economy at one end to absolutely unfettered markets at the other. Responsiveness entails movement by a set of actors – politicians – or a change in policy orientation in the same direction as the movement by an actor located at a previous stage in the chain of representation. For example, we can say that the policy orientation of a country is responsive to its politicians if it moves in the direction of free markets after a set of politicians with more market-oriented preferences assumes office.[1] Capturing levels of congruence,

---

[1] In the existing literature, conceptual definitions of responsiveness are typically intuitive, but they frequently vary in important ways. Often this variation is a function of the nature of the empirical data the authors bring to bear on their explanations of the determinants of responsiveness. We are no different. Note that our definition of responsiveness means that some instances in which congruence increases will be labeled lack of responsiveness. This could occur when two distant actors converge toward the middle of some dimension. We will return to this distinction when we interpret the results of our empirical tests in Chapters 9–11.

in particular, requires that all of the points we are interested in – citizens' preferences, politicians' preferences, and policy orientations – be located on the same scale. We will talk a bit more about how we have achieved that later in this chapter, and we will talk about it at length in Chapter 6.

Normatively speaking, in an ideal world citizens should be able to elect officials as delegates or agents that share their preferences over policies – especially fundamental policies like whether the nation's economic life should be largely regulated by the state or instead governed by free exchange in the marketplace. We refer to this correspondence among preferences of citizens and politicians as *citizen-to-politician congruence*. What is more, when citizens' moods about the balance to be struck between those two hypothetical poles change, we would like the moods of the politicians they choose to shift along with them. We refer to this follow-up shift in the moods of politicians after a shift in the moods of citizens as *citizen-to-politician responsiveness*. Likewise, if this chain of representation is to remain unbroken, we would like politicians to be able to adopt policies that reflect their preferences or moods, the ones they share with citizens, regarding the state-to-market balance the nation should follow. We refer to this as *politician-to-policy congruence*. Again, when politicians' moods about the balance to be struck between the two hypothetical strategies of total state control and absolutely free markets change, we would expect the policies they implement to reflect that change in preferences, a notion that we refer to as *politician-to-policy responsiveness*. Taken together, then, a polity that produces both types of congruence and both types of responsiveness would produce policies that always and everywhere reflect the will of the people.

While we might want all representative democracies to work well, as students of formal democratic institutions we reason that not all constitutional configurations may be equally adept at delivering on these goals of representation. First, as we will describe in detail later, the electoral rules linking citizens and politicians may make representation more or less difficult to achieve. Furthermore, these rules may have differential effects on the extent to which a pivotal politician – we focus on the median member of a legislature,[2] as his or her support is necessary to obtain majority support for a policy (Downs 1957) – is congruent with and responsive to the median citizen. These rules may also have differential effects on the extent to which the distribution of policy moods corresponding to the entire citizenship of a country is reflected in the distribution of economic moods held by all policy-makers. Some electoral rules may excel at promoting median-to-median representation, while others may be better at delivering close and tethered distribution-to-distribution congruence.

Likewise, in terms of the importance of institutional designs, not all PMPs look alike. We focus on relatively less studied separation-of-powers (presidential) systems, and the variation across even this one class of democratic regimes

---

[2] The median legislator has preferences such that at most half of her colleagues are more "rightist" and at most half of her colleagues are more "leftist."

is enormous to the point of being bewildering. Some decision-making processes, including legislative cameral rules and constitutionally allocated powers, would seem to favor the legislative branch when it comes to enacting policies that reflect the preferences of its members. Other institutional arrangements appear as if they were designed to assure that directly elected executives will be endowed with a nearly unilateral ability to pick the policies that they prefer most. Still other PMPs leave legislators and presidents with relatively balanced sets of powers, suggesting that the location of policies on the state-to-market continuum will end up being a compromise between the desires of a citizenry's multiple agents.

We do not live in an ideal world. Our findings suggest that representation is complicated – and not always normatively satisfying. In Chapter 9 we show that the connection between the economic moods of citizens and politicians is, on average, lower than we might expect based on simulations of what different electoral rules could actually provide. We find that citizens choose legislators who are more congruent with and responsive to their preferences *when* the incentives for strategic coordination imposed by electoral rules are at their clearest – demanding either the highest levels of coalescence or very little at all. Presidents on the other hand are "wild cards." They are most congruent with the median citizen when electoral rules are strongest, but they are systematically less congruent with the median citizen than the typical median member of a legislature. Strong or constraining electoral rules are associated with higher levels of responsiveness for both legislators and executives, making it more likely that their economic moods will shift in the same direction as the policy mood of citizens; again, we observe that legislatures tend to be more responsive to citizens than executives.

In Chapter 10, we also find that policies that are agreeable to all "veto players" – the lower house median, the upper house median (in bicameral systems), and the president, all actors whose consent is in principle required to implement new laws (Tsebelis 2002) – are most likely to get enacted in systems that provide presidents with strong powers. In terms of congruence between policy orientation and politicians' preferences (many-to-one congruence), it is in these same strong-president systems that the distribution of preferences held by all members of the legislature are least likely to be reflected in policy. Responsiveness of policy orientation to politicians' preferences, too, is associated with strong presidents.

Given that we find that politicians are congruent with and responsive to citizens only when facing specific sets of electoral incentives and that policy orientations are only responsive to politicians when presidents wield sufficient policy-making powers, any close link between citizens and policies is bound to be limited to specific democratic institutional designs. While we uncover significant nuances in these links, Chapter 11 presents evidence in support of the conclusion that, while strong presidents make policy congruent with politicians' preferences, it is in these systems that policy is least congruent with citizens' preferences. This is not surprising given our finding that president-to-citizen congruence was on average even lower than (median) legislator-to-citizen congruence. However, as with policy-to-politician responsiveness, policy is more likely to move in the direction of a shift in citizens' economic moods when presidents are strong. Of course, moving in the same direction as, and actually being proximate to, are not the same thing.

In sum, it seems that in separation of powers systems the legislative branch is more likely to be congruent with the policy moods of citizens. Unfortunately, from a normative perspective, it is when presidents are at their strongest that policy gets made. Those policies might follow the lead set by shifting public sentiments but, given a generalized lack of congruence between presidents and median citizens, the policy orientations in place at any given moment will likely be distant from the position preferred by the median citizen.

1.2 A CHAIN OF REPRESENTATION

We envision representative democracy as a chain (Powell Jr. 2000). As we depict it in Figure 1.1, the chain has three stages joined together in succession by two linkages. At the first stage in this chain are citizens in a given country with a particular distribution of preferences over the types of policies they would like to see implemented.[3] We often think of preferences over policy as falling along a single dimension, the ends of which we label "left" and "right." We will adopt this conception, but, because we are focusing on economic policies we will often identify the ends of the spectrum as "state" and "market," denoting how economic outcomes should be produced – through state intervention into the economy or through free-market forces. This collection of citizens chooses a set of politicians to represent them (at the second stage in our chain).

The institutional contexts within which citizens make their choice about who they would like to see in office vary dramatically from democracy to democracy as the electoral rules under which they make this selection can be designed differently. The electoral rules are the first institutional linkage in our chain, linking together citizens and their preferences over policies with politicians. Electoral rules vary from those that are highly constraining to those that are very permissive. Constraining rules may limit the choices that elites put on offer, with fewer parties, and therefore fewer policy platforms, entering the political fray. Permissive rules, on the other hand, will encourage elites to enter with multiple parties staking out a variety of policy positions. In short, we expect electoral rules to have an effect on whether the distribution of the preferences of citizens are reflected in the distribution of the preferences of the politicians

---

[3] See Powell Jr. and Vanberg (2000) on the importance of using survey responses as opposed to votes as a measure of citizens' preferences. The main concern is that votes, especially in what we dub strong systems (see Chapter 7), reflect strategic, rather than sincere, behavior. That is, voter choices may not reflect their most preferred outcomes, but their least disliked option.

who represent them. We elaborate at length on our expectations regarding the relationship between electoral rules and congruence between citizens and policy-makers in Chapter 7.

Elected politicians must then design and implement the policies that constitute the third and final stage in the chain. We are interested in separation of powers or presidential systems. In these systems, politicians bargain with one another within a chamber – unicameral systems – or chambers – bicameral systems – and across chambers and branches – legislative and executive – in order to arrive at policy decisions. The politicians at the second stage of our chain are connected to the policies at the third stage of our chain by a set of institutions we will refer to simply as the PMP. The institutions that form this second linkage empower lower houses, upper houses (where they exist), and presidents relative to one another in the process of adopting their most-preferred policies. We will describe these individual powers and how they are put together in a variety of different combinations in Chapter 8.

To the extent that politicians share the preferences of the citizens who chose them, we can capture the degree of *politician-to-citizen congruence*. Similarly, to the extent that the policy orientation of a country at a particular point in time is ultimately placed at a point on the state-to-market continuum near the one preferred by the median politician, we can capture the degree of *policy-to-politician congruence*. If, over time, the distribution of citizens' preferences on the state-to-market continuum changes and the distribution of politicians' preferences on the same continuum follows them to some degree, we can can capture *politician-to-citizen responsiveness*. Similarly, if the median politician's preference on the state-to-market continuum changes over time and policy follows him or her to some degree, we can capture *politician-to-policy responsiveness*. In Section 2.1 we will provide a closer look at our understanding of the chain of representation, especially as it pertains to alternative visions of voters: (i) as actors that are forward-looking selectors of agents or (ii) as actors that are backward-looking evaluators of representatives' behavior (Fearon 1999). These depictions of democracy are related to whether politicians have fixed preferences in office based on what they promised during the last campaign or whether their preferences evolve in an effort to anticipate what voters will desire in the next election.

1.3 POINTS AND DISTRIBUTIONS

We will consider representation in terms of correspondence both between distributions and between individual points (Achen 1978, Cox 1987, Golder and Stramski 2010). At Stage 1 in our chain, we are interested both in the preferences of one citizen, usually the one occupying the median position among all citizens, and in the distribution of preferences across a sample of many citizens. We want to know how these preferences compare with the preferences of one politician – a pivotal one in an assembly, such as the median legislator, or the lone executive – and with the distribution of preferences of the many politicians who occupy a legislative chamber at Stage 2. Finally, at Stage 3 in our chain of representation is a single policy orientation, rather than a panoply of issue-specific policies. We want to estimate whether this policy orientation – more toward the state of market ends of the continuum – is congruent with key individual politicians and with the distribution of many politicians and whether it responds to changes in their locations and spread. Ultimately, we will examine the relationship between points and distributions of preferences held by citizens and the country's policy orientation in any given year. It is the representative connection between Stages 1 and 3 that concerns us most, although we believe strongly, and show throughout the book, that the overall link between Stages 1 and 3 cannot be understood without considering the politicians (and their powers) at Stage 2.

High-quality representation hinges on the ability of politicians and citizens to solve coordination challenges. The strength or weakness of an electoral system, determined largely by district magnitude and less so by seat allocation formulas and thresholds, determines the severity of the punishment for a failure to coordinate (Cox 1987). When coordination succeeds in either constraining or permissive systems, a centrist candidate (relative to the distribution of preferences among voters) is likely to win, making proximity between elected politicians and the median voter very high (Cox 1987, Downs 1957, Duverger 1959). However, many-to-many proximity may remain low in strong systems as voters distant from the median are unable to put like-minded politicians in office.

When coordination fails under very strong, constraining rules – like single-member districts decided by plurality, including those used to elect presidents – this failure can lead to the election of candidates whose positions on the balance to be struck between state and market is very far away from the preferences of the median voter. If voters are sincere and any kind of overcrowding of candidates occurs in the middle of the state-to-market continuum, extremists in either the left or right may be victorious as centrist voters spread themselves too thinly over too many candidates. In more permissive systems the same fate *might* ensue, but the congestion of candidates in the center of the spectrum would have to be significantly greater. As district magnitude (i.e., the number of seats contested in a district) increases, the number of positions that seat-winning parties can take increases as well. This also means that, as magnitude increases, the gaps between positions taken by parties decreases, making it likely that more voters will find a potentially viable party nearby. In other words, as district magnitude increases, parties have incentives to disperse more-or-less evenly across the state-to-market continuum, likely improving many-to-many representation (Cox 1987, 229–230).

When it comes to thinking about the relationships between policy-makers' preferences and policy, we focus on one-to-one and many-to-one representation.

There are reasons, exogenous to electoral rules and PMPs, to expect policy movement to be constrained. Thus, regardless of who gets into office and what kind of policy-making powers they possess, it is unlikely that we will find policies that exactly mirror those of pivotal politicians. Still, even if representation is not perfect, we still might expect some level of responsiveness – that is, policies may move up and down the state-to-market continuum in the same direction as key politicians, even when they do not reflect their preferences exactly.

Theories of legislative decision-making and interbranch relations point to the importance of pivotal players – the median legislator, a single executive. We will be able to locate the lower house median, the upper house median, the president, the policy status quo, and newly implemented policy orientations on a single state-to-market continuum. Thus we will be able to measure the distance between any one of these actors and previous and current policy. We can use these distances to assess the impact of policy-making powers on politician-to-policy correspondence.

In Section 2.2 we will return to our expectations about the quality of representation that democracies can obtain. We will explain there how we establish baselines against which to evaluate citizen-to-politician and politician-to-policy congruence. Implicitly, much of the existing literature takes perfection to be the yardstick against which empirical findings should be judged. We will show that perfect congruence is highly unlikely even in the best scenarios and that comparing empirical findings against more realistic baselines is possible through the use of computer simulations.

1.4 LOCATING ECONOMIC PREFERENCES AND POLICIES

As we will discuss in much greater detail in Chapter 3, we scoured surveys of citizens – from the AmericasBarometer (AB) and LatinBarometer (LB) – for questions related to their preferences for more state intervention into the economy or for freer markets. The surveys span the period from 1996 to 2014. The subjects covered included respondents' preferences about privatization of state-owned companies, the promotion of free trade and utilities regulation, and government intervention to assuage socioeconomic inequality and to protect the poor, the unemployed, and pensioners from adverse market outcomes. From these responses we can infer the economic mood in a country, identifying the position of the median respondent and the distribution of responses around him or her.

Similarly, we were able to use surveys of lower house members conducted by the Parliamentary Elites of Latin America (PELA) project at the University of Salamanca to capture the moods of politicians regarding the balance between state intervention and free markets. We discuss the questions and describe politicians' moods in detail in Chapter 4. The surveys began in 1993 and are conducted once every legislative term in almost every country in the region. Like surveys of citizens, the questions put to politicians touched on a wide variety of economic areas, including taxes, tariffs, state ownership of companies, exchange rates, and privatization.

As with citizens, we can identify the moods of pivotal members of congress and we can capture the dispersion of moods held by members of the deliberative body. We also use survey responses of lower house members to estimate the moods of members of the upper house (where they exist) simply by reweighting responses by a factor based on the difference between party seat shares across both chambers. We discuss the assumptions that are required to accept this method in Chapter 4. Taking even more liberty with the data, we use lower house members' self-placements on a left–right continuum along with their placements of the country's president on that same scale to approximate responses to questions like: "If the president were to answer 'Are you more in favor of state regulation of the economy or in favor of a market-based economy' how do you think he or she would have responded?" From these approximate answers, we obtain a presidential economic mood. We explain in much greater detail in Chapter 4 how we capture politicians' economic moods. The key for now is to understand that we have done our best to locate the economic preferences of key politicians across chambers and branches on a scale that allows us to examine their moods relative to the moods of the citizens whom they represent. Fortunately for us, some of the questions posed to politicians were very similar to the questions posed to citizens. These "bridging questions" help us locate citizens and politicians on the same state-to-market dimension.

Many studies of representation are content to stop far short of looking at the actual policies implemented by elected officials, focusing, for example, on promises made by politicians in speeches or manifestos. Perhaps especially in separation of powers systems, there is often a significant disjuncture between what politicians promise they will deliver and what actually emerges from the PMP. As a result, we sought a means to characterize policies that were ultimately implemented, as opposed to those that were originally promised. We use an augmented version of the Structural Policy Index compiled by the Inter-American Development Bank (IADB) to capture the location of economic policy itself. In Chapter 5 we will explain in detail how, based on observations of several individual policies on a number of issue areas, we estimate a summary location for economic policy, what we refer to as *policy orientation*, on the single state-to-market dimension. We started with data curated by the IADB and have added new information to extend coverage of the original series to recent years. We have also added new indicators to capture policy issue areas that were not originally considered, especially regarding the degree to which a country is open to capital flows across borders. The data include a number of indicators loosely grouped in five categories, each of which captures an important policy area: taxes, trade, labor markets, finance, and public/private ownership of utilities and large companies. Latin American governments have pursued enormous reform efforts in each of these five different areas as the region, with notable exceptions, moved away from the old paradigm of state-led import-substitution industrialization through the "Washington Consensus" set of market-oriented policies of the 1990s and more recently to a set of somewhat more mixed policies balancing state intervention and free markets more evenly.

None of these efforts would bring us any closer to exploring the possibility of congruence without certainty that policy outputs and policy moods are placed on the same "scale." In Chapter 6 we will explain our solution to the challenge of putting all of these measures at each of these stages of the chain of representation – citizens' preferences, politicians' preferences, and public policy – on a single, fully comparable dimension. Without this step, our subsequent efforts to measure the quality of representation would be significantly hampered. With all the foundational components captured on a single dimension, we will be able to pinpoint the relative locations of key concepts of interest, including the locations of the policy mood of the median citizen; the policy moods of the median member of congress, in the lower or single chamber and in the upper chamber; the policy mood of the president; the policy orientation implemented in any given year; and the policy that had been the status quo prior to policy-makers' most recent decision.

1.5 INSTITUTIONAL LINKAGES

As we noted briefly earlier, there are two sets of institutional linkages holding our chain of representation together. The first linkage is made up of aspects of the electoral system. It connects the preferences of citizens to the preferences of politicians. The second linkage is composed of the powers that are wielded during the policy-making process (PMP). It connects the preferences of politicians to the policies actually implemented. Ultimately, we seek to determine whether these linkages systematically affect the translation of preferences at one stage to the outcome of interest at the next stage.

In Chapter 7 we detail the components of electoral systems that we suspect determine whether the distribution of preferences over the state versus the market that we see among citizens is reflected accurately in the distribution of preferences over the state versus the market that we observe among politicians. If populations are homogeneous in terms of their preferences over policy outcomes, variation in electoral rules across those populations will have little impact on the reflection of voters' preferences in the preferences of the representatives selected. However, as preference heterogeneity increases, the importance of electoral rules as incentive structures that favor certain choices increases as well. A voter may identify a preferred candidate – one who reflects the voter's preferences over policy outcomes nearly perfectly – seemingly making vote choice easy. However, if the voter determines that his or her preferred candidate cannot attract sufficient support from other voters to win office, the voter's utility will be maximized by looking for another – not quite as preferred – candidate who can plausibly win. We will refer to electoral rules as "constraining" when they encourage a diverse citizenry to think long and hard about which candidates are viable. We will refer to electoral rules as "permissive" when the bar for obtaining viability is lower, diminishing voters' need to assess whether they should strategically defect from their preferred option.[4]

The major families of electoral systems – majoritarian, mixed, and proportional – are defined primarily on this dimension of electoral system strength: from strong or constraining systems to weak or permissive ones (Cox 1987, Leys 1959, Sartori 1968). While an electoral system family is a nice first cut at categorizing electoral incentives, there is a great deal of variation in rules even *within* these families, as we will show in Chapter 7. To capture the relative strength of electoral systems, we will describe how our cases vary in terms of *district magnitude, seat allocation formula,* and *legal electoral threshold.* District magnitude, as noted earlier, is the number of seats that need to be filled in a given district. The seat allocation formula is the rule that translates votes into seats. Legal thresholds are lower bounds, in terms of votes received, that must be cleared in order to win a seat.

We think that electoral incentives work both on party elites and on voting citizens. When elites are deciding whether or not to enter the race or, put another way, determining what mix of policy positions they wish to claim as their preferred outcomes, they will need to make projections about the relative strength of other potential entrants and how those relative strengths will play out in terms of electoral viability *given* the strength or weakness of the electoral system. Once some number of entrants has put on offer some distribution of advertised policy preferences, voters must compare candidate offerings and then go through strategic calculations regarding candidate/position viability. On the one hand, as we will discuss at much greater length in Chapter 7, we think that under many circumstances electoral rules should not have a significant effect on the distance between the preferences of the median citizen and the preferences of the median politician (one-to-one representation). On the other hand, we expect that permissive or weak systems will be superior at producing a distribution of politicians' preferences that more truly reflects the full distribution of voters' preferences. In separation of powers systems, where bargaining occurs within chambers, between chambers, and across branches, the full distributions of policy preferences are of theoretical interest.

In Chapter 8 we detail the components of PMPs that we suspect determine how the economic preferences of politicians combine to generate the policy orientations adopted in each country. Given that Latin American polities have separation of powers systems, we encounter multiple actors, each with their

---

[4] The strength of electoral laws is central to Huber and Powell Jr.'s (1994) majoritarian and proportional visions of democracy.

own preferences over economic policy, who may be pivotal in any given case. Our expectation is that in cases where politicians across chambers and branches share preferences, any variations in the rules surrounding the allocation of powers in the PMPs are unlikely to impact politician-to-policy correspondence. However, when there is preference disagreement within chambers or across branches, the policies ultimately adopted will reflect who is most empowered by the rules of the PMP.

In many cases, a gain in power in the PMP for the president is a loss in influence for the legislature. The powers are zero-sum. In other instances, a gain for one does not by definition signal a loss for the other. In consequence, we cannot simply take a ranking of presidential powers and assume that more powerful presidents all face equally powerless legislatures. In theory, both branches can be lacking the powers most conducive to adopt a policy at the ideal point of the key decision-maker or, conversely, both branches can be fully endowed with such powers. Our individual indicators of policy-making powers are from Negretto (2014) and Pemstein et al. (2017). Let us first very briefly outline legislators' policy-making powers, and then we will quickly define presidents' policy-making powers. Again, these will all be described in much greater detail in Chapter 8.

We can think of legislators' policy-making powers as contributing two key aspects to ensuring that policy reflects the median legislator's ideal point. Some powers have to do with *information gathering*. Information gathering is important because it allows policy-makers to know when a piece of legislation – a proposed policy – reflects their preferred outcomes. The second set of powers relates to the ease of *engaging in collective action*. Constitutions determine not only whether a legislature has a particular power, but also whether that power can be wielded by a majority, simple or absolute, or whether some preponderance of consensus must be expressed to make use of a power.

We use the other indicators that make up Negretto's index to capture presidents' legislative powers. Following Mainwaring and Shugart (1997), we distinguish between *proactive* and *reactive* powers. Proactive powers aid the president in changing the status quo, moving policy from its current point on the state-to-market continuum to a point relatively preferred by the president. Reactive powers aid the president in protecting the current status quo, making it difficult for even a determined median legislator to move policy from its current point on the state-to-market continuum to a point closer to the median's preference. None of these powers exist in isolation. In fact, it is important to point out that it is consideration of them in conjunction that allows us to talk about policy-making "processes." We conclude Chapter 8 with a system-level look at legislators' policy-making powers and presidents' policy-making powers in combination. In this way we can see in which polities the scales of influence over policy outcomes are clearly tipped in favor of the legislative median's preferences, where they are clearly tipped in favor of the president's preferences, and where the powers deployed in the PMP do the most to create balance between the separate powers.

Identifying and then coding electoral rules and policy-making powers across eighteen countries over an extended period, as we have briefly described here, is an obvious first step in any effort to capture the incentives provided by institutional linkages. In Section 2.4 we provide some more information on how we aggregate from the incentives of individual features of electoral incentives and the dozens of powers at the disposal of politicians while making policy to a single classification of electoral laws and a single classification of PMPs. In Chapters 7 and 8 we will carry out these aggregations and detail their results.

1.6 STRUCTURE OF THE BOOK

We have provided in this chapter the theoretical motivation behind our work and given a brief overview of how we will proceed empirically. In Chapter 2 we return to each of the aspects of our approach in greater detail in order to highlight how this manuscript is unique, or at least uncommon. We make the case for why our operationalization of key concepts is superior to measures often used in the existing literature. We also illustrate how it is that we tackle the entire chain of representation despite some of the challenges and compromises this entails. We conclude the chapter by putting our work in the context of other recent works on related topics. We make the case that, while our sustained focus on congruence and responsiveness differs from other significant works, there are connections to be made between what we do here and those working on public goods provision, certain types of government performance, mandate switching, interbranch stalemate and political crises, and the legitimacy of democracy as a form of government.

In Part I of the book we will describe the stages in our chain of representation. In Chapter 3 we detail how citizens across the region have responded to questions from the LB and AB surveys about their preferred balance between state intervention and free markets – Stage 1 in our chain of representation. We provide some tables and figures with descriptive statistics on responses to a subset of all the economic policy questions that will go into our analysis. We then report aggregate forms of those individual responses, displaying a set of scores that we refer to as the citizens' "mood" regarding economic policy. These policy moods provide the answer that we seek to a simple question: on balance, does the citizenry prefer more market or more state? We use these moods to identify the policy preferences of the median citizen, and the distribution of moods to reflect on the heterogeneity of these preferences.

In Chapter 4 we basically carry out the same exercise but using surveys conducted in each lower house once per legislative term by the PELA project. This is Stage 2 in our chain of representation. Again, we can take an individual member's responses to multiple questions about the balance he or she would like to see struck between the state and the market in a given policy area and aggregate those into an assembly's policy mood. We use these lower chamber results to impute moods for upper chambers simply by accounting for differences in party sizes across the two chambers. We recognize that this method requires several assumptions, and we discuss those openly in Chapter 4. We conclude by providing figures depicting the locations of the policy moods of median representatives, senators, and presidents across countries and over time.

In Chapter 5 we describe, update, and augment the components of the IADB's Structural Policy Index that we use as the measure of Stage 3 in our chain of representation. We track policies on taxes, trade, labor markets, finance, and public/private ownership of utilities and large companies annually for every country in the region. We will briefly outline how others have used the components to create an index that can capture the location of policy in each of these five areas or, with still further aggregation, identify a single point on a state-to-market continuum for the country's entire basket of economic policies. We learn a great deal from these previous efforts, but we report the results of our own original aggregation designed specifically for examining questions of representation. The chapter includes several figures depicting approximately two decades of policy change across the region with widely varying degrees of state intervention, neoliberal market governance, and mixed policy orientations. Despite all this variation, trends are visible that reflect the common international economic realities confronted by most countries in the region and, to a certain extent, shared international prescriptions for how to address them.

Having described the three stages of our chain of representation, in Chapter 6 we explain the methodology we developed for locating citizens' moods, politicians' moods, and policy in a shared, unidimensional policy space. The moods and policy indices reported in Chapters 3–5 were derived in common, not separately from the inputs at any one stage in the chain. In other words, for example, the moods of lower house members regarding the balance to be struck between state and market were actually estimated in conjunction with estimates of the moods of citizens and the location of policies adopted. This, of course, is central to our ability to examine congruence and responsiveness. We will explain this in much greater detail in Chapter 6, so suffice it to say here that we build on a pioneering model by McGann (2013) to obtain policy mood scores, and add to it a graded-response model that helps us infer country policy orientations at various points in time. The linchpin of our strategy to place policy orientations and policy moods on the same scale is an argument about the comparability of two specific policies and two specific survey stimuli. We explain with great care how careful statistical modeling along with judicious use of prior information help us achieve such comparability.

Part II of the book contains only two chapters, each one devoted to one of the sets of institutional linkages that bind our stages of representation together. Chapter 7 develops the rationale for why some electoral systems might be better at producing congruence between the moods of politicians and the moods of citizens – our Linkage I. We talk about electoral rules as "strong" or "weak" or, interchangeably, as constraining or permissive. Beyond the traditional families of electoral rules – majoritarian, mixed, and proportional – we look at specific rules regarding district magnitude, seat allocation formulas, and legal thresholds. Permissive rules encourage voters with heterogeneous economic policy preferences to vote sincerely, casting ballots for candidates with similar stated policy preferences. Strong or constraining rules, on the other hand, may encourage voters to cast a vote for a candidate holding noncongruent views on the economy if those voters believe that he or she is the closest *viable* candidate. Thus, constraining rules might lead to the election of a chamber whose distribution of preferences is less heterogeneous than that of the population it was chosen to represent.

In Chapter 8 we look at Linkage II, the powers held by legislators and executives as they seek to implement their policy moods over state versus market into actual policy. While power for one chamber or for one branch often means a concomitant loss of powers for the other pivotal players, there is not always a zero-sum allocation of might. Consequently, we look at legislators' powers and presidents' powers separately. For legislators, we distinguish between powers that allow them to collect the information necessary to draft (or at least recognize) policies that are congruent with their preferences, and the powers, exercised through collective action, that allow them to pursue those policies once they have been identified. Presidents' powers to influence the location of economic policies are divided into proactive powers that aid the president in directly changing the status quo and reactive powers that help them protect the status quo.

In Part III of the book we attempt to determine how strong the chains of representation are in the separation of powers systems of Latin America. In Chapter 9 we look at the first half of the chain – the impact of Linkage I on congruence and responsiveness between Stages 1 and 2. More specifically, we test whether politicians' preferences or moods regarding state versus market really are a function of citizens' preferences or moods over the same issue *in interaction with* the electoral institutions linking the two. Specifically, we evaluate whether the locations of policy-maker preferences match those of citizens, and whether changes in citizen preferences indeed move policy-makers in a similar direction. The chapter begins with a discussion of ways to measure representation and a descriptive exploration of the evolution of representation across time in the region. Using multilevel models, we then focus on evaluating how representation varies as a function of electoral systems, and how the effect of changes in citizen moods on policy-maker moods is mediated by those same electoral institutions.

In Chapter 10 we look at the second half of the chain – the impact of Linkage II on the quality of representation between Stages 2 and 3. More specifically, we test whether economic policies that determine the balance between the state and market in structuring the economy are a function of politicians' preferences or moods over the same issue, and whether the effects of the latter are, in turn, a function of the policy-making powers linking the two. The chapter begins with a discussion of the challenges in measuring congruence between policy-makers' preferences and policies in separation-of-powers systems, and offers a general sense of how the region is doing in this respect using the results of a simulation. Following that, the chapter discusses models of politician-to-policy congruence and responsiveness that mirror the structure of Chapter 9.

We attempt to evaluate the effects of the entire chain in Chapter 11, where we look at the relationship between citizen moods (Stage 1) and their countries' policy orientations (Stage 3). We try to figure out the impact that both electoral rules (Linkage I) and PMPs (Linkage II) have on the connection between policy moods and policy orientations. Following the standard organization of each chapter in Part III, we first discuss the time trends of different types of citizen-to-policy representation, and then estimate parameters of multilevel models of representation.

In our brief concluding chapter – 12 – we remind readers of our findings regarding the impact of the interaction of preferences and institutions on policy. We also revisit some of the reasons why our approach to the challenges of studying representation is novel and lay out an agenda for future research.

2

Our Solutions to the Challenges of Studying the Chain of Representation

In Chapter 1 we gave a broad overview of our goals in this book. This chapter will be structured somewhat similarly, but we provide some additional, more detailed information about our approach in an effort to define our particular contribution and what makes this book unique, or at least uncommon among others like it.

There is after all an expansive literature on whether politicians accurately reflect the interests of their constituents (e.g. Grofman 2004, Huber and Powell Jr.'s 1994, Powell Jr. 2004, Powell Jr. and Vanberg 2000). Some of it relies on election results to observe the revealed preferences of citizens – the first stage in the chain. However, election results are not just an expression of sincere preferences. They are also a strategic reaction to the rules used to translate votes into seats. Those rules are our Linkage I, and we wish to assess the linkage's impact on the relationship between the preferences of citizens and the preferences of politicians. Therefore, one of our contributions, although clearly not one that is entirely unique to this book, is to use survey responses that precede and are relatively free of any incentives imposed by the electoral system.

There is also an expansive literature on interbranch relations and on the role of pivotal players in the policy-making process (PMP). Much of this work focuses on parliamentary systems where the executive branch has its origins in the legislative branch and the two must enjoy mutual confidence. We focus on relatively understudied, with the exception of the United States, separation-of-powers systems, which adds a layer of complication – but also of interest – to our contribution.[1] While electoral systems and PMPs across democratic regime

---

[1] Other works on presidential systems that touch on part of the questions we deal with here include Alemán and Schwartz (2006), Mainwaring and Shugart (1997), Morgenstern and Nacif (2002), Palanza (2018), Saiegh (2011), Shugart and Carey (1992).

types share many features, we are compelled to account for politicians and their powers in more than one branch, and even across chambers within the legislative branch, in a way that scholars focusing on unicameral parliamentary systems (or on systems that are treated *as if* they were unicameral), for example, might not. The separate origins and survival of the two branches brings to office actors whose powers and incentives to represent constituents vary across time and space.

Given all the powers at the disposal of policy-makers and given their complex interactions, one fruitful strategy would be to hone in, perhaps even through the use of formal models, on the theoretical impact of a single policy-making power. Instead of artificially isolating a single tool, we attempt to account for as many of the tools available to legislators and presidents as we can, including their varying abilities to be informed about a proposed policy's impact, their differential capacities to draft legislation that reflects a preferred position, and the variegated paths that they can take for implementing those preferred policies. As we noted in Chapter 1, these tools can be used to protect the existing status quo or to change it, and later in this chapter we will briefly explain how we decided to aggregate individual powers held by multiple actors into a single PMP. These decisions about characterizing the PMP will be on open display in detail in Chapter 8.

2.1 A CLOSER LOOK AT THE CHAIN OF REPRESENTATION

We do not concern ourselves with the origins of citizens' preferences. This question, while obviously important, is simply beyond the scope of our project. Family, friends, employers, coworkers, parishioners, priests, and many others may influence what one comes to believe about politics in general, and about the balance between state and market in particular. We recognize that political elites may shape the preferences of the citizens who eventually decide whether they remain in office or are replaced. A two-way causal relationship or some kind of feedback loop between the preferences of citizens and the preferences of politicians is entirely possible. We have to let our account start somewhere and are content to simply begin by taking citizens' preferences as given. Technically, we treat citizens' preferences as exogenous.

Different visions of democratic representation vary in their assumptions about the nature of the relationship between voters and politicians (Fearon 1999, Mansbridge 2009, Miller and Stokes 1963). We can start by assuming that citizens will, if they can, elect politicians who share their preferences over policy outcomes. This is based on what is commonly called a *selection* model of the relationship between constituents and their representatives. Candidates take a stand in support of a particular package of policies and a voter looks for a (viable) politician backing the policies he or she most prefers (Bianco 1994, Kingdon 1973, Miller and Stokes 1963). In a *promissory* form of representation, the elected politician has a normative duty to act on the authorization given at the previous election (Mansbridge 2003). If the policies the successful candidate backed during the preceding campaign are the candidate's sincerely preferred policies and he or she continues to back them throughout the term for internal reasons, we talk about a *gyroscopic* form of representation (Mansbridge 2003).[2] If we assume that representation takes either a promissory or a gyroscopic form, we can capture politicians' preferences once and act as if they represented the politicians' preferences during the entire term for which they were elected.

A *sanction* model, on the other hand, focuses on the representative's desire to avoid punishment at the next election (Fiorina 1974, Mayhew 1974). This model is compatible with an *anticipatory* form of representation, when the elected official seeks to estimate what the winning mix of policy positions will be at the next election (Mansbridge 2003). If this is how politicians reason, then we might expect that their preferences expressed near the beginning of a term will not accurately reflect the preferences they express at the end of the term. To account for this possible form of representation, we will also take politicians' preferences measured near the beginning of the term and allow them to evolve gradually toward their best estimate of what voters will be looking for at the next election.

Rather than choosing between a selection model and a sanction model, we will allow each of them to inform our analysis. On the one hand, we will make use of a measure of politicians' preferences captured early during their terms in office, and, on the other hand, we will consider a measure that allows those early preferences to evolve smoothly toward the measure of preferences taken at the beginning of the next term in office. As we will see later, assuming that politicians' preferences are fixed as opposed to assuming that they evolve can have an impact on conclusions drawn about the relationship between policies implemented and the preferences of politicians.

2.2 CONGRUENT WITH AND RESPONSIVE TO WHOM?

When looking at the relationship between voters and politicians, we will examine one-to-one (median-to-median), many-to-one, and many-to-many congruence and responsiveness. In settings where plurality rules are employed, including those used to allocate one seat in a single-member district, a focus on the one-to-one relationship between the pivotal median voter and the single elected official has received the most attention (Achen 1978, Cox 1987, Huber and Powell Jr.'s 1994). However, the electoral systems that we encounter in Latin America are extremely diverse, and systems with single-member

---

[2] The term refers to the fact that the elected official, like a gyroscope, rotates on his or her own axis.

districts decided by plurality are in fact rare. In cases that employ some form of proportional representation, the privileged place of the median voter in determining outcomes is not as obvious. We expect that in those instances the fuller distribution of voters' preferences will influence the composition of the set of politicians chosen in a given district. As a result, when looking at citizen-to-politician congruence and responsiveness, we will also account for the national distribution of citizens' preferences over state intervention versus the free market and the distribution of preferences across the legislative chamber or chambers on that same dimension. We ask how close these distributions are (is there congruence?), whether they move together (is there responsiveness?), and whether any of these dynamics are a function of the electoral institutions that link citizens to politicians.

As we will explain in greater detail in Chapter 7, our reasoning is that highly constraining (strong) and highly permissive (weak) electoral rules may be roughly equal at promoting the reflection of the preferences of the median citizen in the median politician's preferences – with perhaps a slight edge going to strong systems (Cox 1987, 226)[3] – but that permissive systems will excel at many-to-many congruence and responsiveness (Kang and Powell Jr. 2010). The many-to-many relationship may be critical for understanding representation because of the intracameral, intercameral, and interbranch bargaining over policy that per force may end up involving actors other than the legislative median.

We will also focus on one-to-one congruence and responsiveness when considering presidents. Individual presidents are frequently chosen by plurality in single-member districts, sometimes in one round, sometimes in two. Thus, the rules for selecting them are not equally constraining, and we will examine whether some forms of choosing presidents are better at assuring that the president's preferences will reflect the preferences of the median citizen.

Strong systems are likely to bring to office a group of politicians whose state-market preferences are relatively tightly bunched. Who is privileged in terms of policy-making powers – the legislative branch or the executive – will affect whose preferred policies are adopted, but we do not expect policy to move drastically if politicians have relatively similar preferences. As we noted earlier, permissive or weak systems are likely to bring to power a group of politicians with a wider array of preferences than those chosen in constraining or strong systems. Formally or informally, coalition-building will be necessary in multiparty settings. For example, presidents may cobble together support for their programs from disparate groups in the legislature (Palanza 2018, Saiegh 2011, Soroka and Wlezien 2015). In this process, it is possible that the center will get left out of government formation. As a result, median

---

[3] See Grofman (2004) for an argument about why we should not expect convergence to the median in a two-party system, and see McDonald, Mendes, and Budge (2004) on the claim that permissive systems lead to higher one-to-one congruence.

policy-maker to policy orientation – one-to-one – congruence might be lower in weak systems (Cox 1987, 237). On the other hand, if the center is critical for building support for a particular economic program, then weak or permissive systems should generate high levels of congruence (Blais and Bodet 2006). Clearly, the expectations regarding congruence in separation of power systems are complicated, but we attempt to account for institutional variations across those systems.

We do something unique when evaluating levels of congruence and responsiveness – both between citizens and politicians and between politicians and policy. We use a simulation-based approach to establish a baseline against which to judge observed quality of representation. In the absence of such a baseline, the yardstick, implicit or explicit, is a system that would magically produce perfect congruence everywhere and at all times (and therefore perfect responsiveness as well). Against that benchmark, Latin American legislators and presidents look horrible – but so would politicians in any other democracy. Simulating levels of congruence and responsiveness is our way of recognizing that no system is ever likely to deliver perfection. We begin by drawing random samples of citizens' preferences over economic policy from a population that we assume has normally distributed preferences. We make similar assumptions when choosing the state-market location and number of parties that enter an election. We then simulate citizen choices based on two simple spatial behavioral models, one that allows them to choose a sincerely preferred party and another one that allows them to eschew their most preferred alternative for a proximate and viable party. Using thousands of simulated votes, we feed the results of these hypothetical elections through different electoral systems – with varying district magnitudes, seat allocation formulas, and legal thresholds – to produce sets of elected policy-makers. Comparing the preferences of these elected policy-makers with the originally sampled preferences of our hypothetical citizens allows us to establish realistic levels of congruence and responsiveness. These simulation-derived levels then serve as a benchmark against which we can compare observed levels of congruence and responsiveness across countries and over time.

When considering congruence and responsiveness between policy-makers and policies, we go a step further and simulate policies chosen by elected policy-makers. To do so, we first identify the median policy preferred by the legislature and combine this preference with that of the elected president to produce a policy that is the weighted average of the two. In simulations, we vary the relative weight of the executive vis-à-vis the legislature from legislative advantage in policy-making to dominance of the executive. Armed with both a set of simulated preferences of policy-makers and simulated locations of policies adopted, we again compute our measures of congruence and responsiveness on these two inputs. The resulting distances provide a feasible benchmark against which to evaluate observed levels of congruence and responsiveness at this stage of the chain of representation. Again, rather than assuming perfect congruence and responsiveness as an appropriate yardstick, our approach is to establish some kind of plausible baseline regarding congruence and responsiveness against which to compare observed levels.

2.3 A COMMON SPACE FOR PREFERENCES AND POLICIES

We have noted more than once that measures of congruence, in particular, require that preferences and policies be located on a common scale. Without a common metric, any claims about the proximity of or distance between preferences or between preferences and policies are virtually meaningless. Our book contributes what we see as an innovative and creative way to put citizens, politicians, and policy on a single state-to-market continuum. Like others do, our approach begins with "bridging questions," identical or nearly identical questions that are posed to citizens, politicians, and, yes, the "economy." Fortunately, AB and LB share a number of very, very similar questions that are repeated in surveys across time and place. For example, a question repeated regularly asks: "The state, and not the private sector, should own the most important enterprises and industries in the country. How much do you agree with this statement?" Another item that was posed across eleven surveys over time asks respondents whether they agree with the following statement: "The market economy is most suitable for the country." Other questions were used much less often but were still useful in our efforts to capture the mood of the population regarding the balance between state and market. For example, in 2008 and 2011, respondents across all countries were prompted to answer whether higher education (*universidades*) "should mostly be in State hands" or "in private hands." When necessary, we inverted the scales of the responses to make sure that they always ranged from a desire for more state intervention at the lowest end of the scale to a desire for freer markets at the high end.

Several studies of representation, despite making references to veto players and separation of powers, proceed as if all democracies were unicameral. Undoubtedly, this is a result of the dearth of information we have about upper chambers, where they exist. We seek to avoid this problem by imputing the preferences of senators from the directly measured preferences of deputies. We assign the preferences of deputies to their copartisans in the upper chamber and then calculate quantities of interest regarding the upper chamber by reweighting preferences based on party vote shares in the senate. While we recognize that this is not a perfect solution, we believe this approach allows us to generate valid measures of the policy mood of the median senator in systems with upper chambers. Similarly, presidents are not surveyed regarding their preferences over the state and the market. So, in an even greater leap of creativity, we devise a procedure to deduce how members of a legislature might respond to questions like: "If the president had been asked about the need for more privatization, how do you think she would have responded?" This method is based on lower house members' self-placement and placement of the president on a left–right continuum, as we explain in Chapter 4. In this way, we get executives' "responses" to the same questions posed to legislators, and with these responses in hand we then construct policy moods for presidents.

When moving on to the location of policy, we again guarantee that the scales – the scale where the preferences of citizens and politicians are located and the scale where policy is set – point the same way, with larger values corresponding to pro-market positions. Second, to guarantee that these scales have similar "length" – that is that they are commensurate, such that the same number conveys identical meaning regarding the level of reliance on state versus market – we impose an additional restriction, forcing two pairs of policies/stimuli to perform as "bridges" between the policy moods of policy-makers and citizens, on the one hand, and the policy orientations of countries, on the other. These bridges capture actors' opinions on the extent to which privatization has been a beneficial process in Latin America and on the appropriateness of cross-border capital mobility; on the policy side, we gauge the level of state ownership of productive assets and the degree to which capital can in fact move across borders. By assuming that each of these pairs of policies/stimuli have identical power in discriminating across the state/market preferences of actors and the state/market orientation of policies, we are in a position to locate policy orientations and policy moods on an identical scale. Again, we will have much more to say about this in Chapter 6.

As we have noted previously, it is central to testing our theoretically motivated questions that we *not* use votes cast in elections to fill public offices as a measure of citizens' preferences. We theorize that the number of parties that enter a race, their placement on the ideological spectrum, and the distribution of voters with respect to parties contesting an election are all in part a function of the electoral rules in place that encourage more-or-less strategic behavior on the part of entering elites and voting citizens. Thus, votes cast in elections to fill public offices seldom correspond to sincere preferences over policy outcomes, but are instead an expression of a preference for one policy maker over another *given* what is on offer and how the voter anticipates that other voters will behave when casting their ballots. It is this constraining or permissive impact on preferences that we will test in Chapter 9, and we could not test it with votes because these already reflect that impact.

Likewise, given our research questions, we would not want to use roll call vote results as a direct measure of elected officials' preferences over policy. We argue that the content of policy options on which representatives make a decision is a function of the institutions that define the PMP. For example, some constitutions set aside proposal powers in certain areas to one branch or the other, and these powers may constrain the options legislators get to vote on (in favor of the preferences of the actor with proposal power). Likewise, agenda control granted to chamber leaders may mean that some legislators will find that their preferred policies are never proposed on the floor. Alternatively, it is possible that, without staff support or ample investigative powers, officials will err more often in identifying the policy that will lead to their most preferred outcome when it comes to balancing the state and the market. In Chapter 10 we measure the impact of these variations in the allocation of policy-making powers on the translation of officials' preferences into implemented policies, and we could not do this with roll call vote results because they already reflect that impact.

For the location of policy we augment the IADB's Structural Policy Index (Lora 2012). The index is built on dozens of individual policies grouped into five important policy areas: taxes, trade, labor markets, finance, and public/private ownership. To put policy in the same space as citizens' and politicians' preferences, we treat the location of individual policies as responses to questions "posed to the economy," as it were, regarding its "preferences" over state intervention or market freedom. We treat policies regarding privatization and the freedom of capital flows as bridges to questions posed to citizens and politicians about their preferences over these same policies. With this final innovative assumption – some might say, leap of faith – we have the measures we need to calculate citizen-to-politician, politician-to-policy, and citizen-to-policy congruence.

2.4 INSTITUTIONAL LINKAGES

Our chain of representation is held together by two sets of institutional linkages. Citizens are linked to politicians by the electoral rules that govern the choice of the latter. Politicians are linked to policy by the powers deputies, senators, and presidents bring to the struggle to craft policy. For both institutional linkages, we start with detailed information about their component parts and then develop a theoretically justified means of aggregating them into a single, linkage-specific score.

District magnitude is the number of seats to be awarded in a given district in a single election. We average this number across districts – not always as easily as this simple statement suggests – to obtain one part of our system-level indicator of permissiveness (many seats to hand out) or constraint (few seats to award). The seat allocation formula – the formula used to translate votes into seats – furnishes a second indicator. The permissive formulas reward relatively low vote-getters, while the constraining ones reward relatively high vote-getters. Finally, electoral thresholds in place in some systems provide a third indicator. They establish a floor, in terms of percentage of the vote won, to obtain even a single seat. The higher the threshold, the stronger the system. As we will show later, some systems are uniformly constraining, some are uniformly permissive, and most send a mixed signal to entering elites and voting citizens about how coordinated their behavior must be.[4]

---

[4] Our primary sources for coding these aspects of electoral systems are Bormann and Golder (2013), Carey and Hix (2011), Inter-Parliamentary Union (2017), Reilly, Ellis, and Reynolds (2005), and various websites of electoral authorities in the countries themselves.

To aggregate these component parts of electoral systems into a single measure of strength – constraint or permissiveness – we use a Classification and Regression Tree (CART) model. We use the relationship between votes and seats in a simulation exercise to calculate the proportionality of results of every election for lower houses, upper houses, and presidents in the region during the period under study. In these simulations, we allow the possibility that voters choose their preferred candidates sincerely, based exclusively on their own preferences, or strategically, based on their anticipation of which candidates are viable. We rely on the CART model to tell us which combinations of district magnitudes, seat allocation formulas, and legal thresholds are associated with more or less disproportionality, averaging over sincere and strategic behavioral rules. We will explain this procedure in much greater detail in Chapter 7, but suffice it to say here that the exercise generates clusters of electoral systems that institutionalize similar incentives for coalescing behind fewer or more parties.

Our second institutional linkage corresponds to the powers available to politicians during the PMP. Placing oneself on an ideological spectrum ranging from 1 – most left – to 10 – most right – answering a question about whether the tax rate should be higher or lower than it was last year, and casting a roll call vote in support of a piece of legislation all involve reflecting on one's own ideal point across several scales. That mental exercise is aided by information. As a result, we used data across chambers regarding the amount of staff support for members, the level of development of the committee system, and the ability to question executive branch officials. Obviously, if the hurdle for collective action is some super-majority, rather than a simple or even absolute majority, the median's preferences will not likely prevail even if a legislative chamber is endowed with a power. To get at this aspect of legislators' policy-making powers, we used information such as the requirements to amend the constitution, the power to make spending changes, provisions that restrict the introduction of legislation in certain areas, and the level of consensus necessary to overcome a recalcitrant president (veto override).

Fortunately, our desire to take bicameral systems seriously is easier for Linkage II than Linkage I. While Pemstein et al. (2017) asks experts to classify several powers of the legislative branch generally, it also asks multiple questions where experts score lower and upper chambers separately. Thus, when we cluster legislative policy-making powers, we attribute the general powers to both chambers but can attribute varying levels of some specific powers to each branch separately.

As we noted in Chapter 1, we followed Mainwaring and Shugart (1997) in examining both presidential powers to change the status quo – proactive powers – and presidential powers to protect the status quo – reactive powers. We drew on some of the components of Negretto's (2014) index, but not on his overall index of presidential powers for a couple of reasons. First, some of the ingredients in the index are better, to our way of thinking, attributed to legislatures than presidents since they correspond to an absence of presidential power. Second, we ran our own clustering exercise also, so that we can incorporate the powers drawn from Pemstein et al. (2017) that we alluded to earlier.

The proactive powers for which we account allow the president the first chance to move economic policy on the state-to-market continuum, or at least to prod the legislature to make a move. Decree authority is a clear example of the former, but decree authority varies widely across constitutions (Carey and Shugart 1998). Some presidents clearly do not have a constitutionally allocated ability to issue decrees with the force of law, but, among those who do, the status of decrees that do not receive subsequent support from a congressional majority varies. Examples of the ability to prod the legislature to move include the ability to call special sessions – which often entails the right to define the subject matter to be dealt with during the session – or the ability to declare a bill initiated by the executive branch "urgent," moving it to the top of the legislature's agenda.

The reactive powers for which we account capture both the ability to prevent the legislature from considering changes to some policies and the ability to vastly reshape the legislature's preferred policies. As an example of the former, some constitutions give the executive the exclusive right to propose changes in some areas of policy. As long as the executive does not broach the subject, the status quo is safe. Regarding the latter, one can imagine a bill passed by the legislature that contains changes to the policy status quo of which the president approves but that also contains changes of which he or she does not approve. If a president can partially promulgate a bill, putting into force only those initiatives where he or she agrees with the congressional median, the president can protect the status quo in areas where the branches disagree.

It is important to stress again that we do not approach policy-making powers as a zero-sum game where any loss (or gain) in power for the legislature is equivalent to a gain (or loss) in power for the president. Clearly, in theory, we reason that there are frequently trade-offs. However, we allow for independence of powers across veto players. At the end of Chapter 8 we conduct an original clustering exercise using lower/only house powers, upper house powers, and presidential powers. The results depict three types of PMPs – systems where the legislature seems to be relatively empowered, systems where the legislature and executive seem relatively balanced in terms of powers, and systems where executives seem armed to be relatively more successful at dictating the location of the policies adopted.

2.5 SOME CONNECTIONS LEFT UNMADE (AT LEAST FOR NOW)

In this book we have endeavored to remain clearly focused on how formal democratic institutions affect representation (Powell Jr. 2000). In this particular chapter we sought to offer some details of our approach that we think make clear the multiple, original contributions of this book to the literature on congruence and responsiveness. Despite the temptation to veer off and pursue dozens of interesting tangents that occurred to us or were suggested by others, we think we have remained true to our intent. That said, we want to wrap up this chapter by suggesting some of these "tangents" and how we, or perhaps others, could, in the future, use what we have done here to step beyond our focus in order to fruitfully pursue other important research questions.

Achen and Bartels (2017) probably would have forewarned us that our search for evidence that citizens select representatives based on shared preferences over important policies that those representatives then dutifully implement was an exercise in futility. We would like to claim that our results constitute solid evidence to the contrary, but that would not be entirely accurate. If voters intend to choose politicians based on their shared preferences, we will show that, when it comes to elected assemblies, some electoral systems appear to make that choice easier than others. Congruence is never perfect, but it is greatest when electoral incentives are either clearest about the need to coordinate carefully or clearest about not having to coordinate much at all. However, we also find that putting into office presidents who share the preferences of the median voter is relatively uncommon. The impact of this difference in preferences over economic policy is accentuated by our finding that policy is most responsive to politicians' preferences when presidents are endowed with significant legislative powers. So, while we are not ready to abandon entirely a model of representative democracy where voters steer the direction of policy through elections, we will provide plenty of evidence that, to the extent they do, it is no straightforward process that characterizes most separation of powers systems on a regular basis. Again, we find that, given the right electoral incentives, the preferences of legislators will reflect the preferences of voters, but those legislators are not often effective at moving policy to their preferred location.

Our focus on congruence and responsiveness comes at the expense of attention to other laudable outcomes, like the pursuit of public goods by elected officials rather than particularistic payoffs and self-enrichment, an outcome that Besley analyzes in *Principled Agents?* (Besley 2007). It is certainly possible to reimagine our analysis in these terms. Our theorizing about institutional linkages does not attempt to deduce their roles in providing transparency and accountability per se, but future work could certainly seek such explanations. For example, we will show that very constraining and very permissive electoral systems lead to greater congruence between citizens and elected assemblies. Electoral systems that provide heterogeneous citizenries with middling incentives to coordinate fare less well in these terms. Similarly, we will show that PMPs with balanced powers across branches struggle in terms of politician-to-policy responsiveness. It seems plausible to hypothesize that we might find similar relationships between institutional linkages and the provision of public goods or the absence of malfeasance.

Similarly, while we use a state-to-market continuum to locate the preferences of citizens, the preferences of politicians, and the policies adopted, it is not explicitly our goal, as it was for Persson and Tabellini in their *The Economic Effects of Constitutions*, to explain which institutions lead to big governments, high levels of corruption, or larger budget deficits (Persson and Tabellini 2005). Again, one could hypothesize that institutional linkages among citizens, politicians, and policy should have an impact on these outcomes. Here, however, we have confined ourselves more closely to the question of whether citizens get the policies they want. We do not ask who wants what, when, and where. We take the preferences of citizens as an exogenous starting point – whether they want state-run economies or unfettered markets – and then seek to determine how democratic institutional designs impact the likelihood that citizens get the politicians and policies they want.

As we noted earlier, we will show that, on average, the presidents that get elected across systems and over time do not closely share the policy preferences of the median voter. Unlike Stokes in her work on *Mandates and Democracy*, we do not claim to have evidence that candidates for the presidency are dissimulating during their campaigns only to reverse course once in office, although that is certainly a possible explanation for some of our findings (Stokes 2001). Previous research has shown that the historical reputations of political parties are not good predictors of the economic policies their presidential candidates will enact once in office (Johnson and Crisp 2003), and our results, while not directly testing this idea, are consistent with that conclusion. We do not reveal the preferences of presidents through their pronouncements on the campaign trail nor through the historical reputations of their parties – and we certainly avoid revealing the preferences of presidents based on the policies that are implemented under their watch. Instead, we ask the elected members of lower houses to help us identify how presidents might answer survey questions about their preferences over specific economic policies.

Yet another theme we do not pursue here is whether a lack of congruence between politicians, particularly presidents, and citizens leads to political crises. Pérez-Liñan documents how several directly elected presidents have been removed from office through impeachment procedures – and others jailed after their terms in office are complete (Pérez-Liñan 2007). It seems reasonable to hypothesize that the design of electoral systems – our Linkage I – can increase or decrease the distance between the preferences of congress and the president. Executives are chosen through relatively strong or constraining electoral systems while some legislatures are chosen through very weak or permissive systems. One might hypothesize that wide variation in electoral systems within a country might generate presidents with relatively little support in congress, perhaps making their impeachment more likely.

At the risk of suggesting that the contributions made by this book are exceedingly narrow, we will point out one more interesting questions we could have pursued but chose not to. Based on work by Booth and Seligson, we know that support for democracy varies across citizens in any given country, but disaffected citizens, rather than supporting coup plotters or resigning from the political arena entirely, tend to pursue political participation through peaceful means other than the ballot box, including communal development and the strengthening of civil society (Booth and Seligson 2009). It seems reasonable to hypothesize that sustained periods of lack of congruence between voters and their elected representatives or between voters and enacted policies might become a source of disaffection. If this is so, our work will reveal the kinds of institutional designs – electoral systems (Linkage I) and PMPs (Linkage II) – that will minimize that lack of congruence. It is possible, then, that political reforms might ameliorate disaffection and boost regime support.

Despite all these "missed opportunities" in terms of theoretical connections left unexplored, we stand by our decision to keep our focus tightly on how formal, democratic institutions affect representation conceived of as congruence and responsiveness. While our focus is tight, the undertaking remains gargantuan, and we think that readers will find all the remaining chapters of this book necessary to our goals; we also hope that readers find fulfillment in our attempt to methodically build toward a set of important questions. In this chapter we sought to introduce several innovative solutions to the challenges of studying representation that will be discussed more thoroughly throughout the rest of the book. We hope this conclusion to the chapter serves to set our project in a broader landscape of important debates that the book addresses – or at least has the potential to address.

PART I

STAGES

3

Stage 1: Citizens' Preferences

In Chapter 1 we laid out a general causal map of the chain that links citizens to policy-makers in representative democracies. Our "big picture" interest is on the degree to which the policies enacted by Latin America's democratic governments over the past two decades have been in line with the preferences of the citizens they represent. Because citizens' preferences (Stage 1) are the starting point in the chain depicting how representative government is supposed to work, our inquiry starts with a detailed description of the "policy moods" of Latin American citizens throughout the period under observation. In subsequent chapters we will provide descriptions of the other stages along the chain – the policy moods of Latin American policy-makers and the broad economic policies that they have implemented over the past two decades.

We start in Section 3.1 with an overview of the data on which our analysis is based, followed by a presentation of policy moods for all countries in our purview in Section 3.2. Section 3.3 addresses questions of validity of our measures by comparing policy moods against alternative scales that attempt to capture attitudes toward economic policy among citizens. We employ these policy moods to throw further light onto recent debates about the character of citizen preferences in Latin America (cf. Baker and Greene 2011, Remmer 2012, Wiesehomeier and Doyle 2013). We are normatively agnostic about what constitutes "good" or "morally appropriate" preferences, which means that we are not interested in chastising Latin American citizens for displaying too much of a predilection for market solutions or for favoring too much state regulation. That said, we want to explore what the policy mood scores that we derive say about the economic preferences of Latin American citizens, as this has been an extremely important debate in the analysis of the rise and fall of a "pink tide" – that is, the election and defeat of leftist governments in most major countries – over the past decade and a half. A thorough description of how the policy mood of Latin American citizens has waxed and waned between a preference for market versus state intervention constitutes our main substantive contribution to those debates.

In turn, our main technical contribution is a method that allows us to place citizens, policy-makers, and policies on the same scale. The details of this method are far too consequential to discuss in a cavalier way, but they can also be terse. Rather than interrupting the descriptive narrative that we lay out in Chapters 3–5, we postpone our presentation of the intricate details of this scaling method until Chapter 6.

3.1 DATA COVERAGE FOR CITIZENS' PREFERENCES

In this chapter we provide the reader with a full portrait of the kind of data that we have at our disposal, describing the mass surveys of citizens on which we base our work. We describe the numerous survey questions that we use to construct the "policy mood" of citizens in eighteen Latin American countries from 1996 through to 2014. Recall that we conceive of this policy mood as a continuum on which individuals can locate their own preferences regarding how the economy ought to be run. Individuals prone to prefer heavy government guidance of the economy naturally locate themselves on the state end of this continuum, while those that would leave economic governance to the free play of market forces place themselves on the market extreme.

The policy moods that we build are summary representations of the general affect that citizens express toward pro-state or pro-market economic policy as distilled from their opinions about and attitudes toward a number of policy questions. We indistinctly refer to these policy questions – the building blocks of all policy moods in our analysis – as "items" or "stimuli." That is, policy moods are latent dimensions that we cannot directly observe. They are instead constructed from observable items. When it comes to obtaining information on policy items or stimuli, scholars have access to a number of survey instruments that have been collected since the early 1990s. In particular, we make use of the LB and AB survey collections. LB has produced surveys of citizens in Latin American countries since the early 1990s, but the very early ones lack information useful for our purposes; we thus consider surveys from 1996 to 2012.[1] Altogether, LB has made available up to 281 unique country/year surveys throughout this period, which reduce to 230 when we limit our purview to the eighteen countries in our analysis. These surveys include a broad set of stimuli that we could in principle consider; we count sixty-five different items related to economic policy that were asked to at least some Latin American respondents at least once in the 1996–2012 period. The questions themselves

---

[1] In addition, we understand that the earlier LB respondent samples were not nationally representative, but were biased toward urban environments.

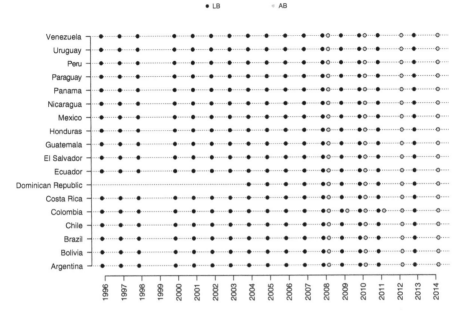

FIGURE 3.1. Availability of citizen survey data across countries and years. The figure depicts, for every country in our sample, the years in which LB (dark circle) and AB (light circle) surveys were fielded and are at our disposal. When both surveys were fielded, circles appear side by side.

are not always consistently worded, and, even when they are, not a single one of them is asked in each and every one of the 281 LB surveys.

Similarly, the AB project has produced a large number of high-quality nationally representative samples of citizens' dispositions since the early 2000s. Unfortunately, the series on attitudes toward economic policy that is most relevant to us first appeared in 2008. This makes for a comparatively short series, with six consistently worded questions that specifically ask the opinions of citizens about the desirability of state intervention in the economy. For the most part, these questions are available in seventy-four unique country/year AB surveys up to 2014. Figure 3.1 summarizes graphically the surveys at our disposal.

The Appendix contains the exact wording of all the questions that we employ, and Table A.1 in Online Appendix A contains a country-by-country breakdown of available stimuli. Previous attempts to build summary representations of citizen preferences – that is, something akin to policy moods – have broken down upon realization that it is impossible to find a large number of identically worded stimuli throughout time and across countries, a point made clear from a cursory look at the Appendix. Fortunately, the methods that we use in Chapter 6 to derive "policy moods" are relatively forgiving and allow us to work with sets of questions that are not identically worded. As we explain in Chapter 6, the most important reason why these methods are "forgiving" is that we work with aggregate responses, as opposed to individual-level responses. For our scaling method to work, we do require (i) as many items as we possibly can obtain that can be interpreted as stemming from an underlying economic policy mood, and (ii) that these items are repeated in at least two different surveys within each country with at least similar wording (we elaborate on the rationale behind these requirements in Chapter 6). Many of the stimuli that we analyze have informed previous scholarly working on economic policy reform in Latin America (e.g., Baker 2009). However, many others, as far as we know, are used in such an endeavor here for the first time.

The first requirement forces us to start from the largest possible number of unique questions in both the AB and LB series. All of these questions are at least loosely connected to what we see as an economic policy dimension running through countries in our observation set. We understand citizens as political actors capable of locating their own preferences along this dimension, and thus able to choose between state- and market-based answers to questions of economic distribution and efficiency. We cast a wide net, including questions related to feelings about privatization of state-owned companies, the need for governments to temper socioeconomic inequality, and the appropriateness of free trade and regulation of utilities, among others.[2] After applying this first cut, we are left with forty-nine distinct stimuli. Unfortunately, many of these forty-nine stimuli appeared exclusively in a single round of either the LB or AB surveys, which means that, by our second criterion, we cannot include them in our analysis. The remaining stimuli are worded very similarly across surveys; six of them, those from the AB series, are identical across surveys. In a few instances, we took the liberty of pooling questions that, although not identical, referred to a similar underlying policy position. For example, `privatization.beneficial` pools together different questions from AB and LB.[3]

---

[2] We omit questions concerning regional integration or questions about the desirability of collaboration with international financial organizations. Although one could argue that these items provide a glimpse into how respondents feel about states and markets, we decided that the wording of these questions made them too remote from an everyday understanding of economic policy to merit inclusion; moreover, we just do not see these questions as connected in an obvious way to pro-state or pro-market impulses.

[3] In AB, question `ros1` reads: "*El Estado, en lugar del sector privado, debería ser el dueño de las empresas e industrias más importantes del país. ¿Hasta qué punto está de acuerdo o en desacuerdo con esta frase?*" ("The state, and not the private sector, should own the most important enterprises and industries in the country. To what degree do you agree with this statement?"). In contrast, LB asks a similar question in a couple of different formats, for example by asking respondents whether they agree with the statement: "The privatisation of state companies has been beneficial to the country" (alternatively labeled np14b (1998), p16st.a (2000), p15sta (2001), p22sta (2002), p26st (2003), p40stc (2005), p54sta (2007), and q81st.d (2009). Again, we refer the reader to the Appendix.

After taking both requirements into consideration, the stimuli available for analysis are much reduced, but still plentiful enough to allow us to measure citizen policy moods across time and space. Figure 3.2 shows the distribution of stimuli throughout time for two of the countries we inspect, Argentina and the Dominican Republic. Note for starters that, although LB surveys exist for 1997, none of the items considered in this round are useful to us because they are not repeated in any other survey, not even in a loosely similar manner. In consequence, we only have information for 1996, 1998, and the years 2000 through to 2014. Argentina represents the modal case in terms of data availability. In this country, we consider information from twenty-four distinct stimuli, each of which was asked at least in two different years. The stimuli that were asked most often include `privatization.beneficial` (asked in twelve different survey waves), `market.best` (eleven waves), `privatization.improved.quality` (nine), and `state.limited .scope` (seven) (see the Appendix for the exact wording). A number of stimuli were asked only in a couple of surveys, often in consecutive survey waves – `state.not.in.telecom`, `state.not.in.petrol`, `capital .mobility.good`, `labor.migration.good`, `state.not.in.water`, and `encourage.fdi`. In fact, with the exception of Colombia and the Dominican Republic, all of the countries that we observed had the exact same stimuli available at the exact same time as Argentina. Colombia, which is not portrayed in Figure 3.2, had information available for all the stimuli and years for which Argentina had information, on top of which it adds five AB items for two additional years (2009 and 2011). The policy items available for the Dominican Republic are sparse, mostly because we lack a number of LB surveys for this country. As a consequence, we only have measures of the policy mood of Dominican citizens from 2004 onward.

Aside from the data requirements mentioned earlier – that is, as many stimuli as possible, observed at least in two different waves – our scaling method requires that we make three small, more technical, decisions. First, notice from our shorthand labels that we preprocessed *all* responses across *all* surveys such that agreement with the underlying question would correspond to *pro-market* positions. We believe that our decisions on which responses correspond to pro-market positions are fairly conventional, but the reader should independently ascertain the accuracy of this statement. For example, the label `privatization.beneficial` suggests that individuals that reported higher scores on the underlying question are more likely to have a better opinion of economic activity when industry and services are in private hands. In contrast, labels such as `state.not.in.pensions` suggest a reversal of the original scale, that is, questions captured by this label originally asked respondents whether they agreed with the statement that the state should guarantee pensions for retirees, which is *not* a pro-market position. Since a high score in the original scale would have denoted agreement with a pro-state rather

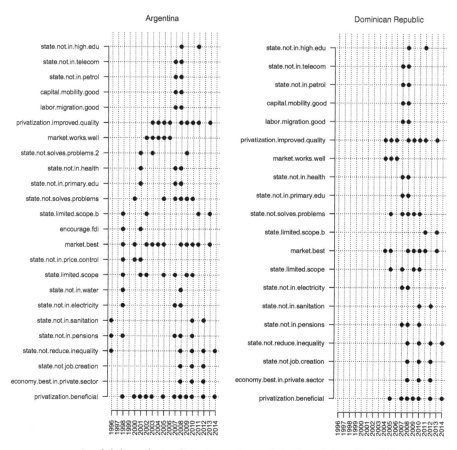

FIGURE 3.2. Availability of stimuli in Argentina and the Dominican Republic. As an example, and for each of the survey items (or *stimuli*) we consider, the figure shows years in which they were asked in Argentina and the Dominican Republic. Instances in which a stimulus is available are indicated with a solid circle.

than a pro-market position, we simply preprocessed this variable by reversing its polarity. This decision does not introduce any extraneous elements into the original LB and AB data.

Second, for reasons that will be clear in Chapter 6, we do not work directly with individual-level data. Instead, we consider *aggregate* information about the fraction of respondents within a survey that register a pro-market response. We follow a very simple rule of thumb: all respondents with answers greater than the midpoint of the response scale are considered to be pro-market. For example, if the scale takes on integers from 1 to 6, the midpoint is 3.5; thus, respondents with values of 4, 5, and 6 are coded as having registered a pro-market response. Wherever the midpoint is an actual value of the scale (for example, 4 is the midpoint of an integer scale from 1 to 7), we simply apportion half of the respondents that report a midpoint value to the pro-market end, and half to the pro-state end. As we built these percentages, we made sure to use the sample weights provided by both LB and AB to ensure that the respondent samples are nationally representative. For example, responses in Argentina 2011 to item market.best – which captures agreement with the statement "The market economy is the single system in which Argentina can become developed" – break down as follows: 61 individuals answer "1," 383 "2," 672 "3," and 84 "4," which suggests that 63 percent $((672+84)/(61+383+672+84))$ approve of the notion that Argentina can only develop through the market; after applying sample weights, this percentage becomes 63.45 percent (we seldom see dramatic changes after applying survey weights). To round up this example, Tables 3.1 and 3.2 reproduce all of the aggregate input data that we use to estimate the policy moods of Argentine citizens between 1996 and 2014.

Third, our analysis is slightly complicated by the existence of individual-level missing values in all data sets. As a rule of thumb, we eschewed stimuli with very high levels of missingness. At the same time, when missingness is not pervasive, we have preferred to impute missing values as opposed to listwise-deleting all respondents with missing items. Imputing missing values allows us to avoid bias in the estimation of the percentage of individuals that support pro-market statements, conditional on a *missing at random* assumption. That is, imputation prevents potential biases in our estimates if, for example, missingness patterns were not completely random (completely random missingness is a tall assumption that is seldom satisfied). To be clear, we carry out multiple imputation of missing values at the individual level on a survey-by-survey basis; as predictors available for imputation, we used respondents' answers to *all* available policy items in the survey. Furthermore, we included a number of socioeconomic status indicators (income, education, urban/rural environment, age, employment status, occupation, gender) and respondents' self-placements on the left–right ideological spectrum, wherever they were available, as additional predictors alongside the respondents' policy views.[4]

---

[4] We used amelia to carry out imputations for the citizen surveys (Honaker, King, and Blackwell 2011). We hasten to add that our final, complete data sets average over imputed values, which means that we ignore uncertainty introduced by the imputation process. Although this is not ideal, adding uncertainty from the imputation process would have required working with several complete data sets, which adds a layer of complication to our data-intensive analyses. In any case, most quantities of interest we care about are observed at the "group" level (the population of citizens in a country, policy-makers in an assembly), so the additional uncertainty that stems from the imputation process at the individual level would have been "smoothed over" anyway as we move to a higher level of aggregation.

TABLE 3.1. *Aggregate information from mass surveys in Argentina; twenty-four stimuli observed throughout 1996–2014 (part I)*

	1996	1998	2000	2001	2002	2003	2004	2005	2006
state.not.in.high.edu	—	—	—	—	—	—	—	—	—
state.not.in.telecom	—	—	—	—	—	—	—	—	—
state.not.in.petrol	—	—	—	—	—	—	—	—	—
capital.mobility.good	—	—	—	—	—	—	—	—	—
labor.migration.good	—	—	—	—	—	—	—	—	—
privatization.improved.quality	—	—	—	—	—	25.61	20.77	36.99	46.17
market.works.well	—	—	—	—	2.29	15.43	18.16	27.74	37.88
state.not.solves.problems.2	—	—	—	12.55	—	0.00	—	—	—
state.not.in.health	—	—	—	3.24	—	—	—	—	—
state.not.in.primary.edu	—	—	—	4.17	—	—	—	—	—
state.not.solves.problems	—	—	57.34	—	—	—	—	51.04	—
state.limited.scope.b	—	60.17	—	—	—	—	—	—	—
encourage.fdi	—	66.08	—	59.93	42.30	—	—	—	—
market.best	—	69.50	63.86	—	52.84	70.15	67.22	64.60	—
state.not.in.price.control	—	77.50	65.56	61.89	—	—	—	—	—
state.limited.scope	—	57.75	—	48.28	38.77	—	—	47.46	—
state.not.in.water	—	38.00	—	—	—	—	—	—	—
state.not.in.electricity	—	45.42	—	—	—	—	—	—	—
state.not.in.sanitation	8.67	—	—	—	—	—	—	—	—
state.not.in.pensions	1.25	0.00	—	—	—	—	—	—	—
state.not.reduce.inequality	13.68	—	—	—	—	—	—	—	—
state.not.job.creation	—	—	—	—	—	—	—	—	—
economy.best.in.private.sector	—	—	—	—	—	—	—	—	—
privatization.beneficial	—	44.17	27.77	17.73	14.02	11.83	—	26.57	—

TABLE 3.2. *Aggregate information from mass surveys in Argentina; twenty-four stimuli observed throughout 1996–2014 (part II)*

	2007	2008	2009	2010	2011	2012	2013	2014
state.not.in.high.edu	—	0.00	—	—	8.69	—	—	—
state.not.in.telecom	23.32	25.58	—	—	—	—	—	—
state.not.in.petrol	10.05	12.08	—	—	—	—	—	—
capital.mobility.good	56.95	64.42	—	—	—	—	—	—
labor.migration.good	72.58	36.00	—	—	—	—	—	—
privatization.improved.quality	—	31.75	26.10	31.89	39.36	—	27.28	—
market.works.well	—	—	—	—	—	—	—	—
state.not.solves.problems.2	—	—	13.06	—	—	—	—	—
state.not.in.health	21.38	0.00	—	—	—	—	—	—
state.not.in.primary.edu	20.39	0.00	—	—	—	—	—	—
state.not.solves.problems	39.73	7.38	46.59	29.68	—	—	—	—
state.limited.scope.b	—	—	—	—	36.03	—	23.34	—
encourage.fdi	—	—	—	—	—	—	—	—
market.best	—	62.75	50.51	67.60	63.45	—	55.73	—
state.not.in.price.control	51.86	—	—	—	—	—	—	—
state.limited.scope	—	—	67.80	77.42	—	—	—	—
state.not.in.water	—	13.75	—	—	—	—	—	—
state.not.in.electricity	14.74	18.08	—	—	—	—	—	—
state.not.in.sanitation	—	—	—	13.33	—	6.02	—	—
state.not.in.pensions	18.67	0.00	—	14.50	—	—	—	—
state.not.reduce.inequality	—	8.81	—	15.07	—	8.73	—	12.20
state.not.job.creation	—	14.83	—	15.57	—	11.57	—	—
economy.best.in.private.sector	—	9.62	—	14.61	—	9.62	—	—
privatization.beneficial	20.39	28.11	23.06	29.34	—	29.73	—	31.81

3.2 CITIZEN POLICY MOODS IN LATIN AMERICA, 1996–2014

We consider the "revealed" policy mood of citizens to be the most relevant normative benchmark for assessing whether good representation – congruence and responsiveness – is achieved (Golder and Stramski 2010, Powell Jr. 2000), and in later chapters we analyze the distance between the opinions of democratically elected representatives and those of the citizens they represent for clues to potential failures of representation. For now, our point of departure is Figure 3.3, which displays the estimated policy moods of the median citizen in each country (the labeled gray dots) along with a smooth estimate of the overall "Latin American policy mood" (the continuous black line with a nonparametric confidence envelope), throughout the period of observation. Low values of the policy mood on the y-axis correspond to pro-state options. The most striking pattern in this figure is the degree to which policy moods move together *across* countries. Indeed, the estimated between-year variance of these series is 4.5; in contrast, we estimate within-year variance at around 0.12. This means that the variation in policy moods of all countries within a given year (within-year variation) is much smaller than the variation across time that we find in the average Latin American policy mood (between-year variation). Put differently, the policy moods of the citizenries of eighteen Latin American countries tend strongly to move together through time. This strong co-movement across countries is not an artifact of our model, as we see an identical pattern when we estimate eighteen different policy-mood models, one for each of the eighteen countries (results not shown).

That a strong regional pattern would underlay country-specific policy moods is at first surprising. After all, why would the policy moods of citizens in eighteen countries as diverse as Guatemala and Uruguay, for example, tend to move together through time? The most important worry, one we address later, concerns the possibility that this strong pattern is produced by our method, rather than by the data we explore. Consider however that this finding is in line with evidence studied by Baker, who explicitly prefers not to display reports of spread around a central Latin American tendency "because cross-national heterogeneity … is minimal" (Baker 2009, 98).[5] More importantly, diverse as the region is, its countries continue to be affected by common economic developments throughout the world. For example, when the *Tequila* crisis erupted in Mexico in 1994, Argentina and others suffered economically through a contagion effect that was unlikely to be a consequence of bilateral connections with Mexico and more likely to be a consequence of assumptions held by foreign investors about the basic economic similarity of Latin

---

[5] Some of the data that Baker analyzes are also included in our indices – this is the case of the LB rounds from 1995 to 2006 – which might explain why neither of us find much cross-national heterogeneity. However, Baker also makes use of surveys that we have not included in our measure of policy mood, including information from a 2003 Globescan survey, a 1998 *Wall Street Journal* survey, and three waves of World Values Surveys.

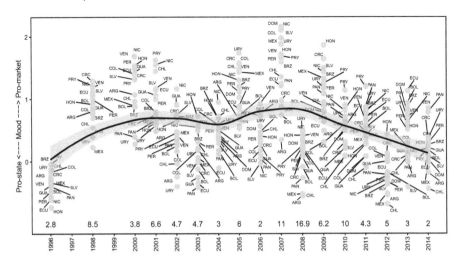

FIGURE 3.3. Policy moods of the median citizen in eighteen Latin American countries. The figure depicts the estimated policy moods of the median citizen in each country (as labeled gray circles) along with a smooth estimate of the overall "Latin American policy mood" (continuous black line with confidence envelope) over time. Point estimates are stacked on each of the years of observation, with labels arranged to as to improve their readability. Higher values indicate more pro-market moods.

American countries. More recently, almost all Latin American countries benefited throughout the 2003–2012 decade from the boom in raw material exports fueled by China's furious demand. Given shared economic performance, it is thus less strange that we find what we would characterize, for lack of a better term, as a "meta policy mood" running throughout the region.

The second pattern that stands out in Figure 3.3 is the oscillation of policy moods between state and market at different points during the past two decades. We observe that the general Latin American mood is pro-state at the beginning of the period that we inspect. Later on, during the "lost half-decade" of 1998–2003, the policy mood turns from slightly pro-market again to more pro-state positions during a period that pundits and scholars identify as the beginning of a pink tide in Latin America, with successive presidential victories for leftist parties in Argentina, Brazil, Chile, Uruguay, and Venezuela. In contrast, we see a buoyant pro-market policy mood in 2004 through 2007, as the pink tide has gathered full force in the region and Latin American governments claim credit for delivering sound rates of economic growth. Although this might appear surprising, it is consistent with research that finds that electoral support for leftist parties does not necessarily follow from massive conversion to socialism in Latin America (Baker and Greene 2011). Instead, governments of the partisan left clearly cohabited with some measure of mass pro-market sentiment in almost all countries. Then a sudden

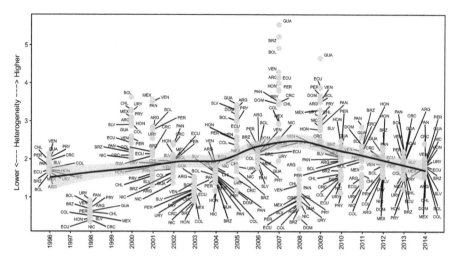

FIGURE 3.4. Heterogeneity of citizen policy preferences in eighteen Latin American countries. The figure shows the estimated standard deviations of citizen mood distributions (as labeled gray circles), taken to indicate heterogeneity in said moods, over the period of our study. The figure also overlays a smooth trend of average heterogeneity in the region (continuous black line with confidence envelope). Point estimates are stacked on each of the years of observation, with labels arranged so to improve their readability. Higher values indicate more heterogeneity.

and drastic drop in pro-market sentiment during the global economic slump of 2007–2008 – a drop masked by "smoothing" of the regional trend – ushers in a protracted turn from markets at the beginning of the second decade of the new millennium as the period of fast economic growth tied to raw material exports to China came to an end. The question we undertake in Part III of the book is whether these policy moods of citizens are reflected in the policy moods of elected representatives and especially in the policies they implement.

Our scaling model produces a number of additional quantities that we also exploit in our theoretical analyses in Part III. One of these quantities is the "spread" of the distribution of citizen preferences. Whereas the policy mood captures the "location" of citizen preferences – that is, the degree to which a representative citizen, the median citizen in our case, is pro-state or pro-market – the spread suggests how close or far apart a typical citizen is from the views of that representative citizen. This spread is in fact a measure of "heterogeneity" of preferences – that is, of relative lack of consensus around the views of the median citizen. Although we avoid a long discussion about these quantities here (and refer the reader to Chapter 6 for the technical details), we summarize in Figure 3.4 our estimates of heterogeneity throughout time and across the region. The continuous black line (and corresponding confidence envelope) is a non-parametric estimate of overall heterogeneity in the region, while the labeled gray dots correspond to heterogeneity in a given country and year. The one discernible pattern we detect is that heterogeneity increased between 2007 and 2009, right at the time of the great global recession; outside this period, the pattern that we observe is one of relative stability throughout time.

3.3 HOW DOES OUR "POLICY MOOD" COMPARE WITH OTHER INDICES?

Our citizen policy moods are based on a particular model specification (see Chapter 6) that also allows simultaneous estimation of the policy moods of policy-makers (Chapter 4) and the policy propensities of Latin American governments (Chapter 5). Here, we compare our policy mood scores to two other measures available in the literature that seek to characterize the aggregate location of Latin American voters. We do not expect these measures to convey identical conclusions about citizen attitudes in Latin America. For starters, some of these alternative measures are based on different sets of questions that do not even aim to explicitly capture the attitudes of citizens toward economic policy. However, we do expect a modicum of similarity, especially with Aldrich–McKelvey (A–M) scores, which would furnish evidence that our policy mood estimates are informed mostly by underlying data and less so by modeling assumptions. We compare our policy moods against two alternative measures: A–M scores and voter-revealed positions. We discuss these alternative methods briefly.

Aldrich and McKelvey developed a model not unlike factor analysis that allows researchers to map a set of observed graded responses (stimuli) onto a single latent dimension by assuming that stimuli are affine transformations of the latent dimension plus random error.[6] The model assumes that a common dimension underlies the positions of all respondents, and that the observed responses of individual respondents are distorted measures of this common dimension. Albeit a relatively early development in efforts to infer ideological positions, this model continues to be one of the best scaling tools in the discipline due in no small part to its ability to handle a phenomenon known as differential item functioning – namely, the very real possibility that a statement like "Private enterprise is indispensable for the development of the country" might mean different things to different people (King et al. (2003), Saiegh (2009)). Poole (1998) more recently generalized a version of the A–M method that works well in the presence of missing values and multidimensional latent spaces. We estimate A–M scores for all country-years for which we can use at least *two* different items; note that, rather than starting from aggregate percentage data, as we do with our

---

[6] Y is an affine transformation of X if $Y = a + bX$ for any real numbers a and b.

own model, A–M scores are computed directly from individual responses.[7] We use country-year median A–M scores to compare against our policy moods.

Rather than using responses to survey items, scholars have also employed aggregate electoral returns to infer the degree to which an electorate is "leftist" or "rightist." Based on Kim and Fording (1998), Baker and Greene (2011) combine publicly available information about vote shares for candidates and parties in national presidential and legislative elections, on the one hand, with expert placements of political parties on a left–right spectrum, on the other, to derive a weighted average that represents the degree to which a country's electorate veered to the left at a particular point in time. For example, if vote shares for three parties are 0.5, 0.3, and 0.2, and the average expert places these parties at 3, 5, and 7 on a 1–10 left–right scale, then the voter-revealed leftism score for this particular election would be $(0.5 \times 3) + (0.3 \times 5) + (0.2 \times 7) = 4.4$. One limitation of this measurement approach is that information is available only during election years, which are few and far between. A second weakness is that we often find among Latin American citizens relatively low correspondence between left–right self-placement and economic policy positions (Kitschelt et al. 2010, Zechmeister 2006, Zechmeister and Corral 2010). A final and more consequential drawback is that citizens' policy moods are estimated from the very policy positions offered by political parties; in contrast, we want to estimate citizen and policy-maker moods separately, from independent data, although we certainly aim to identify these moods on the same scale so as to assess how close or far apart they are. Be this as it may, we follow Baker and Greene (2011) and calculate voter-revealed positions for legislative and presidential elections. Note that we shift the polarity of this measure to construct voter-revealed "rightism" scores that correspond more closely to our policy mood scores (where higher values in principle indicate pro-market attitudes).

Figure 3.5 compares these two alternative summaries of public opinion to our policy mood measure in the eighteen Latin American countries on which we focus. Within each plot, the main series (in black) corresponds to the policy mood of citizens based on our model. To complete this series, we interpolated point estimates for the years 1997 and 1999, which appear in gray.[8] The alternative measures are plotted alongside these policy mood scores. In an effort to facilitate graphical comparisons across scales, we have standardized A–M scores (i.e., these measures have been rescaled so that they have mean 0 and standard deviation 1), and we have rescaled voter-revealed rightism to vary from -2 (100 percent vote share going to parties with an extreme leftist

---

[7] We use the blackbox function in R (Poole et al. 2016). Details appear in Online Appendix A.

[8] We use a cubic spline interpolation routine from the zoo library in R (Zeileis and Grothendieck 2005).

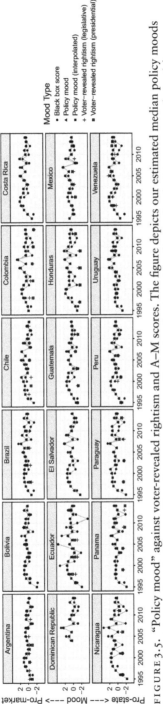

FIGURE 3.5. "Policy mood" against voter-revealed rightism and A–M scores. The figure depicts our estimated median policy moods (solid squares) interpolated using a cubic spline over the span of our time-horizon. The figure also depicts measures derived from alternative measurement models, including interpolated A–M black box scores (solid circles) and moods derived from both legislative (crosses) and presidential vote shares (crossed boxes) (i.e., so called voter-revealed rightism scores).

47

expert score of 1) to 2 (100 percent vote share going to parties with an extreme rightist expert score of 10).

It is important to underscore that when we compare the policy moods of Latin American citizens against alternative measures we are in fact employing different yardsticks. The A–M scores are most similar to our policy moods in both *substantive* and *methodological* terms. Methodologically, both A–M and our model are scaling techniques that reduce observations on a very large number of variables to a handful of scores that correspond to latent unobserved dimensions. The similarities end there, as the statistical models on which these scales depend, as well as the estimation algorithms that produce the actual scores, are very different; more importantly, A–M is based on individual-level responses, whereas the starting point of our own model are data aggregated at the country-year level in the form of "pro-market response percentages." Substantively, both the A–M and the policy mood scores are estimates of the *economic policy preferences* of a representative centrist citizen; this similarity is aided by the fact that we use similar policy questions as inputs into both methods.[9]

In contrast, *voter-revealed rightism* is different in that it does not aim to summarize a series of policy attitudes and stances, but rather the placements of Latin American citizenries on an ideological continuum that may or may not be related to economic policy. *Voter-revealed rightism* uses vote shares of political parties to weight left–right scores assigned by experts. Admittedly, *left* and *right* are commonly employed labels that in principle should correspond to economic policy stances, although this correspondence tends to be low among Latin American citizens. The broad consensus is that the label *left* corresponds to policies that promote state intervention, whereas *right* refers to market-oriented policies. However, the meanings of *left* and *right* can vary across time and place, and often include policy matters beyond the economy (issues of morality, attitudes toward the environment, etc.) and even broader non-policy pronouncements (the left advocates "social justice," the right promotes "family values"). Consequently, we would not expect as tight of a correspondence between *voter-revealed rightism*, on the one hand, and A–M scores or policy moods, on the other (cf. Bauer et al. 2017, for a recent analysis of the semantics of left and right). We still compare our policy moods against *voter-revealed rightism* because such measures are often employed in analyses of democratic representation.

How then do these indices fit together? Table 3.3 compiles correlation coefficients among these different scales based on pairwise complete observations. The differences are telling. On the one hand, the correlation between policy

---

[9] We do not use an identical set of policy questions because the flexibility of our model allows incorporation of a much larger set of stimuli. Thus, instead of the twenty-four policy items that we use to build our policy mood scores, we rely on a smaller subset of thirteen of these items to estimate the A–M scores (see Table A.1 in Online Appendix A).

TABLE 3.3. *Pairwise-complete correlations among three different scales*

	Policy mood	A–M score
A–M score	0.73	—
Voter-revealed rightism	0.12	0.16

moods and A–M scores is high and statistically significant at conventional levels (0.73, SE: 0.04). This is expected, as both measures rely on a similar set of stimuli to infer economic policy stances of Latin American citizens. Note, however, that the A–M and policy mood scores follow from two very different scaling algorithms, connected only by the philosophy of accounting for variation in a large number of stimuli using one latent dimension. We consider this high correlation index to be evidence that both of these methods recover actual information about policy moods from the collection of stimuli that we feed into the algorithms.[10]

In contrast, we only observe a small, though still positive, correlation between *voter-revealed rightism* and policy moods (and a similarly small positive correlation between *voter-revealed rightism* and A–M scores). We are not the first to uncover a disconnect between the concepts of left and right, on the one hand, and the economic policy positions of individuals in Latin America. One potential reason for this disconnect might be that the semantic contents of "left" and "right" vary from country to country – and even within countries – and may capture public opinion with respect to noneconomic policies and traits (Bauer et al. 2017, Benoit and Laver 2007). It is entirely possible that our measures of the economic policy mood fail to correlate with left–right scores because Latin American citizens may use these labels to describe their attitudes toward noneconomic concerns such as minority rights, questions of sexual morality, or other "culture war" issues (Zechmeister 2006, Zechmeister and Corral 2010).

Furthermore, recall that *voter-revealed rightism* scores are based on the knowledge of country experts about the stances, mostly in terms of economic policy, that Latin American political parties take. But they also depend on vote shares, that is, on observed voting behavior by citizens, a component that is

---

[10] Incidentally, we calculated A–M scores multiple times based on a number of alternative rules: (i) running blackbox on a pooled data set containing all eighteen citizenries, so that country-specific policy moods were forced on the exact same metric; (ii) running blackbox on country-specific citizen sets, as we do with the McGann mechanism, but then carrying out a Procrustes rotation so that all citizen scores would line up as closely as possible to the scores of Argentina; (iii) running blackbox on country-specific citizen sets, but leaving country-specific policy moods unrotated. The resulting time-paths remain very similar to each other regardless of the algorithm that we use. See Online Appendix A for an explanation of blackbox and the Procrustes rotation method.

farther removed from citizens' economic stances. In other words, individuals that would never self-describe as rightists but happen to vote for a party that experts consider to be on the right of the political spectrum end up increasing the voter-revealed rightism score. Furthermore, although the economic stances of political parties surely have an impact on the electoral choices of the citizenry, electoral choice is also determined by a number of additional factors, such as perceived valence or charisma of candidates, incumbent effects, or corruption scandals.[11] For this reason, constructs like voter-revealed rightism could well end up being too far removed from the actual economic policy opinions of citizens that we are interested in.[12]

We have ample confidence in the validity of "policy moods" as a measure of preferences over economic policies – state or market – as a result of their relatively high correlation with the A–M scores. In turn, we prefer our model to A–M for a number of reasons: (i) it is based on more responses to stimuli about a wider array of economic policies, (ii) it is based on clear micro-foundations about citizen beliefs that yield a larger number of inferences about the location and distribution of policy moods, (iii) it depends on aggregate information that is less noisy than individual information, and (iv) it allows us to set *opinions* on economic policy and observed *implementations* of economic policy on the same scale, as we detail in Chapter 6. Our fundamental aim is to determine how institutional linkages in the democratic process affect the translation between citizens' preferences and enacted policy. What is it about the institutional designs of separation of powers systems that makes policy more-or-less congruent and responsive? We have thus built an instrument that is best suited to capturing citizens' preferences over economic policies.

---

[11] To wit, Baker and Greene (2011, 71) report a mild correlation (−0.22) between a measure of "mass support for the market" and their index of *voter-revealed leftism*. This is a correlation coefficient of magnitude similar to the one we report here. See Warwick and Zakharova (2013) for an explanation of why Kim–Fording voter-revealed measures of ideology may misrepresent median citizen preferences (see also Stevenson 2000, 624).

[12] In addition to A–M scores and *voter-revealed rightism*, we also used self-reported left–right stances of respondents as an alternative yardstick. At the aggregate level, this measure correlates very poorly not only with policy moods and A–M scores, but even with *voter-revealed rightism*. The problem extends to individual-level data, as the average within-country correlation between left–right self-placement and A–M scores is 0.04 (the interquartile range is −0.02 to 0.09, and, although the maximum correlation is 0.27, the minimum observed correlation is −0.18.) Thus, even at the individual level we see that knowing a respondent's self-reported left–right score tells us basically nothing about the respondent's inferred policy positions. In other contexts (e.g., in European politics [cf. Stevenson 2000] or among politicians in Latin America) there may be a shorter distance between the left–right self-placement of individuals and their economic policy attitudes, but there is too much of a distance between these constructs among Latin American voters to make left–right self-placements valuable to our enterprise.

3.4 CHAPTER SUMMARY

We started this chapter by presenting the attitudinal stimuli that we use to understand how Latin American citizenries think about the choice between "state" and "market" when it comes to economic policy-making. We thus inspected citizen policy moods in Latin America, providing a sense of how these have moved over the almost two decades that go from 1996 to 2014.

With the policy moods we have inferred, we could in principle reflect on a number of descriptive characteristics. For example, we find that the country with most variation in citizen policy moods is Mexico (the variance of its policy moods is 0.58), whereas Bolivia is the place where citizen moods vary the least (variance is 0.19). The Dominican Republic in 2007 is the country that reaches the maximum pro-market policy mood, whereas the lowest, most state-centric policy mood obtains in Mexico in 2008. On average, Argentina tends to be the least pro-market citizenry (0.26), whereas Honduras, Nicaragua, Paraguay, and Venezuela have, on average, the highest pro-market policy mood scores. These scores naturally change year after year, and, as a cursory look at this list suggests, they are probably not always reflected in the preferences of policy-makers. Colombia, Costa Rica, Nicaragua, and Uruguay have the lowest levels of preference heterogeneity, whereas Argentina, Bolivia, Guatemala, and Venezuela appear to have much higher heterogeneity. These and other characteristics of citizen moods can be easily expressed, but we obviously mean to employ them to analyze patterns of congruence and responsiveness in the region.

In the next chapter, we introduce the data that we employ to estimate the policy moods of Latin American legislators. Because our theory about institutional mediation in the chain of responsiveness requires that we measure the policy preferences of other elected policy-makers, we will explain how we also produce policy mood estimates for senators and presidents.

4

Stage 2: Policy-Makers' Preferences

Just as we described the policy mood of citizens in Chapter 3, in this chapter we present an overview of the policy moods of Latin American policy-makers. A quandary we confront is the paucity of data from which we can extract policy moods. This obstacle is more formidable when we consider politicians relative to citizens. To see why, consider that we need policy mood estimates for three different sets of actors: deputies (lower or only house members), senators (upper house members), and presidents. Estimating the policy moods of legislators in unicameral systems or in lower houses in bicameral systems is relatively easy, as we take advantage of the frequent surveys of Latin American lower or only house members made public by the Parliamentary Elites of Latin America (PELA) project. These surveys sample members of congress from across the region every legislative term and contain attitudinal information about their preferences over economic policies (among many other things).

Unfortunately, we lack similar information about the attitudes of senators and presidents in Latin America. As we hinted at earlier, inferring the policy moods of these actors requires that we embrace a number of additional assumptions. In order to estimate the policy moods of senators, we essentially assume that these actors have attitudes and beliefs that are similar to those of their lower chamber copartisans, then take account of variations in the seat shares that parties hold in the upper house and lower house in order to estimate senatorial policy moods. A different set of assumptions underscores our estimates of the policy moods of presidents. As we detail later, we use legislators' left-right placements of the executive along with their own left-right self-placements to infer the policy moods of presidents. We hope to convince the reader that these assumptions, while admittedly not innocuous, are also not too heroic and lead to plausible estimates of the policy moods of actors who are not surveyed directly.

While we did avoid making similar assumptions to capture the moods of citizens, the analysis of political elite attitudes based on the PELA surveys offers some relative advantages too. In the PELA surveys, question wording is more consistent across countries and across waves than is the case with the AmericasBarometer (AB) and LatinBarometer (LB) citizen surveys used in Chapter 3. Furthermore, the PELA surveys contain, comparatively speaking, a much larger number of stimuli directly related to economic policy. We open with a review of the surveys and items at our disposal in Section 4.1 before proceeding to a description of the policy moods of Latin American deputies, senators, and presidents in Section 4.2.

Before starting in earnest, we make one last clarification about the terms we employ. The names of legislative chambers vary across the unicameral and bicameral systems of Latin America. For the sake of consistency, we will use "house" to refer to lower or only chambers and "senate" to refer to the upper chambers of bicameral systems. We will use "representatives" or "deputies" interchangeably to refer to members of a lower or only house. We will use the term "senators" to refer to members of the upper house. We use the terms "members of congress" (MCs) and "legislators" to refer to all members of the legislative branch, either in lower or upper houses.

4.1 DATA COVERAGE FOR POLICY-MAKERS' PREFERENCES

Just like with citizens, politicians' policy moods can be understood as latent dimensions that synthesize the opinions of individuals regarding whether governments should rely on state intervention or market allocation to generate superior economic outcomes. Although we cannot observe policy moods directly, we can derive them from the analysis of the attitudes and opinions that politicians hold in a number of more specific policy areas. Under the original guidance of Manuel Alcántara at the University of Salamanca, the PELA project has published to date seventy-nine legislative surveys, with a handful more on the way. Throughout the past two decades, these surveys have been timed to maximize coverage of parliamentary elites. As a rule of thumb, a PELA team has visited the lower or only chamber of every new congress elected in Latin America since the mid-1990s with the goal of interviewing a sizable sample of legislators.[1]

---

[1] We cannot always tell whether PELA respondent samples are drawn randomly from lists of all available legislators. Our understanding is that the Salamanca teams interview as many legislators as they can, especially in the smaller legislatures in the region. The original sampling procedure appears to have been a snowball technique in which each respondent suggested a number of legislators that could be further interviewed. This process led to samples that did not always mirror the actual distribution of seat shares in the national assemblies (seat shares appear in Table B.2 in Online Appendix B). We guard against obvious size mismatches between samples and populations by weighting observations up or down based on partisanship (see fn. 3).

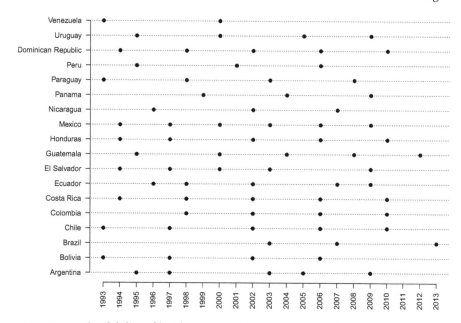

FIGURE 4.1. Availability of legislator survey data across countries and years.
The figure depicts, for each country in our sample, the years in which PELA surveys were fielded.

Figure 4.1 depicts the timing of the surveys available to us. As is obvious from the graph, the main distinction between the citizen data of Chapter 3 and the legislative surveys we inspect in this chapter is that the latter are not collected simultaneously across countries. The reason is that collection times depend on country-specific electoral calendars. We can rely on about four to five surveys in most countries during the period 1993–2013, with a minimum of two surveys in Venezuela – which the Salamanca team would not visit again after 2005 – and six surveys in Mexico – which was regularly visited every three years upon installment of a new congress. On average, we avail ourselves of 4.2 surveys per country. Consequently, the amount of information that we can use to build legislators' policy moods is much more sparse time-serially than the amount of information available to infer citizen moods, for which we basically have annual policy mood scores in each country. In contrast, the policy mood of house members (and, as a derivative, of senators and presidents) can only be measured at the *congressional session* level. Table B.1 in Online Appendix B lists the timing of the surveys and the congressional sessions for which these surveys provide information.

Regarding the economic policy stimuli on which we base our inferences about the policy moods of legislators, we adhere to the same rules of thumb that determined which items we could use to infer citizen policy moods. First, we base the legislative policy moods on as many economic policy questions as possible, subject to the constraint that the questions have to be repeated at least in two different surveys within a country. Second, again as with questions put to citizens, we recode all original responses so that larger numbers correspond to pro-market positions, after which we carry out multiple imputation at the individual level to work with complete data.[2] Third, we aggregate the complete responses at the congressional session level, calculating the percentage of legislators that register a pro-market response for each available policy stimulus. As we did for our citizen samples, we weight individual responses so that the aggregate information (i.e., the *weighted* percentage of legislators that register a pro-market response) will more closely resemble the opinions of the assembly as a whole, placing particular care to avoid overrepresentation of parties with a disproportionately large number of respondents. The weights that we employ simply correct a party's share of sample respondents by a factor that reflects the party's seat share in the legislature (house and senate seat shares appear in Table B.2 in Online Appendix B).[3] These *weighted pro-market percentages* constitute the raw inputs that we use to estimate legislator policy mood scores, as we will detail in Chapter 6.

To give the reader a sense of the types of questions that are available in the PELA legislative surveys, Figure 4.2 shows the stimuli at our disposal for Brazil and Mexico (in general, there is ample consistency in item availability across countries and years). Mexico is a good example of the type of data found in the Salamanca surveys. Note first that many of these items have labels that are identical to the ones we employed in the analysis of citizens in Chapter 3. We hasten to emphasize that the questions that correspond to these labels, although equivalent in spirit to those in the mass citizen surveys, are not always worded in an identical manner. Exact wordings for all the items that we employ appear in Appendix A.

We can make use of up to fifteen potential items, even though no single survey asks all of them. For example, the survey collected in Mexico in 2000 contains a maximum of fourteen items, but the number of available items is much smaller in other rounds. For 2009, for example, we can only use six

---

[2] We carry out multiple imputation based on the chained equations routines of van Buuren and Groothuis-Oudshoorn (2011). As predictors, we include available legislator responses to the policy items under analysis, plus legislator self-placement on a left-right ideological scale, and legislator placement of the country's president on the same scale. Contrary to the multiple-imputation routine for citizens, we do not include legislators' socioeconomic information in the predictor set. Whereas socioeconomic information is valuable in helping us predict attitudes and opinions of citizens, this kind of information is seldom useful in predicting the attitudes and opinions of professional politicians; in contrast, politicians are more adept than citizens, at least in Latin America, at mapping policy attitudes on shared understandings of left and right, as we argue later. We use one full set of individual-level data for each legislature, which ignores imputation uncertainty while keeping data management simple.

[3] For party p in legislature l, the weight w that we use is $w_{pl} = c_{pl}/s_{pl}$, where c is party p's *seat share* in legislature l and s is party p's *sample share* in the survey that corresponds to legislature l.

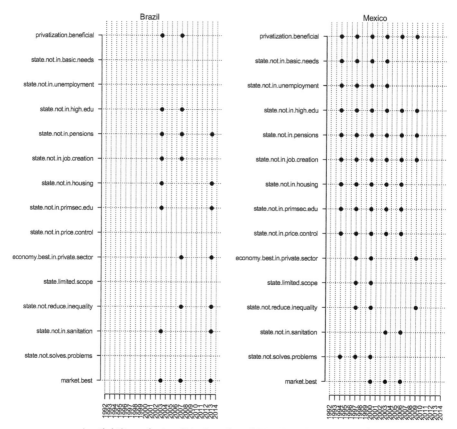

FIGURE 4.2. Availability of stimuli in Brazil and Mexico. As an example of data availability, the figure depicts the PELA survey items (or *stimuli*) available to us for Brazil (left panel) and Mexico (right panel). Instances in which the stimulus was available in a given year are indicated with a solid circle.

questions. The items that are more consistently asked across time and countries are `privatization.beneficial`, `state.not.in.high.edu`,[4] `state .not.in.pensions`, and `state.not.in.job.creation`, which are asked in all six survey waves. In the case of Brazil, a few items like `state.not .in.unemployment`, `state.not.in.price.control`, and `state.not .in.basic.needs` are asked only in one survey, and it therefore is impossible to use them to infer how policy moods change throughout time (consequently, we omit these items in Figure 4.2). Elsewhere, we have at the very least six items per year on which to base our legislative policy mood scores (the average number of available items per survey across all surveys is 9.86).

___

[4] This particular abbreviation stands for "the state should not be involved in the provision of higher education."

The PELA surveys are a veritable treasure trove of information on the attitudes and beliefs of Latin American legislators. They contain a much larger array of policy items than the ones included here, including a number of stimuli that collect information on legislators' dispositions toward regional integration, government collaboration with international financial institutions, the ability of trade agreements to promote job creation, the role of imports in fostering or hindering the national economy, and the desirability of wooing foreign capital. All of these are economic policy items in their own right. We exclude them from our analysis because we could not always find similar stimuli among citizens and because they tend to be asked more sporadically. The fifteen items that we inspect, in contrast, are asked repeatedly across countries and years and, for the most part, find similar correlates among items in the mass opinion surveys of AB and LB.

4.1.1 Inferring the Issue Stances of Other Political Actors

One of our main contributions is the comparative examination of separation-of-powers or presidential systems. A full inspection of the chain of responsiveness that ties citizens to policies requires that we infer policy moods not only for members of a single chamber, but also for members of the other chamber, if there is one, and for the executive too. This is a seemingly impossible task given that we lack survey responses for members of upper chambers and presidents. To address this serious limitation, we need to make a number of auxiliary assumptions about the similarities between the issue stances of house members, on the one hand, and the issue stances of senators and presidents, on the other.

The Policy Moods of Senators. Nine countries – Argentina, Bolivia, Brazil, Colombia, Chile, the Dominican Republic, Mexico, Paraguay, and Uruguay – have bicameral legislative systems. Peru and Venezuela abolished their upper houses in 1992 and 1999, respectively – meaning Peru's upper house was abolished before the beginning of the PELA surveys. For Venezuela, in contrast, we could have used PELA information to make inferences about the policy mood of the upper house elected in that country in 1993 – this was the next-to-last upper house elected in the country before the 1999 Bolivarian constitution eliminated this body. Unfortunately, our algorithm to calculate policy moods requires that we have policy items for at least two different years, and the only other Venezuelan survey that we have is from the unicameral legislature elected in 2000. We thus decided to drop Venezuela's Senate from our analysis altogether. Otherwise, our method of obtaining policy moods for Latin American upper houses will be identical to the one we use to elicit policy moods for lower houses, starting from *weighted pro-market percentages* – that is, aggregate information about the shares of senators that support a pro-market stance on a given issue area. In fact, the only difference is that we build weighted pro-market percentages using weights based on the relative seat shares of parties in the *senate*, instead of the seat shares of parties in the *house* (these appear in Online Appendix B; in Table B.1 in that appendix, we also note which surveys correspond to which senatorial terms).

Thus, in order to infer the policy moods of upper houses, we have to explicitly embrace the assumption that the policy opinions of senators are similar to those of their copartisan legislators in the house. It is difficult to assess the verisimilitude of this assumption. On the one hand, one can certainly point to differences in the voting behavior and pronouncements of senate and house members in countries like the United States to suggest that even members of the same party may hold contrasting views on any given policy area. However, differential voting behavior across chambers in the United States may be a function of strategic responses to differences in the ideological make-up of the constituencies that these politicians represent, rather than honest disagreements in attitudes, beliefs, and worldviews from members of the same party.

On the other hand, one would expect self-selection of politicians into different political parties to engender organizations made up of relatively like-minded senators and deputies, especially in parties that have a clear programmatic profile. And even if political parties lack a clear programmatic profile, we would anticipate ideological incoherence to be equally manifest in lower and upper houses, again suggesting little difference in the overall issue stances of deputies and senators that belong to the same party. It was, after all, the perceived similarity in the opinions and beliefs of members of lower and upper houses, among other arguments, that led to the elimination of upper houses in Peru and Venezuela in the 1990s. These countries moved toward unicameralism based on the notion that the upper house duplicated the make-up of the lower house. In evaluating this argument, Carey (2003) suggests that the old Peruvian Senate and Congress showed similar degrees of malapportionment, and therefore may have represented similar constituencies, whereas in Venezuela the party composition of both chambers was so similar that they may have even had identical ideological profiles.[5] In view of this evidence, we think it reasonable to assume that copartisan legislators and senators subscribe to similar views, and we build senate policy moods based on this assumption.

The inferred policy moods of lower and upper houses are based on the same data and only differ in the weighting scheme – the party seat shares – that we use to build them. The correlation between senate party seat shares and house party seat shares based on 274 parties with representation in the senates of nine countries is 0.86. Only one country – the Dominican Republic – shows marked systematic disparity in party seat shares in upper and lower houses, as can be seen in Figure 4.3. Despite any differences in the ways in which upper and lower houses are elected, the strong correlation in party seat shares indicates that

---

[5] For several elections after the reestablishment of democracy in 1958, Venezuelan voters cast a single, "fused" ballot (or "small card") to elect members to both the Chamber of Deputies and the Senate. Thus, candidates for the lower house and the upper house of the same party had no electoral incentive to distinguish themselves from one another (Crisp 2000).

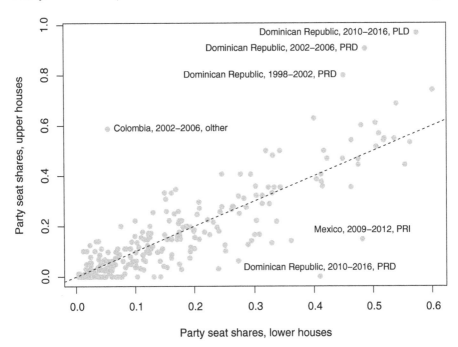

FIGURE 4.3. Discrepant seat shares in upper and lower houses. The figure depicts the strong relation between party seats shares in the lower and upper houses of bicameral countries in our sample. The 1-1 correspondence line is dashed, and party legislature instances that deviate from that 1-1 relationship are labeled, along with their country of origin. PLD, Partido de la Liberación Dominicana (Dominican Liberation Party); PRD, Partido Revolucionario Dominicano (Dominican Revolutionary Party); PRI, Partido Revolucionario Institucional (Institutional Revolutionary Party).

parties with large seat shares in one chamber are likely to have a similarly large seat share in the other, even after accounting for the fact that upper houses are generally more disproportional than lower houses. Combining our assumption that copartisans across chambers share positions on economic policy with the highly correlated electoral performances of parties across chambers, it is easy to see that the policy moods of these different bodies will be very similar to each other.

Aside from mild differences in party shares across lower and upper houses, a second component introduces some variation in the policy moods of these bodies. Because the terms of upper and lower houses do not always coincide (the former tend to be longer), we find senate terms that overlap with two house terms and for which we then have information from two different surveys. In our data set, this happens for the Mexican senates in 2000–2006 and 2006–2012. We estimate two policy moods for each of these senates, but we then combine them into a single average estimate of the policy mood for the entire period (i.e., six years) that the senate is in a particular session. This coding decision does not change substantively our estimates of the policy moods of the Mexican Senate.

Presidential Policy Moods. Clearly, we also need to measure presidential policy moods to analyze congruence and responsiveness in separation of powers systems. Strictly speaking, we would require information about presidents' stances and opinions on economic policy issues in order to arrive at inferences about presidential policy moods. The quandary we face is that presidents are not regularly surveyed. In fact, they are not surveyed at all: there is, to our knowledge, no systematic compendium of the economic policy opinions of recent Latin American presidents. Recent scholarship resorts to party policy programs and campaign documents to infer presidential moods, as in the Comparative Manifesto Project (see, inter alia, Budge and Klingemann 2001). Unfortunately, the available corpus of campaign programs in Latin America is too limited to make this a practical option. Arnold, Doyle, and Wiesehomeier (2017) carry out text analysis of inauguration and state-of-the-union speeches to infer presidential moods, but the moods derived from these data appear to be too driven by a strategic logic of compromise, rather than by sincere stances on issues, which is what we seek to obtain by considering anonymous surveys. Presidential positions on a number of issues could arguably be obtained from campaign pronouncements, but these would also be affected by strategic posturing (in fact, Stokes [2001] describes "policy switches" – a marked lack of correspondence between campaign pronouncements and policy-making of elected presidents – as an important phenomenon in Latin America in the early 1990s).

In short, we simply lack information about the policy stances of presidents similar to the information that we employ to build legislators' policy moods. To obtain some insight into the opinions and issue stances of presidents, we exploit information provided by legislators about their perceptions of the president's left-right position. Because we also have access to the legislators' own left-right self-placements, we can use these items to "bridge" the legislators' policy opinions and the policy opinions of the president. To do so, we use left-right placements to predict the president's opinions from the issue-stances of legislators, then aggregate these opinions into *weighted pro-market percentages* where the weights correspond to the proportion of legislators that would presumably see the president as holding a pro-market stance on a particular issue.

An example will make this procedure transparent and also provide readers with a better sense about the limits of this approach. Consider the 2000 round of the PELA survey in Mexico, which has a sample size of 124 legislators. Each of these respondents expresses an opinion on fourteen policy items. Each respondent also furnishes information about self-placement on a left-right scale and about their perception of the president's location on that same scale. Our procedure requires that we first regress responses to *each* policy item, observed across 124 legislators, on left-right self-placements; we then use the estimated coefficients from this regression model to predict the president's opinions on policy items based on the legislators' perception of the president's left-right position. In Mexico 2000, a regression of, say, `market.best` on left-right self-placement yields least-squares estimates of $\hat{\alpha} = 3.39$ (SD $= 0.37$) for the intercept and $\hat{\beta} = 0.25$ (SD $= 0.07$) for the slope coefficient.[6] Our prediction of legislator *i*'s assessment of the president's opinion on `market.best`, call it $\hat{y}_i$, is then $\hat{y}_i = \hat{\alpha} + \hat{\beta} \cdot$ president LR placement$_i$.

In this fashion, we obtain 124 predictions, one from each legislator, about the Mexican president's `market.best` score. From these opinions, we can then obtain a "pro-market percentage" – that is, the proportion of legislators that "score" the president as having a pro-market opinion on the policy item `market.best`. The president has a pro-market opinion when this inferred score is larger than the sample average for the item in question (this is the same procedure that we followed for the case of citizens and legislators, except that in those cases we used the exact midpoint of the scale, rather than the observed sample average, as the cutoff point). This percentage, along with thirteen other percentages corresponding to the other policy stimuli in this particular PELA survey, are the ones we use as input to elicit the policy mood of Mexico's president ca. 2000. We follow the same procedure to build *weighted pro-market percentages* of all other presidents during the period under observation.

Building *weighted pro-market percentages* for presidents in this way requires that we buy into two assumptions. First, we must believe that a legislator's self-assessed position on a left-right scale is a good indicator of her policy stances. We argued in Chapter 3 that left-right self-placement is seldom a good predictor of policy stances among Latin American *citizens*, but our expectations are different when it comes to politicians as these are generally more capable of elaborating on the correspondence between left and right and a notional economic-distributive divide (see fns. 2 and 6). Second, we must also believe that legislators are capable of locating presidents on the same left-right scale where they place themselves. We do not have reasons to expect that legislators would be systematically "wrong" in placing presidents in positions where they do not belong (a right-wing president perceived as left-wing), although we do

---

[6] We do not concern ourselves with the fit of the regression (which in this case is $R^2 = 0.9$), nor with the statistical significance of the predictors. The auxiliary regressions we run serve the exclusive purpose of furnishing guesses about the president's opinions. Be this as it may, the pooled correlations between `left.right` and the policy items that we inspect are always positive, as one would expect if politicians were adept at using the concepts "left" and "right" to summarize their economic policy stances: 0.10 (`state.not.in.sanitation`), 0.36 (`state.not.in.price.control`), 0.12 (`state.not.in.primsec.edu`), 0.17 (`state.not.in.housing`), 0.17 (`state.not.in.job.creation`), 0.16 (`state.not.in.pensions`), 0.19 (`state.not.in.high.edu`), 0.26 (`privatization.beneficial`), 0.11 (`state.not.solves.problems`), 0.27 (`state.not.reduce.inequality`), 0.24 (`state.limited.scope`), 0.25 (`economy.best.in.private.sector`), 0.16 (`state.not.in.unemployment`), 0.16 (`state.not.in.basic.needs`).

find that, compared to "rightist" members of a legislature, legislators that self-place as "leftists" tend to place executives slightly more to the right.[7]

Finally, as was the case with senators, there are a number of presidents whose terms overlap with two different legislative terms, and for whom we can therefore use information from two different legislative surveys. This is the case for executives in Argentina (1995–1999), El Salvador (1994–1999 and 1999–2004), and Mexico (1994–2000, 2000–2006, and 2006–2012). We estimate two policy moods for each of these executives, but we then combine them into a single average estimate of their policy mood, just as we did in the case of the Mexican Senate. As was the case with the policy moods of senators, this coding decision does not change markedly our inferences about the policy moods of presidents.

4.2 POLICY-MAKER POLICY MOODS IN LATIN AMERICA, 1993–2013

As we did in Chapter 3, we first inspect aggregate information about the policy stances of Latin American policy-makers, that is, we show what the average Latin American representative, senator, and president policy moods look like. Consider Figure 4.4(a); labeled gray dots correspond to the point estimates of the policy moods of seventy-six lower or only houses in Latin America between 1993 and 2013, while the overlaid continuous black line traces the smoothed "overall policy mood" of Latin American house members during the period under inspection (we add a 95 percent uncertainty band around this regional policy mood). Each point estimate can best be thought of as the policy mood of the "median legislator" in one lower or only house, and we present median legislators across the full set of Latin American assemblies for which we could examine data during the two decades following 1993. As was the case with citizens, we notice that between-year variance is much larger than within-year variance (1.05 and 0.15, respectively), which confirms the impression one obtains from the graph that moods tend to cluster tightly within years.

However, we can also see that, in stark contrast with the long up-and-down pattern in the policy moods of Latin American citizens that we found in Figure 3.3 – which veered from state protectionism to market enthusiasm to state protectionism again – there is a strong overall trend among deputies toward the pro-state pole of the continuum, with a slight leveling of the mood toward the end of the observation period (most likely driven by the rather marked pro-market tilt that we estimate in the 2011 Brazilian Congress). Whereas the mood was more hospitable to pro-market positions at the beginning of the observation period in the mid-1990s, the typical Latin American *median legislator* is less pro-market by 2010. The aggregate "turn" away

---

[7] There is basically no correlation between self-placements and president placements along a left-right scale, as one would expect (the correlation coefficient pooled across all surveys is 0.07).

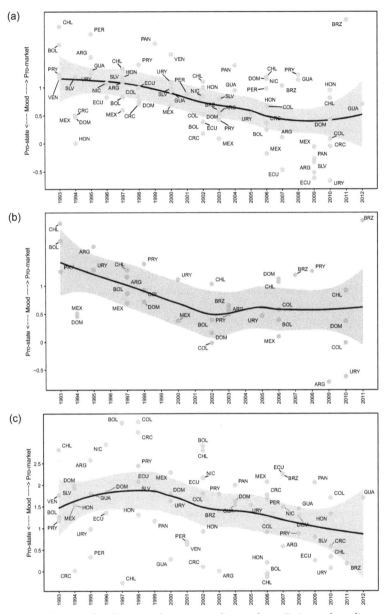

FIGURE 4.4. Estimated policy moods among policy-makers. Estimated median policy moods of (a) seventy-six lower houses, (b) thirty-seven senates, and (c) sixty-nine presidencies in eighteen Latin American countries, from 1993 through 2013. Moods in a given year are shown as solid gray circles, labeled so as to improve readability. The continuous black line (along with nonparametric uncertainty band) traces the smoothed "overall policy mood" of Latin American policy-makers during the period under inspection. Higher values along the vertical axis indicate more pro-market moods.

from markets that we observe in the figure takes the form of a gradual shift. This gradual shift contrasts with the common narrative of a sudden "pink tide" that swept Latin American politics following the election of Chávez in Venezuela in 1998; according to this narrative, that election ushered in an abrupt indictment of the "neoliberal" policies adopted in Latin America during the 1990s. An indictment it may have been, but a panoramic view suggests that it was not an abrupt one, and that it followed an anti-market trend in legislative policy moods that had started before 1998.

This same pattern of gradual but continuous change away from decidedly pro-market positions characterizes the policy moods of the median senators in those countries with bicameral arrangements (Figure 4.4(b)). We detailed earlier why, given both data availability and methods, on the one hand, and substantive knowledge of partisan politics in the region, on the other, similarity across chambers was to be expected. Indeed, there is a strong regional pattern in the senate policy moods, with much of the variation in the data obtaining from the temporal trend in policy moods away from the "market" end (between-year variance is 0.86), and much lower variation across countries within the same year (within-year variance is 0.14), which is similar to the house policy moods depicted in Figure 4.4(a).

We do see more contrast when we consider estimates of the policy moods of Latin American presidents. First, notice that variation in the policy moods of presidents is as likely to come from year-to-year movements that are identical across countries as from country-to-country differences within the same year (between- and within-year variances are 0.95 and 0.78, respectively). That is, knowing the policy mood of Chile's president in 1993 is about as helpful for predicting the policy mood of Chile's president in 1997 as it is for predicting the policy mood of Paraguay's president in 1993. It is useful to reflect on what this means: in separation of powers systems, voters can elect presidents that often present starker, more differentiated positions against or in favor of the market than the "average" position of copartisan candidates to congress or senate, which likely explains why we have high within-year variation. Furthermore, in looking at presidencies and legislatures, we compare an *individual* executive against a *collective* legislature whose composition rarely changes drastically from one election to the next. In other words, substituting a leftist for a rightist president has a large impact on the presidential policy mood, whereas substituting a majority leftist for a majority rightist legislature may not produce that much of a change in the legislative policy mood, which after all corresponds to the mood of the median legislator.

Second, an obvious secular tilt away from the market pole in the regional presidential mood starts only relatively late, compared with what we see among legislatures. By the end of the observation window the general mood is certainly less pro-market than at the beginning of the observation period, but in between the general mood veered in a pro-market direction during the late 1990s. At the same time, most of the presidents that made up the "pink tide" are correctly identified as having pro-state policy moods. This is the case of the presidents of Argentina, Bolivia, Brazil, Chile, Peru, Uruguay, and Venezuela. The presidents of Colombia and Mexico, the two largest countries in the region where a leftist party had not yet been able to capture the presidency by 2017, are estimated as holding pro-market moods. But we also observe a few estimates that we find mystifying. For starters, the position of the Venezuelan president in 2001 (Chávez) is estimated as about as leftist as that of the Chilean president in 2010 (Piñera, who was the standard bearer of a right-wing coalition). Some cherry-picking of these results is likely to turn out other estimates that do not always correspond to the reputations of presidents among experts. This might introduce grave concerns about the validity of our inferences regarding presidential policy moods. However, we show below that, despite these occasional awkward estimates, there is a relatively high correspondence between inferred policy moods of presidents and expert assessments of where their parties should be placed on a left–right continuum. We also speak more to the advantages of basing executive policy moods on the opinions of contemporaneous politicians, rather than on expert placements of presidential parties, which are an obvious alternative.

4.2.1 Representatives

We see greater diversity at the country level in the paths that policy moods take through time, at least more so than in the citizen policy moods of Chapter 3, which were relatively homogeneous across countries. Consider the country-specific plots in Figure 4.5. The segments in these plots correspond to point estimates of the house, senate (where appropriate), and president policy moods based on data from the PELA surveys that we described in Section 4.1. Start with the lower or only house point estimates, marked in a medium shade of gray: each segment covers the entire period through which the corresponding legislature was in place; the black line within the segment provides a point estimate, and the width of the bar corresponds to the interquartile range of the posterior distribution of the policy mood for the legislature, which is a measure of uncertainty about this estimate. Next to these segments we have included the name of the largest party in the legislature, along with its corresponding seat share, for easy reference. One can see that the policy moods in legislatures like those in Argentina, Bolivia, or Uruguay follow a path that coincides with the overall pattern presented in Figure 4.4. These are legislatures in which a pro-market policy mood for the median legislator in the mid-1990s eventually gives rise to a more accentuated pro-state sentiment. A second pattern obtains in legislatures like those of the Dominican Republic or Nicaragua, where the policy mood of the median legislator remains mostly static through time. In Brazil, in contrast, the policy mood appears to move toward pro-market positions in the legislature that started in 2011. This may seem paradoxical, given that this was the first term in power of President Dilma Rousseff, from

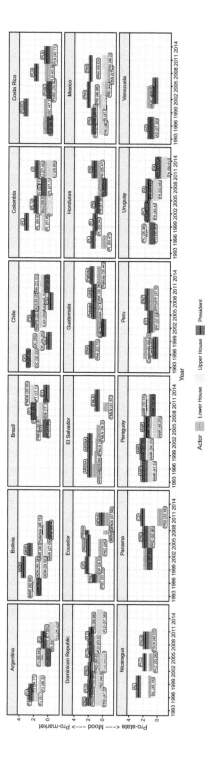

FIGURE 4.5. Policy moods of policy-makers in eighteen Latin American countries. Each plot contains the estimated policy mood of a country's president (dark gray), lower house median legislator (medium gray), and upper house median senator (light gray). The black line within each graph is the median – and the gray segments correspond to the interquartile range – of the posterior distribution of each actor's policy mood.

the leftist Partido dos Trabalhadores; consider though that this party, despite having the largest contingent in Brazil's Congress, held a relatively modest seat share (17.1 percent), which means that it is reasonable to expect that the median legislator may be far away from the policy sentiment of the Partido dos Trabalhadores (Workers' Party).

As was the case with the policy moods of citizens, one major challenge is to assess the verisimilitude of the policy mood scores we have generated for Latin American legislatures. The most obvious concern is that the scores might be artifacts, rather than informed by the survey responses of legislators. A quick look at the *weighted pro-market percentages* that constitute the raw inputs in our analysis suggests that most legislatures have indeed seen a sustained pro-state turn among their members, which is duly reflected in Figure 4.4. For example, in Argentina, the average proportion of respondents that chose pro-market responses across available stimuli in 1995, 1997, 2003, 2007, and 2009 were, respectively, 0.48, 0.35, 0.33, 0.33, and 0.28. Corresponding to these decreasing proportions, we estimate the legislative policy mood in Argentina for these years as 1.54, 1.10, 0.54, 0.11, and −0.51. Except for 2009, these were all legislatures in which the Peronist Justicialista party had either an outright majority of seats or a plurality so large as to be functionally equivalent to an outright majority (the party still held the largest plurality, at about 34 percent, in 2009). However, these scores line up well with common knowledge about the ideological factions within the Peronist party that supported Presidents Carlos Menem (up to 1999), and Néstor Kirchner and Cristina Fernández de Kirchner (2003–2015).

As a second example, we see a pattern in Mexico where average pro-market proportions moved up and down from 0.39 (1994) to 0.35 (1997), 0.37 (2000), 0.32 (2003), 0.25 (2006), and finally to 0.34 (2009). During this period, however, the corresponding policy mood estimates for the lower house are 0.48, 0.60, 0.69, 0.09, −0.18, and −0.05 (starting in 1997, no political party had a majority presence in the lower chamber; the PRI would eventually lose its plurality to the Partido Acción Nacional (National Action Party) in 2003). Mexico's case shows that the policy moods of deputies can move with some independence of the weighted pro-market percentages on which they are based. As pro-market responses decreased from 1994 to 1997, the policy mood between these two years actually moved rightward – that is, toward the market pole of the policy continuum. Our modeling choices explain this and other similar results: increments in weighted pro-market percentages may be produced (i) by rightward shifts in the policy mood of the median legislator and/or (ii) by an increase in the spread of preferences around the policy mood of the median legislator, what we call *legislative heterogeneity* (in Chapter 6 we detail how our model allows estimation of separate "heterogeneity" parameters). In the case of Mexico, our estimates suggest that heterogeneity decreased markedly in the Mexican legislature in 1997 and 2000, and increased after 2003 (estimates of heterogeneity for the

(a)   (b)

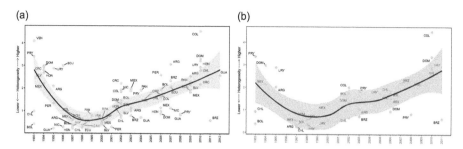

FIGURE 4.6. Average heterogeneity scores in Latin American lower and upper houses. The figure depicts estimated levels of mood heterogeneity (labeled gray circles) among Latin American (a) lower and (b) upper houses, along with a smoothed regional average (solid black line with confidence bands).

years 1994, 1997, 2000, 2003, 2006, and 2009 are 2.4, 0.67, 0.55, 2.13, 1.23, and 2.02). The policy moods that we estimate then account for the possibility that, while a minority of members become more extreme in one direction, our policy mood will still be dictated as pro-state or pro-market given the location of the median member. We will go into more detail over this advantageous characteristic of our modeling strategy in Chapter 6.

Consider then the overall patterns of legislative heterogeneity that we uncover among Latin America's legislatures. Figure 4.6(a) portrays the overall level of heterogeneity among Latin American legislatures. The plot suggests that the increase in within-legislature heterogeneity that characterized Mexico at the end of the 2000s was in fact a more general phenomenon throughout the entire region. Latin American legislatures appear to be relatively consensual at the turn of the century (the nadir of heterogeneity obtains around 1999), only to see consensus dissolve with the rise of the pink tide during the early 2000s. In any case, this exercise reveals that the model-based inferences that we make about policy moods are consistent with the information contained in the raw data input. More importantly, these estimates of legislators' policy moods and levels of heterogeneity provide a sense of the *average location* and *spread* of their individual policy moods. As we explain in Chapter 1, these estimates help us build one-to-one and many-to-many measurements of policy congruence between citizens and legislators.

Beyond assessing whether our estimation strategies recover data-based policy moods (as opposed to moods driven entirely by modeling assumptions), we can also consider how the policy mood scores for legislators fare against alternative yardsticks of legislative opinion. Similar to the exercise we presented in Chapter 3, we can compare legislative policy moods against A–M scores and measures of "revealed rightism" based on expert party placements on a left-right dimension. Figure 4.7 shows these comparisons; in these plots, each dot corresponds to a different lower house (i.e., observations are at the legislative session level).

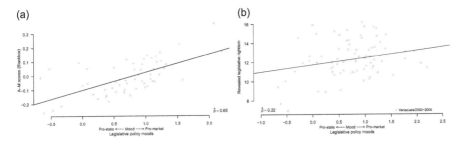

FIGURE 4.7. Legislative policy moods and alternative measures of policy preferences. The figure compares point estimates of the moods of the median legislators against two alternative descriptions of the location of the median policy preference. (a) shows a strong positive correlation with A–M scores, whereas (b) suggests a much weaker correlation with an index of legislative "revealed rightism."

Consider Figure 4.7(a), where we observe a high positive correlation between A–M scores and legislative policy moods ($\hat{\rho} = 0.63$, SE: 0.1). This is not a surprising outcome, as A–M scores are similar to the legislative policy moods on substantive and methodological grounds.[8] Still, the methods underlying A–M and our own model are sufficiently different that their ability to return very similar orderings of legislatures across a state-market spectrum is reassuring. The second yardstick we consider is a measure of revealed rightism that we develop based on Baker and Greene (2011). Here, we simply use the legislative seat shares of political parties as weights for expert placements of these same parties on a left-right scale, generating one "center of ideological gravity" score for each legislature in our sample; this measure ranges theoretically from 0 (most leftist) to 20 (most rightist), but in practice we only see scores between 6.9 and 16.2. The degree of correlation between "revealed rightism" and our legislative policy moods is now much lower, but still positive and statistically significant ($\hat{\rho} = 0.22$, SE: 0.11). This correlation remains low even if we omit the highly leveraged and highly discrepant observation on the lower-right corner of Figure 4.7(b) – this corresponds to Venezuela 2000–2005, a lower house with a relatively pro-market policy mood even though its degree of revealed rightism, which combines expert placement of political parties with the observed seat share of legislative parties, is very low.

4.2.2 Senators

Figure 4.5 also plots policy moods in the region's senates, along with credible intervals, for the nine Latin American countries that have an upper house (these appear in the lightest shade of gray). We observe a few lower and upper chambers with drastically different party seat shares. In Colombia 2002,

---

[8] See our discussion about this similarity in Chapter 3 and an explanation of A–M scores in Online Appendix A.

for example, the Uribista party controlled 36 percent of seats in the lower chamber, but only 14.2 percent in the senate; similarly, the Conservative party obtained 28.9 percent in the lower house and 12.7 percent in the upper house. The estimated ideological distance between these two bodies in Colombia is, consequently, about the largest that we find in our set. But the more general finding is that the estimated policy moods of lower house members and upper house members are pretty similar; we noted before that this was also true for the average policy moods of lower and upper houses across the entire region. Consider, for example, the almost identical policy moods of both Uruguayan chambers in 1995. It is not very surprising that their policy moods are similar, since the three major parties held similar seat shares in both bodies (31 and 29 percent for the Broad Front, 32 and 35 percent for the Colorado party, and 31 and 32 percent for the National party). This general correspondence between the policy moods of senators and legislators is not entirely surprising. Over the entire set of upper house–lower house combinations that we inspect, the average difference between a party's upper house seat share and its lower house seat share is about 8 percentage points, which explains why our method to elicit senatorial policy moods returns estimates that are very similar to those of legislative policy moods.[9] This basic similarity extends to our findings about heterogeneity of policy moods among senators. Figure 4.6(b) displays the longitudinal pattern of heterogeneity across Latin American senates, which is very similar to the one we uncovered for lower and only houses.

4.2.3 Presidents

The final piece of information in Figure 4.5 concerns presidential policy moods, which are captured by the dark gray segments. We annotate each segment with the name of the party to which the president belongs, so that the reader can easily ascertain whether the same party controls a congressional plurality or majority along with executive power. Figure 4.5 suggests that executives tend to lean rightwards, and in fact it is the case that, among a group of executives and lower houses with overlapping terms, whose moods are easy to compare, a majority of presidents (thirty-four out of fifty-two) have policy moods to the right of the median legislator.

Contrary to the policy moods that we derive for upper houses in Latin America, we can compare the presidential policy moods against some yardsticks. The easiest and most obvious comparison is against the left-right placements of the parties to which Latin American presidents belong, as assessed by experts. Based on information put together by Baker and Greene (2011), Figure 4.8 plots our measure of the policy moods of executives against presidential party expert

---

[9] Because positive/negative party seat share differences tend to cancel out across houses, we calculate the square root of the average squared difference for all parties in a senate. The mean of these statistics is 0.079 (SD: 0.06).

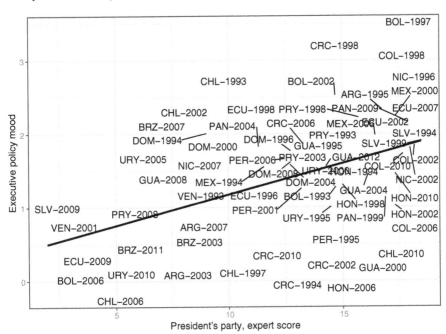

FIGURE 4.8. Presidential policy mood scores and presidential party expert scores. The figure depicts point estimates of the policy moods of sixty-nine Latin American presidents compared with expert left-right presidential party placement scores.

placements. Although the correspondence between these two series might not appear to be extremely tight, their correlation is relatively high (0.41, SD: 0.11) and statistically significant at conventional levels. Consistent with this high correlation index, the top three administrations that we identify based on executive policy moods – Hugo Bánzer in Bolivia (1997–2001), Miguel Ángel Rodríguez Echeverría in Costa Rica (1998–2002), and Andrés Pastrana in Colombia (1998–2002) – have an average left-right ideological score of 16.3, which means that they are also coded as relatively "rightist" based on presidential party expert placements.

On the other side of the ideological divide, our executive policy moods coincide with presidential party expert placements in suggesting that the presidencies of Evo Morales in Bolivia (2006–) and Michelle Bachelet's first presidency in Chile (2006–2010) are leftist. Furthermore, although we pick Hugo Chávez's first presidency as relatively leftist, he only ranks as the seventeenth most leftist president in the set of administrations that we inspect, while being one of the top three leftist presidents based on expert party placements. Occasionally, our executive policy moods differ very markedly from an assessment of the degree of rightism of presidents based on their party's expert score. Consistent with this view, we see Manuel Zelaya's policy mood as extremely leftist, when the expert placement score of his party would put him in the center-right. Zelaya, president of Honduras between 2006 and his unconstitutional removal in 2009, was certainly elected on a conservative platform, but his embrace of the Bolivarian Alliance for the Americas sponsored by Chávez's Venezuela ushered in a number of policies more traditionally identified with the left. This unanticipated leftward shift illustrates an advantage of our measure, namely, that it is based on assessments of the president's policy positions by other contemporaneous politicians. Admittedly, this presumed advantage cuts both ways, as Chávez's original economic policy positions may not have appeared as particularly leftward to a legislature made up almost entirely of Chávez's ideological brethren. As we noted earlier, president's are not bound by norms of party discipline and others have noted that party reputations and presidential actions often do not jibe (Johnson and Crisp 2003, Stokes 2001); all told, we prefer to err on the side of presidential policy moods based on contemporaneous assessments by other politicians than by expert assessments of party reputations.[10]

4.3 LEGISLATIVE PARTY POSITIONS

The thrust of our theory concerns the ways in which the policy moods of citizenries lead to policy implementation through the consecutive filters of electoral rules and institutions that pattern the balance of power between executives and legislatures in separation-of-powers systems. Both in measuring congruence and, especially, in our assumptions about how policy-makers interact with one another, we decidedly embrace a view of politics in which pivotal actors, such as median voters and median legislators, hold the key to understanding which policies are implemented. This approach is reminiscent of Krehbiel's *pivotal politics*, a theory that underscores the powerful influence held by legislators that occupy "pivotal" positions in the legislative process (Krehbiel 1998). For example, when the median legislator and the president hold wildly differing views on a particular issue, the policy preferences of the

---

[10] We tried two additional comparisons. First, we calculated voter-revealed rightism scores composed using presidential candidate vote shares, rather than legislative vote shares, as weights. Although positive, the correlation between the series is much lower (0.2) and not statistically significant. Voter-revealed rightism scores, however, reveal more about the electorate than about the left-right ideology of elected presidents, and they can only be a proxy for the latter under certain restrictive conditions (Warwick and Zakharova 2013). Second, we used an alternative yardstick from Arnold, Doyle, and Wiesehomeier (2017), who study policy compromise based on presidential annual speeches to congress. Since their scores are based on text analysis of an ample array of words, we reproduced their analysis based exclusively on a "bag of words" containing terms that alluded to an economic-distributive divide. The correlation between the executive policy moods and the positions of presidents on this notional economic-distributive divide at the beginning of their terms is 0.16, but is not statistically significant (SD: 0.16).

legislator whose participation is required to build a veto-proof coalition become increasingly relevant to understand what policy may end up prevailing over the status quo.

One important implication of a pivotal-politics approach to legislative decision-making is that political parties become irrelevant in understanding policy implementation. In other words, if actors such as the median legislator or the veto-proof legislator hold power, political parties become little more than epiphenomena, vessels that do not hold any particular powers over their like-minded members. Although our theory has a strong Krehbielian flavor, we do not entirely ignore the potential roles that political parties play in organizing the legislative process, roles that have been studied in a long and growing literature (see, among others, Alemán and Tsebelis 2011, Cheibub, Figueiredo, and Limongi 2009, Coppedge 1998, Cox and Morgenstern 2001, Morgenstern and Vázquez-D'Elía 2007, Rosas 2005). Some Latin American parties have in fact developed ample capacity to control the voting behavior of their legislative contingents. This means that we should approximate the policy moods of parties as represented by their median member even if only to address potential alternative explanations.

We have repeatedly hinted at our use of a scaling model that uses data aggregated at the country level to help us identify the policy moods of median citizens and legislators. (Again, we postpone further discussion until Chapter 6.) However, we also employed an alternative method to build summaries of the policy views of citizens and legislators – that is, A–M scores. So far, we have only used summaries of these scores aggregated at the country level to verify that our preferred policy mood scores are reasonable representations of the preferences of citizens and politicians. Yet, one characteristic of A–M scores is that they are estimated at the *individual* level, which means that we can also aggregate them to the party level (instead of the national level). We use these party-level aggregates to capture the approximate policy moods of most parties in the Latin American legislatures that we analyze, and we will use these party-specific policy moods to control for potential confounders in our analyses in Part III. Note, however, that in using A–M scores the party median moods are no longer necessarily on the exact same scale we use to locate legislative median moods for the heart of our analysis.

Figure 4.9 presents graphical summaries of these data. Within each of the eighteen plots, we display a number of quantities of interest. Most obviously, the gray acronyms correspond to the A–M scores of the median legislator within a political party; to estimate party positions, we literally line up the A–M scores of all legislators within that party and pick the A–M score of the legislator in the middle of that distribution. In addition, open squares identify the position of the median legislator within the lower or only house. Not surprisingly, even if there are relatively large congress-to-congress movements in the positions of within-party medians, within-legislature medians tend to be more stable.

74

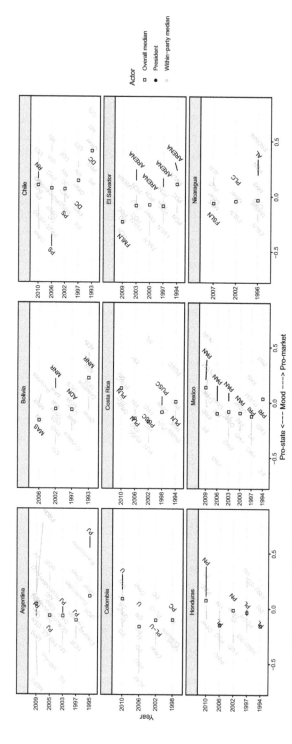

FIGURE 4.9. Policy moods of legislative and party-specific medians. The figure depicts estimates of the policy moods of within-party median legislators (identified by the gray party acronyms) and median legislators in the lower house (black open squares); the president's party is also identified with a black acronym

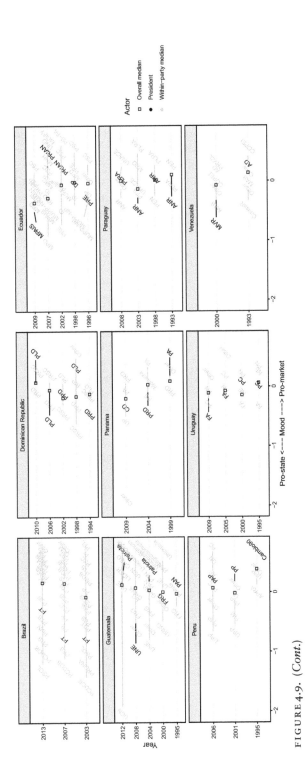

FIGURE 4.9. (Cont.)

Finally, the black acronyms correspond to the positions of median legislators within the president's party.

Following the within-country trajectory of presidential parties (black acronyms) presents an interesting picture of at times radical change in the positions held by the parties to whom Latin American executives belong. Consider El Salvador or Nicaragua, where presidential victories by political parties with origins in the Farabundo Martí and Sandinista armed movements shifted the center of ideological gravity of the executive far away from where rightist parties had previously set it. Needless to say, these movements are more dramatic than those of the congressional medians, which remain for the most part steadfast in these countries during the period we consider.

4.4 CHAPTER SUMMARY

We have presented in this chapter a panoramic view of the policy moods that characterize three important sets of political actors – deputies, senators, and presidents – in Latin America over the past two decades. We have constructed these policy moods to share the same scale on which the policy moods of citizens and the policies implemented by Latin American governments are located. In the next chapter, we describe the information that allows us to build "policy market orientation" scores, which are analogous to policy moods but capture the essence of policy output implemented by governments. Then, in Chapter 6 we discuss the modeling assumptions that substantiate our claim that all of these quantities – policy moods for citizens, deputies, senators, and executives, as well as the policy market orientations of government policies – can be readily compared because they are identified on the same scale.

5

Stage 3: Public Policies Chosen

Having constructed indicators of the policy moods of citizens, legislators, and presidents on a state-to-market continuum, we now turn our attention to the measurement of public policy on that same dimension. As the chain of responsiveness model suggests, good representation ultimately requires a minimum of correspondence between the policies that citizens prefer and the policies that politicians provide. But just as with aggregate measurements of the policy moods of different actors, distilling multifaceted public policy into a single dimension is fraught with complications. We start by looking into previous attempts in the policy literature to build indices of structural policy reform. These attempts provide a very useful departing point, and we veer from them only because of our need to ensure that policies are located on the same state-to-market continuum on which we place citizen and policy-maker preferences.

We do so by repackaging a number of indices corresponding to sixteen different policies into ordered categorical variables. Our decision to aggregate information in this way obeys two reasons. First, we need to model a number of indicators that would otherwise be measured in drastically different ways – some as continuous variables, other as categorical variables – in a relatively uncomplicated manner. Second, we want to avoid the possibility of over-interpreting some of the minute movements that we see in continuous variables; more likely than not, these movements are small adjustments that governments – and, oftentimes, nonelected bureaucracies – make to respond to changing economic realities rather than fundamental changes in an economy's policy orientation. However, the aggregation algorithm that we follow preserves plenty of information about the state- and/or market-orientation of the policies that governments implement in different issue areas. In the last part of the chapter, we provide a glimpse into the policy orientations that different countries have taken at different points in time. More so than the policy moods of citizens or legislators, these policy orientations are strongly patterned and suggest a secular progression toward market-based economic governance as Latin America transited from the old paradigm of import-substitution industrialization to the Washington Consensus. More recently, of course, the so-called pink tide once again popularized state intervention in the economy, which the policy orientation scores that we estimate pick up as a slight dip in the state-to-market policy orientations of a few countries.

5.1 WHAT IS POLICY ORIENTATION?

In this section, we document the steps we take to build a scale that reflects oscillations in public policy between state intervention and market freedom. We find inspiration in a number of related efforts to quantify the amount of "structural adjustment" in Latin America in the aftermath of the turn to markets of the 1990s. Back in the day, the idea that Latin American governments should embrace the Washington Consensus became an important and contested point in the more general debate on how to move away from periodic relapses into recession and to jump start sustained economic growth (Williamson 1990). The basic notion was that Latin American citizenries had been ill-served by the dated postwar model of economic growth led by import-substitution industrialization and that returning to a path of sustainable growth would require adoption of painful but essential market-oriented reforms. The most important components of the so-called consensus included fiscal discipline, trade and capital account liberalization, privatization of state-owned companies, and deregulation of labor and financial markets.

The public policy research community tied to the IADB and the United Nations' Economic Commission for Latin America and the Caribbean responded by promoting a number of measurement efforts to understand the amount of change in "policy outputs" across Latin America (Escaith and Paunovic 2004, Lora 2012, Morley, Machado, and Pettinato 1999). This community sought to understand whether the policy outputs implemented by the region's governments had had any impact on actual economic outcomes like economic growth or employment. Lora (2012) provides the most widely recognized index, one built from information about the policies implemented by governments in the region in five different issue areas: trade policy, financial regulations, tax reforms, state or private ownership, and labor reforms. Morley, Machado, and Pettinato (1999) and, more recently, Fernández et al. (2015) added international financial liberalization, or the lack thereof, as a distinct issue area in the effort to build a comprehensive index of economic orientation.

Our own effort starts from the data curated by Lora (2012). We build on Lora's original collection by updating his series up to 2014, which drastically reduces the amount of missing observations to only a few instances, as can be seen in Table 5.1. The table lists the sixteen indicators that we include in our analysis, pointing out the ones that come from Lora's original list. We exclude

TABLE 5.1. *Sources and time coverage of all indicators included in the policy orientation scale.*

Indicator	Brief definition	Up to	Lora
Trade policy			
Average tariff	Average import tariff (%)	2014	✓
Trade dispersion	Dispersion of import tariffs	2009	✓
Financial policy			
Reserve requirements	Reserve requirement coefficient (%)	2009	✓
Interest rate	Interest rate liberalization (ordered scale from 0 to 3)	2014	✓
Financial transaction	Tax rate on financial transactions (%)	2014	✓
Tax policy			
Value-added tax	Basic value-added tax rate (%)	2014	✓
Personal tax	Personal income tax rate (%)	2014	✓
Corporate tax	Highest marginal corporate income tax rate (%)	2014	✓
Privatization			
Privatization	Privatizations minus nationalizations as a percentage of GDP (cumulative stock since 1985)	2009	✓
Privatized assets	Total value of privatized assets in energy, telecomm, transport, and water, divided by GDP	2014	
Labor			
Job termination cost	Expected cost of firing a worker (months of wages)	2009	✓
Hiring flexibility	Flexibility of legislation on hiring (ordered scale 1–3)	2014	✓
Working flexibility	Flexibility of working hours (ordered scale 1–3)	2014	✓
Social security tax	Cost of social security contributions (%)	2014	✓
Minimum wage	Minimum wage (as proportion of per capita GDP)	2009	✓
International capital openness			
Capital openness	Factor-based index of (lack of) obstacles to international capital transactions (Chinn and Ito 2016)	2014	

a few of Lora's original indicators that we find difficult to construe as having a clear state/market polarity.[1] We also add the degree of openness of an economy to cross-border capital flows as a separate issue area, as suggested by Morley,

---

[1] For example, Lora looks into quality of bank supervision or productivity of the income tax, but we interpret these as indices that reflect bureaucratic capacity or state extraction capabilities more than the state or market orientation of a government.

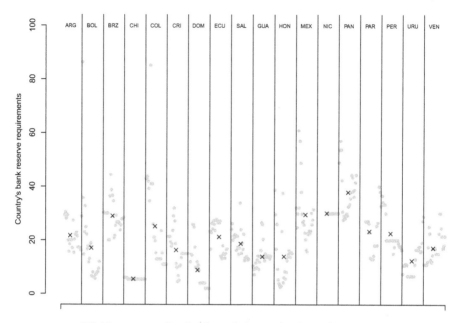

FIGURE 5.1. Within-country distribution of observed values of reserve requirements. Each vertical "slice" contains ordered annual observations of a country's bank reserve requirements (gray dots). The × symbol within each slice captures the country-specific average bank reserve requirement.

Machado, and Pettinato (1999); in this case, we use an indicator of capital openness produced by Chinn and Ito (2016).[2] Online Appendix C includes information about the sources that we employed to update Lora's series.

5.2 TIME TRENDS IN DIFFERENT POLICY-MAKING ARENAS

Before constructing our index of state-to-market policy orientation, we briefly describe how policy has changed in Latin America along each of the six specific areas that we identify in Table 5.1. As we answer this question, we introduce our first coding decision. To motivate this decision, consider Figure 5.1, which portrays reserve requirement rates across space and time. Reserve requirement rates measure the amount of capital that banks are mandated to keep on reserve rather than available for lending. The purpose of these reserves is to withstand liquidity shocks to the banking system that can come, for example, from an unanticipated deposit run on a bank or from a spell of delinquency in bank

---

[2] This indicator is a (principal factor) summary of restrictions on the international sale or purchase of a number of financial assets, as collected in the International Monetary Fund's *Annual Report on Exchange Arrangements and Exchange Restrictions.*

loans. In general, high reserve requirement rates are an indicator of larger state meddling in financial markets because they limit the ability of financial intermediaries to allocate credit based purely on profit motives. Note, however, that, although these rates vary continuously between 0 and about 90, they also tend to be heavily clustered within countries, with Chile consistently imposing the lowest rates and Panama the highest. In some countries, like the Dominican Republic or El Salvador, the rates appear to fall continuously throughout the period under observation, but the modal experience throughout the region is one of reserve requirement rates moving up and down around a country-specific mean (the ×s in Figure 5.1). The reason is that, beyond the pro-state or pro-market inclination of each government, the reserve requirement rate is one of several instruments in the arsenal of macroeconomic counter-cyclical weapons that governments – and nonelected bureaucracies, in this case including a country's central bank and banking supervisors – can deploy to tame or accelerate investment in the short run. Because of this function, it is inappropriate to interpret *small* upward or downward movements in this variable as a signal of a marked change in pro-state or pro-market policy orientation; many of these adjustments should be seen as short-term stabilization measures rather than as radical departures from preexisting public policy arrangements. In the case of reserve requirements, the country-specific averages or, even better, some other partially aggregated measure, would be more likely to provide accurate and sufficient information about the state/market orientation of the government.

Other indicators – for example tax rates or trade tariff-related measures – also invite overinterpretation of small incremental changes. Partly for this reason, we decided to "discretize" all of the indicators in Table 5.1 into a small number of ordered categories; to be clear, a couple of these indicators were already coded as ordered categories, as can be seen in the same table. We are aware that aggregating continuous variables into discrete categories leads to loss of information, and is therefore inefficient, but hopefully our discussion about reserve requirements has convinced the reader that any loss of information is minimal compared to gains in capturing movements that really reflect changing policies. Beyond this reason, we also find it much easier to model a number of outcome variables that are measured in similar ways, as we mentioned in the introduction to this chapter. Statistical models that appropriately deal with mixed continuous and categorical indicators certainly exist, but they are unwieldy and add little to our enterprise, which is to infer policy orientations observed at the country-year level.

While our decision to turn input variables into discrete categories is straightforward, deciding how many categories to include or which cutpoints to adopt to break down these categories is less obvious. In the end, we broke down all continuous outcomes into categorical variables with four different categories (low, medium low, medium high, high). To do so, we first performed a cluster analysis of each continuous indicator in Table 5.1 to select cutpoints that maximized the ratio of between-category to within-category variance in each

TABLE 5.2. *Ratio of between-to-total variance achieved by coding continuous indicators into categorical indicators. We turn all continuous policy inputs into variables with four ordered categories. Information loss is kept at a minimum, as suggested by the high ratios of between-to-total variance.*

Policy	Ratio	Policy	Ratio
Average tariff	0.88	Privatization	0.92
Trade dispersion	0.91	Privatized assets	0.88
Reserve requirement	0.86	Job termination cost	0.9
Financial transaction	0.95	Social security tax	0.92
Value-added tax	0.91	Minimum wage	0.89
Personal tax	0.9	Capital openness	0.97
Corporate tax	0.89		

outcome, thus minimizing the risk that we would inadvertently project our own biases in coding these public policies as more or less pro-market.[3] In fact, we performed five cluster analyses on each indicator, varying the number of desired categories from two to six. We then assessed the lowest number of categories that would account for a substantial amount of variation in each indicator. In all cases, no less than three and no more than four categories captured meaningful variation in all indicators, and we thus opted for the larger number of categories. Table 5.2 shows the ratio of between-to-total variance achieved by our chosen categorizations for thirteen variables. The other three indicators in our analysis are *interest rate liberalization, hiring flexibility,* and *work flexibility,* which were already coded as categorical indicators. (In Online Appendix A, Table C.1 contains summary statistics for all of the indicators, now transformed into categorical variables, and Table C.2 shows the actual ordered categorical values for each of our country-year observations.)[4]

As we suggested in Table 5.1, we can arrange sixteen different indicators among six different policy areas. As a first cut to describe cross-national and longitudinal variation in each of these six policy areas, we display in Figure 5.2 country-specific averages over all policies that belong to each issue area (e.g., the country-specific "trade policy" timeline for Argentina would comprise the year-by-year average of that country's scores on *average trade* and *trade dispersion*). We display in Figure 5.2 a black timeline that represents the regional average trend, laid over (unidentified) country-specific timelines (in gray).

A quick glance at these plots confirms a liberalizing trend across the region in a few issue areas, which should not surprise even casual observers of Latin America over the past three decades. The most dramatic case concerns *trade*

---

[3] We use the kmeans function in R.

[4] In addition, where necessary we inverted the ordered categories so that *higher* values would correspond to *market-oriented* policies for all indexes, as we consistently did with the survey items that we inspected in Chapters 3 and 4.

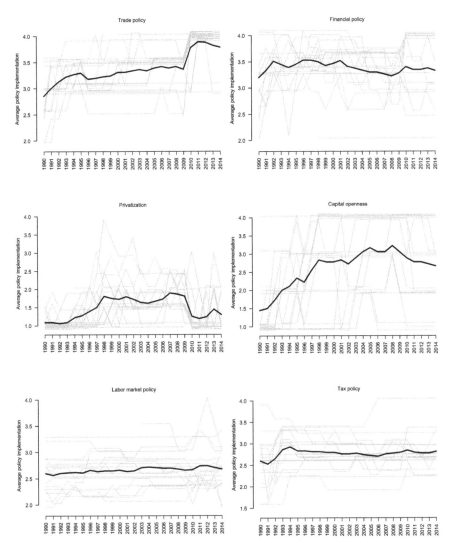

FIGURE 5.2. Average Latin American policy implementation in six different issue areas. The thin gray lines in each plot capture changes in the country-specific sums of all indicators within a particular issue area. The superimposed black line captures the cross-country average of these sums as an overall estimate of regional change.

policy, where we see a steep increase in the number of countries that move up in the two ordered category scales comprised by this issue area (recall that these categories *increase* when countries *reduce* average trade tariffs and the dispersion around these tariffs). Many gains in trade liberalization had in fact occurred between 1985 and the early 1990s – a period not plotted in Figure 5.2 – as some countries within the region dropped tariffs and other obstacles to the free movement of goods and services. This radical shift in trade openness was followed by a period of slower but continuous liberalization that lasted until the first decade of the twenty-first century. More recently, further liberalization under the aegis of center-left governments in countries like Paraguay and Peru increased overall trade openness to the highest level it has ever reached in the region, even after accounting for a slight regression in Argentina, which dropped from a maximum average score of 4 to 3 in 2012, probably as a consequence of attempts by Cristina Fernández de Kirchner's administration to increase export taxes. The *trade policy* series shows strong correlations across countries, as can be surmised by the fact that the within-year variance in the trade policy series of Figure 5.2 is much smaller than the between-year variance (0.16 vs. 1.2).

Within-year cross-country correlations are similarly high for *financial policy*, *privatization*, and *capital openness*, suggesting strong co-movements in these policies across different countries in the region. *Financial policy*, which mostly reflects the elimination of repressive domestic financial regulations, had also increased markedly in the aftermath of the debt crisis of the early 1980s, but stagnated throughout the 1990s and 2000s. At the end of the period under observation, we see a wider spread around the average trend, with a country like Ecuador retrenching swiftly from a high average score of 3.6 in the early 2000s to a low score of 2.5 by 2010 (within- and between-year variances for financial policy are, respectively, 0.23 and 0.16).

In the policy realm of *privatization*, the liberalization efforts of the 1990s led in many countries to massive policies of divestiture of state-owned enterprises in energy, telecommunications, banking, pensions, and airlines, although some of these efforts were later rolled back in countries like Argentina and Venezuela, a trend reflected by a dip in the average timeline around 2008 (within- and between-year variances are 0.26 and 1.4). The time-series information on *capital openness* suggests a trend toward liberalization that culminates around 2008, after which we see regional retrenchment (within- and between-year variances are 1.09 and 4.58). At the same time, we should not discount cross-country variation even within these co-moving series. Brazil has kept ample controls over cross-border capital movements throughout the period under observation, whereas countries such as Peru and Uruguay have been relatively more market-oriented; Argentina and Venezuela progressively imposed capital controls starting in the late 1990s.

In contrast to these series, we observe two issue areas without a common cross-country liberalizing trend: *labor market policy* and *tax policy*. In the realm of *tax policy*, most Latin American countries embraced in the past decades a combination of value-added taxes, which are easy to collect but considered to be regressive, and lowered tax rates for personal and corporate income. Once established, however, tax rates do not tend to jump around in big increments, and tax policy has remained relatively stable within and across countries since the late 1990s (within- and between-year variances are 0.18

and 0.12, respectively). In the issue area of *labor market policy*, we confirm Lora's observation of very little general movement toward deregulation and mostly an incredible amount of path dependence. Many countries display scores that hover around the middle of the scale, but there is enough cross-country variation that within-year variance for this issue area about triples the size of between-year variance (0.11 to 0.04).

5.3 COUNTRY-SPECIFIC POLICY ORIENTATIONS

It should be obvious by now that there are idiosyncratic differences across issue areas. Latin American polities embraced some elements of the Washington Consensus – such as trade and capital openness – with alacrity, whereas in general they failed to enact dramatic reforms in areas like labor market deregulation. Reform efforts have proceeded at markedly different paces in different fronts. We have discussed issue areas separately only because we will want to ascertain soon enough whether a *policy orientation* score can reflect some of these nuances. Indeed, our main contention is that all of these issue areas ultimately provide information about a single, underlying *policy orientation* that goes from heavy state intervention, on one end, to full market governance of a country's economy, on the other.

Based on this contention, we infer scores on a *policy orientation* dimension based on the sixteen ordered categories of Table 5.1. Contrary to our preliminary observations in the previous section, and contrary as well to the way in which Lora and others construct their indexes of structural reform, we eschew additive scores that weight all policy indicators equally. As we will argue in Chapter 6, policy outputs differ in the amount of information they furnish to help us discriminate between the policy orientations of Latin American governments, and consequently there are ample differences in the usefulness of these policy outputs to help us infer policy orientations across countries and throughout time. The model we develop in Chapter 6 allows us to capture the varying discriminating powers of the sixteen policy outputs. Furthermore, recall from Chapter 2 that we embrace the challenge of setting policy orientations on the same scale as the policy moods of citizens and politicians in Latin America. Again, in Chapter 6 we explain in detail how we achieve this purpose. Suffice it to say here that we make a crucial assumption about the comparability of two of our sixteen policy outputs – *privatization* and *capital openness* – with two corresponding stimuli – privatization.beneficial and capital.mobility.good – that are repeatedly asked in the PELA and LB surveys.

How, then, do Latin American governments vary in terms of their *policy orientations* across space and throughout time? The black points and vertical bars in Figure 5.3 collect country-specific estimates of *policy orientations* along with uncertainty intervals (80 percent highest posterior densities) for all eighteen countries in our purview. These *policy orientation* scores are the

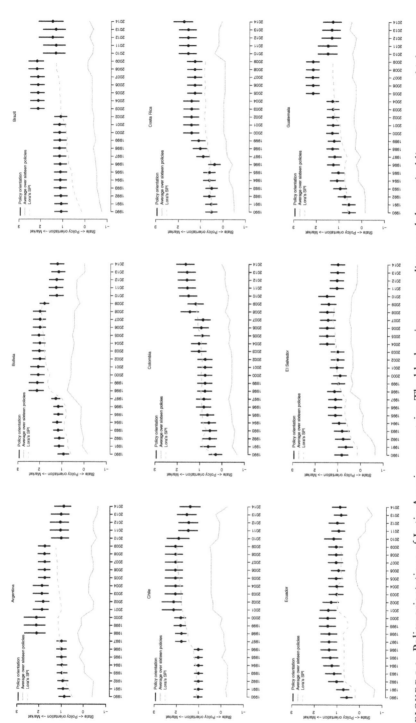

FIGURE 5.3. Policy orientations of Latin American countries. The black points are medians, and the vertical lines 80 percent highest posterior density intervals, of the posterior distributions of policy orientations within each country. The continuous gray line averages over the values of the sixteen items in our policy orientation scale, while the broken gray line corresponds to Lora's structural reform index (rescaled to the −2 to 2 range). SPI, structural policy index.

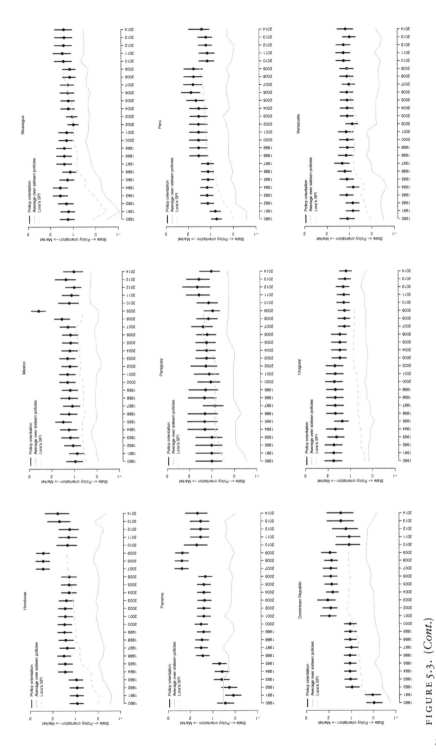

FIGURE 5.3. (*Cont.*)

ones that we analyze in Part IV of the book for evidence of congruence and responsiveness. Because we combine different policy items, and because we rescale and weight these items based on their discriminating power rather than just adding them, our index of policy orientation is different from Lora's. To aid comparison, we added two additional series to the plots in Figure 5.3. The first series is a continuous gray line that simply averages over the values of the sixteen categorical items that we use as inputs in our analysis (these averages are then mean-centered, so that they could be placed in the graph). The second series is a broken gray line that corresponds to Lora's structural reform index, which stops in 2009 and has been rescaled from the unit range to a scale that goes from -2 to 2 (note that there is no structural reform index for Panama). Because both Lora's structural reform index and the simple average both weight all policy outputs equally, there are many similarities in the gray lines (other than, of course, they have different means), so much so that they very often run parallel to each other. The simple average, however, operates on categorical variables, which introduces some variation from the structural reform index.

We bring the reader's attention to three main points. First, the policy orientations that we infer are relatively persistent. Of course governments of different stripes purport to enact policies that are consistent with their ideological views, but at least in the issue areas that we inspect, and based on our codification rules, we mostly see relatively small changes from one year to the next. Once we take into account estimation uncertainty, we could even ignore relatively small fluctuations in year-to-year policy orientations as basically meaningless. One extreme example of this persistence is Paraguay, whose policy orientation appears to be constant and only recently slightly turned toward further market governance. The policy orientation of an economy is very sticky even over the long run.

Second, even with this amount of persistence we recover some of the most obvious trends that have characterized economic policy-making in the region over the past decades. Notice for example that across the region our policy orientation scores recover the mostly upward trend that we had seen in issue areas such as *privatization, financial policy,* and *capital openness.* Colombia is a good representative of this trend. The country enters the period under observation still with relatively low scores, and shows a mild upward trend (most likely resulting from the liberalization of trade under César Gaviria) that becomes stagnant after the notorious expansion in government spending brought about by the policies of Ernesto Samper and Andrés Pastrana. Then, under the presidency of Álvaro Uribe, Colombia's policy orientation contin- ues to climb up toward the market-end of the scale throughout the 2000s, despite the loss of the Liberal Party majority in both legislative chambers. In contrast, our scale also recovers movements toward the state-end of the scale in countries that were part of the pink tide. Argentina under the Kirchners with relatively large Justicialista pluralities in congress, Bolivia under Morales and his very strong Movimiento Al Socialismo legislative majorities, and Ecuador

TABLE 5.3. *Average Latin American policy implementation in six different issue areas. The correlations (with standard errors) capture the degree of within-country association between our policy orientation scores, on the one hand, and the average value of all categories used as input (column 2) and Lora's structural reform index (column 4), on the other.*

Correlation with ...	Average Value		Lora's SRI	
Country	$\hat{\rho}$	SE $(\hat{\rho})$	$\hat{\rho}$	SE $(\hat{\rho})$
Argentina	0.24	0.20	0.69	0.17
Bolivia	0.87	0.10	0.95	0.08
Brazil	0.71	0.15	0.80	0.14
Chile	0.86	0.11	0.95	0.07
Colombia	0.94	0.07	0.83	0.13
Costa Rica	0.92	0.08	0.92	0.09
Dominican Republic	0.72	0.14	0.95	0.08
Ecuador	0.41	0.19	0.39	0.22
El Salvador	0.73	0.14	0.78	0.15
Guatemala	0.66	0.16	0.85	0.13
Honduras	0.63	0.16	0.69	0.17
Mexico	−0.32	0.20	0.07	0.24
Nicaragua	−0.04	0.21	−0.40	0.22
Panama	−0.58	0.17	—	—
Paraguay	0.34	0.20	0.22	0.23
Peru	0.82	0.12	0.93	0.09
Uruguay	−0.45	0.19	−0.61	0.19
Venezuela	0.40	0.19	0.52	0.20
Overall	0.42	0.04	0.60	0.04

under Correa, whose Alianza PAIS turned a strong plurality in 2009 into an overwhelming majority of national assembly seats in 2013 are countries where we see a reorientation toward pro-state policies at the end of the period under observation. We should add to this list Brazil under Lula. This retrenchment has tempered the pro-market impetus seen earlier in the region, but has not returned Latin America to the levels of state intervention witnessed in the 1980s. In Venezuela and in Nicaragua, both before and after the pink tide, we mostly see a pattern of stasis at relatively low values throughout the observation window.

When we compare our index of policy orientation with the average of the categorical indicators on which it is based, the overall correlation coefficient is 0.41 (SE: 0.04). Within-country correlations, however, vary more widely, with a minimum of −0.45 for Uruguay and a maximum of 0.94 for Colombia, as can be seen in Table 5.3. Aside from Uruguay's negative correlation between our index and the simple additive score, we also see negative correlations in Mexico, Nicaragua, and Panama. We observe a similar situation when we compare our index against Lora's structural reform index, for which we only have observations until 2009. Overall, the correlation between our policy orientation scores and Lora's index is tight (0.60, SE: 0.04). When we consider country-by-country information, we observe in Table 5.3 that most correlations are in fact quite high. The only exceptions are Nicaragua and Uruguay, where we see negative correlations between policy orientations and structural reform.

A closer look at Uruguay reveals the reasons why we see such a disparity between structural reform and policy orientation in this case. Note, first, that both average scores and structural reform index are relatively flat for Uruguay in Figure 5.3. An upward trend in the structural reform index exists but is barely detectable in the graph. Consequently, our inference about policy orientation in Uruguay already starts from the knowledge that, in general, stasis is the norm. Add to that the fact that our index weights different items differently. As we show in Chapter 6, items such as *personal tax* or *reserve requirement* correspond to policy areas in which Uruguay moved away from the market-end toward the end of the observation period. This accounts for the slight downward trend in policy orientation that we observe for this country in Figure 5.3.

5.4 CHAPTER SUMMARY

This chapter concludes the overview of the indicators of policy moods – for citizens, legislators, senators, and presidents – and policy orientations that we have constructed. As measures of the stages in our chain of representation, they will help us understand patterns of congruence and responsiveness in further chapters in Part III. We hope to have convinced the reader that our measures of the policy moods of citizens and policy-makers, and our measures of the policy orientations of governments are useful representations of the underlying concepts for which we wish to account. Yet, in order to convince the reader that policy orientations and policy moods are more or less commensurable, we lay out in the next chapter a very detailed account of the logic that we have followed in building our model of policy moods and policy orientations. Although the discussion in Chapter 6 is relatively technical, we believe the payoff of going through the logic of our model is worthwhile in terms of achieving a better understanding of what these economic policy moods and orientations represent.

6

Placing Preferences and Policies on a Common Scale

We described in previous chapters how the policy moods for and against markets of Latin American citizens and policy-makers have waxed and waned over a period of almost two decades. The propensity to enact pro-market public policy (what we refer to as policy orientation) increased in general across Latin America up to around the late 1990s, only to stagnate, and in some cases retrench, after that period. In the chapters ahead, we will explore in more detail how and where the chain of responsiveness that putatively ties public policies to the desires of the citizenry can link them more or less closely depending on how the chain is designed. As we have noted previously, we will investigate whether the policy moods of citizens and policy-makers correlate, as we would expect in systems that promote good political representation, by looking at the effect of electoral rules in fostering or hindering congruence and responsiveness. We will also analyze whether pro-market public policy orientation responds to shifts in the policy moods of legislators, and if these responses are mediated by rules that define the policy-making powers of presidents and legislatures.

To deliver on these goals, we need to show that our estimates of policy moods and policy orientation are more or less comparable. More specifically, we must show that all of our estimates are similarly "scaled," so that a policy mood score of 1.5 and a pro-market public policy orientation of 1.5 represent more or less the same thing: a tight correspondence between, on the one hand, the policy preferences of citizens and policy-makers (their "ideal points," to use the lingo from spatial models of voting behavior), and the actual policy that presidents and legislators implement, on the other. Scaling policy moods and policy orientations would not be problematic (i) if we could pose to all actors identical questions with identical possible numerical responses and (ii) if we could translate actual public policies into the same set of possible numerical responses to those questions. Neither of these steps is feasible given constraints imposed by data availability. We were consequently forced to search high and low for modeling techniques that would address this scaling problem. In this chapter, we carefully explain how we confronted these obstacles and justify all of the assumptions and modeling techniques that we employ.

Our solution to the scaling problem proceeds in two steps. First, we explain in Section 6.1 how we place policy-makers and citizens in a "common space." This step requires making a few assumptions about how different survey stimuli "discriminate" among policy-makers and citizens. Second, in Section 6.2 we address the problem of placing policy orientation on the common space on which the preferences of politicians and citizens are located. Throughout these sections, we will point out additional "clues" that increase our confidence in the appropriateness of our modeling assumptions. We understand that less technically inclined readers may find it difficult to absorb the material presented in this chapter. We beg these readers to bear with us as we endeavor to present our modeling decisions in as an intuitive and conversational a manner as we possibly can. We believe the payoff from reading this chapter will be worth the reader's while.[1]

6.1 A METHOD TO OBTAIN POLICY MOODS FROM AGGREGATE DATA

In this section we document the steps we took to distill thousands of individual responses to multiple survey questions throughout time and across countries into measures of the "policy mood" of citizens, deputies, senators, and presidents. In particular, we strive to convince the reader that our measures are solid summaries of the way in which Latin American citizens and policy-makers perceive the promises and dangers of state intervention or market solutions to their everyday concerns. As is the case with any attempt to extract meaning from data, we cannot make inferences about policy moods without imposing a certain number of assumptions about the ways in which citizens and politicians respond to survey questions. In other words, there is no such thing as "letting the data speak for themselves." However, we want to make sure that our assumptions do not inject too many extraneous elements into our inferences. That is, we want to ensure that our policy mood scores are fundamentally driven by the survey data, rather than by model specification, especially considering that our broad collection effort still yielded a relatively limited amount of data – a small fraction of the amount of data available to scholars interested in questions of representation in, for example, the United States.

The reader may have noticed that our notion of "policy moods" is reminiscent of the idea of a "public mood," which is very much a staple in the analysis of political behavior in the United States. Stimson developed the concept of

---

[1] We warn the reader that some basic knowledge of probability and statistics is helpful in order to follow our discussion. In an effort to facilitate reproducibility of our analyses, all of our code is available on the book's GitHub repository: https://github.com/solivella/ChainOfRepresentation.

public mood, as well as the mathematical apparatus required to build an empirical indicator of this theoretical construct, in his path-breaking *Public Opinion in America* (Stimson 1991). The "public mood" series that Stimson first analyzed has been updated to cover the entire postwar history of the United States, and it is commonly employed as a tool to gauge the *overall* degree of economic "liberalism" or "conservatism" of the American public at any given point in time (see, inter alia, Erikson, MacKuen, and Stimson 2002, Stevenson 2000, Stimson, Mackuen, and Erikson 1995).

We do not use Stimson's algorithm to estimate the moods of Latin American citizens and politicians, but it is illustrative to think through the challenges he first encountered when building a measure of the US public mood, because these challenges are similar to the ones we face. Although work on political behavior in the United States had led to the accumulation of a large number of opinion surveys throughout the postwar era, Stimson realized that many stimuli were asked infrequently, and that very often several survey rounds would go by before a particular item would be asked again in a survey. Furthermore, the stimuli that Stimson analyzed could all be seen as tracers of an economic liberal–conservative attitudinal divide (just as the stimuli we analyze can be mapped onto a state–market divide), but the fraction of responses that one could consider to be "liberal" varied markedly across stimuli. For example, it could well be the case that a much larger fraction of US respondents would adopt a "liberal" position on government intervention to guarantee a pension in old age than to, say, alleviate poverty. Because of this (potentially large) variation across stimuli, and because of the infrequency with which some stimuli were asked, it was difficult to build a measure of the public mood by simply counting the number of individuals that in any given year provide "liberal" answers to a changing number of different stimuli.

Stimson observed that for any proportion I of liberal respondents to a given stimulus that was asked in any two years t and $t + k$, one could build a "dyad ratio" I_{t+k}/I_t to capture year-on-year variation in *aggregate* liberal opinion, that is, in the percentages of individuals that took a liberal stance on a question. For example, I could be the percentage of respondents that favor government spending to alleviate poverty, with observed values $I_t = 69\%$ and $I_{t+k} = 72\%$. The dyad ratio for this item in the period $t + k$ would be $0.72/0.69 = 1.04$. Dyad ratios such as these are comparable across stimuli, as they provide information on whether the public shifts in a more or less liberal direction regardless of the baseline degree of liberalism for each response, that is, regardless of the size of I_t; values larger than 1 correspond to changes toward the liberal end of the ideological spectrum. Stimson then developed a *dyad ratios* algorithm – in essence a time-trend average of all dyad ratios available in a given period – to extract a unique, "smooth" public mood measure that could incorporate information from changing numbers of stimuli throughout time.

Stimson understood that we do not always need to consider individual-level variation in issue positions. For a number of purposes – including an analysis of patterns of representation, congruence, responsiveness, and accountability – the use of aggregate information, as opposed to individual-level information, is not only sufficient, but actually desirable. The desirability of aggregate information is obvious in the case of the United States, the country that Stimson analyzes, and even more obvious in the countries that we study, where survey data is not as abundant and question wording varies tremendously from one survey instrument to the next. Were we to consider individual-level information, we would need to make extremely heroic assumptions about the exact correspondence between two different questions that are not even measured on the same scale and whose wording is only vaguely similar. In contrast, the assumption of similarity that we make when we aggregate responses at the survey level is more plausible.

Consider for example the following statement. Query #1 tells respondents: "On a scale of 1 to 7, where 1 is strongly disagree and 7 is strongly agree, what is your position on the following statement: Governments should regulate prices so that the poor have affordable access to basic foodstuffs." Question #2 asks: "Should governments control food prices? Never, only occasionally, always." The two questions are clearly related, but they elicit responses on different scales and the ways in which they are framed may induce the same individual to answer differently. If we aggregate responses, however, and simply tally the percentage of survey respondents that agree with the liberal answer to questions #1 and #2, many of these microlevel measurement concerns would be assuaged. In other words, not only is the analysis of aggregates desirable for theoretical reasons, but it is also justified on empirical grounds.

Stimson's dyad-ratios algorithm is the foundation of a long research program in American behavior. However, the algorithm is not unimpeachable as a method of inferring public mood scores. McGann (2013) notes that the algorithm may deliver estimates of the public mood that do not follow the central tendency of respondents under certain circumstances. For example, and as we will elaborate further later in this chapter, increased polarization in a legislative body could result in a strongly bimodal distribution of policy preferences, with a vocal minority holding radical positions on the underlying state-to-market continuum, say for increased state governance of the economy. Although the majority continues to hold relatively centrist positions on this continuum, the dyad-ratios algorithm may instead lead to the conclusion that the typical legislator has turned toward the statist pole of the continuum, all on account of how far toward that end the policy preferences of an extreme minority have become.

When everything is said and done, the main problem stems from the fact that the dyad-ratios algorithm is not deduced from clear and explicit assumptions about individual behavior. This is paradoxical given our argument that we do not necessarily care about individual behavior, but rather about aggregate behavior. Yet, in order to develop a sound measurement strategy at the aggregate level, we need to start on solid microfoundations about the presumed behavior of individual respondents. McGann endeavors to provide these microfoundations of a model of the aggregate public mood, and to do so he proposes an estimation technique that purposefully measures the central tendency of the distribution of opinions of a set of respondents based on an explicit and widely used model of individual behavior known as "item-response theory (IRT)."

Consider a respondent – a citizen or policy-maker – who is called upon to answer a survey question on the desirability of government provision of unemployment benefits. On one end of the scale, this respondent would answer "1" if she were in favor of unconditional government support for whomever happened to be unemployed; on the other end, the respondent would answer "7" if she opposed any amount of unemployment benefits of any kind supported by taxpayers.[2] Presumably, the respondent's answer will be driven by an unseen, more fundamental disposition to prefer markets over states in matters of economic allocation. We use Greek letter ζ_i (*zeta*) to capture respondent i's general pro-market proclivity or state–market disposition.

Now, some policy items are so uncontroversial that it would take a real anti-market extremist to provide a "leftist" answer. By now, for example, it seems that the idea that *all* means of production should be owned by the state is so discredited that only a handful of eccentrics on the extreme left would ever profess to support it. Items with such wordings are "easy" to respond to in a pro-market fashion; regardless of their actual pro-market propensity ζ, most individuals will provide responses that are away from the left, that is, most will say that they *do not agree* that *all* means of productions should be state-owned. Thus, the state–market disposition ζ of an individual combines with characteristics of each policy to produce an answer to the corresponding survey question. Think of parameter α_q (*alpha*) as capturing the *difficulty* of item q. Difficulty parameter α_q captures a characteristic of item q, not of the individual, but it is easier to understand what this characteristic is if we think about an individual with "average" state–market disposition, that is, a "centrist": A centrist will find it easy to provide a rightist response to items that have *low* values of α and will find it difficult to provide a rightist response to items with *high* values of α.

Similarly, some items are better than others at helping us *discriminate* among respondents with varying state–market dispositions. For example, knowing that a respondent prefers a market solution to the problem of providing higher education might be less informative about her state–market disposition than knowing that she prefers a market solution to the problem of providing pensions in old age. After all, we can conceive of individuals on both the left and right that may be perfectly content with either private or public high school education; while the same is possible for pensions, we tend to think

---

[2] Notice that we have now reversed Stimson's scale so that larger values correspond to more market-oriented opinions.

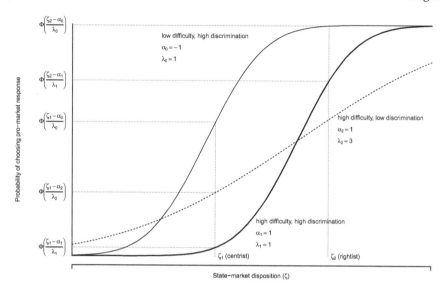

FIGURE 6.1. The core IRT model. The graph shows the probability of choosing a pro-market response (the *y* axis) as a function of state–market dispositions (the *x* axis) and the difficulty and discrimination capacity of three different items (values of α and λ determine the shape of the function linking state–market dispositions to pro-market responses). An individual with "rightist" disposition (ζ_2) is less likely to choose a pro-market response to an item with higher difficulty (α_1) than to one with lower difficulty (α_0). An individual with a "centrist" disposition (ζ_1) is more likely to choose a pro-market response to an item with higher discrimination (λ_2) than to one with lower discrimination (λ_0).

of this as a trait that more closely corresponds to an individual's ideological disposition. For this reason, these two items – higher education and pensions in old age – could well have different discriminating power, which we represent with parameter λ_q (*lambda*). When we put all of these elements together, we can model the probability that respondent *i* will provide a market response to a stimulus as a function of her own individual state–market disposition and the difficulty and discrimination characteristics of the item in question, that is,

$$\text{Pr}(\text{Pro-market response}_{iq}) = \Phi\left(\frac{\zeta_i - \alpha_{qt}}{\lambda_{qt}}\right), \tag{6.1}$$

where $\Phi(\cdot)$ is the cumulative standard normal distribution function that transforms real numbers into a number bound by 0 and 1, as befits a probability measure.[3] The specific function inside $\Phi(\cdot)$ is the basic kernel of an IRT model.

Figure 6.1 puts these elements together. In the figure, we consider two individuals: a "centrist" with state–market disposition ζ_1 and a "rightist"

---

[3] The use of the standard normal cumulative distribution function $\Phi(\cdot)$ (*Phi*) is equivalent to setting a probit link. IRT models often rely on other links, like the extreme-value cumulative distribution function (the logit link). See Johnson and Albert (1999, ch. 6) for a superb introduction to IRT.

with disposition ζ_2. The thick continuous line captures the characteristics of an item with high difficulty ($\alpha_0 = 1$) and high discrimination ($\lambda = 1$), and it can be seen as a function that translates state–market disposition into a probability of choosing a pro-market response. For this high difficulty, high discrimination item, the centrist chooses a pro-market response with probability $\Phi\left(\frac{\zeta_1-\alpha_1}{\lambda_1}\right)$, and the rightist chooses a pro-market response with probability $\Phi\left(\frac{\zeta_2-\alpha_1}{\lambda_1}\right)$. Consider now the probability that this same rightist voter would select a pro-market response to an item with low difficulty ($\alpha_1 = -1$) and high discrimination ($\lambda = 1$), which is $\Phi\left(\frac{\zeta_2-\alpha_0}{\lambda_0}\right)$. The take-home point is that the same individual may choose a pro-market response to one item with very high probability and a pro-market response to another item with lower probability depending on characteristics of the items. More generally, the probability that two individuals would respond in a pro-market fashion depends on their dispositions on the state–market dimension and on the difficulty and discrimination characteristics of the item in question. Note that the state–market dispositions of respondents and the item-specific difficulty and discrimination characteristics are the *individual-* and *item-level* building blocks of our model. These are the basic conceptual inputs that give rise to *aggregate* policy moods.

It would be illustrative, but not particularly interesting, to infer the individual pro-market proclivities of all respondents in an AB sample or of all legislators in a PELA data set. We aim to learn the pro-market proclivity of a specific individual within each group: the median citizen, the median legislator, the median senator, or the president. To move from the individual to the aggregate level, McGann proposes simply averaging over the distribution of ζ in Equation 6.1, that is, finding the "average" mood among the moods of all individuals in group g, in country c, at time t. It is relatively innocuous to think of these individual moods as being normally distributed around a mean μ_{gct} (*mu*), with variance σ^2_{gct} (*sigma*). Thus, McGann further assumes that the Normal probability density function $\phi(\zeta_{igct}, \mu_{gct}, \sigma^2_{gct})$ characterizes the distribution of individual moods. This allows us to derive m_{gcqt}, which is the probability that the "average" individual in group g, in country c, at time t will provide a pro-market response to item q, that is:

$$m_{gcqt} = \int_{-\infty}^{\infty} \Phi\left(\frac{\zeta_i - \alpha_{qt}}{\lambda_{qt}}\right) \phi\left(\frac{\zeta_i - \mu_{gct}}{\sigma_{gct}}\right) d\zeta_i \qquad (6.2)$$

$$= \Phi\left(\frac{\mu_{gct} - \alpha_{qc}}{\sqrt{\lambda^2_{qc} + \sigma^2_{gct}}}\right) \qquad (6.3)$$

Under the assumption that we make of a Normal distribution of ζ, the average mood μ_{gct} will coincide with the opinion of the median individual in the group. Thus, μ_{gct} is also the *median* public mood, which is the quantity of interest in our analysis.

Recall that our data set includes aggregate responses to items that we obtain by counting the percentage of individuals in each group that provide a pro-market response. As we explained in Chapters 3 and 4, all of the items that we consider are captured as ordered responses on numerical scales. To turn these *individual-level responses* into *aggregate-level percentages*, we first recoded all responses so that those larger than the scale's midpoint would be pro-market responses and all those smaller than the midpoint would be pro-state responses.[4] This solves the problem of a relatively small number of respondents skewing central tendencies with extreme positions near one or the other end of the spectrum. We then simply add the number of pro-market responses and divide by the total number of responses in the group to obtain an aggregate percentage (or an aggregate proportion after dividing by 100). Consequently, the main input into our analysis consists of aggregate numbers Y_{gcqt} that correspond to the proportion of respondents in group g – citizens, deputies, senators, or presidents – in country c that provide a pro-market response to stimulus q at time t.

Note two things in particular: First, not all groups g respond to the same questions q, but there are a few questions, including *capital openness* and *privatization*, to which *all* groups respond in one way or another. Second, our use of the term "response" is broad; recall in particular that we lack actual survey responses for presidents, as explained in Chapter 4; whenever we refer to presidential responses, we actually are talking about legislators' views on where their president would stand on a variety of issues based on where they place the president and themselves on a left–right scale. In addition, when senators "respond," these are actually deputy responses reweighted to reflect the difference in party seat shares across lower and upper houses, where the latter exist.

We extend the model proposed by McGann (2013) to recover policy moods from the aggregate quantities Y_{gcqt}. Consider the following equations, which link the aggregate responses Y_{gcqt} to the quantities of interest μ_{gct} (we will carefully explain this model in the following paragraphs):

$$Y_{gcqt} \sim \text{Beta}(a_{gcqt}, b) \tag{6.4}$$

$$a_{gcqt} = b \cdot \frac{m_{gcqt}}{1 - m_{gcqt}} \tag{6.5}$$

Equations 6.4 and 6.5 constitute the core of McGann's model of the public mood, a model that looks forbidding but that we can easily unpack into its main components. As mentioned earlier, the data that we input into this model consist of a large number of observed aggregate proportions Y_{gcqt} (remember that all values Y_{gcqt} are originally percentages, but we can also see them as proportions of pro-market responses without losing any relevant information).

---

[4] For example, if a particular question recorded values from 1 to 7, responses larger than 4 would be pro-market and responses lower than 4 would be pro-state. Responses of 4 would be randomly assigned to pro-market or pro-state.

Each observation Y can be thought of as a draw from a probability distribution;[5] here we assume that these draws come from the Beta distribution, which is commonly employed to model outcome variables that can take on any value between 0 and 1. As is true of any probability model, assuming a specific distribution such as the Beta distribution means that we can characterize the general shape of the distribution by focusing on a small number of parameters. Specifically, the main characteristics of the Beta distribution are captured by two parameters, a_{gcqt} and b. Just as we can summarize many characteristics of a normal distribution by knowing its mean and variance, we could actually say plenty about the expected values of Y_{gcqt} from knowing the values that a_{gcqt} and b take. For example, if a_{gcqt} were 5 and b were 1, we would expect Y_{gcqt} to take on a value close to 1 (more precisely, the expectation of Y_{gcqt} would be 5/6.)[6]

In our context, needless to say, we do not know the values of a_{gcqt} and b. Instead, we observe data Y_{gcqt} and, based on these data, we seek to infer the values of a_{gcqt} and b that are most consistent with these observed data and our prior expectations. Notice that, by Equation 6.5, a_{gcqt} is a function of the odds $\frac{m_{gcqt}}{1 - m_{gcqt}}$, which vary across groups, across countries, across stimuli, and across time. These odds capture *systematic* variation in Y_{gcqt}; *stochastic* or residual variation in Y_{gcqt} is captured in this model by the Beta distribution in Equation 6.4.

What kind of factors would produce systematic variation in these odds? Go back to Equation 6.3, which defines m_{gcpt} and points to four drivers of systematic variation. Two of these drivers vary across time, group, *and* country (μ_{gct} and σ^2_{gct}), whereas the other two vary across stimuli *and* country (α_{qc} and λ^2_{qc}). As we mentioned before, the main quantity of interest is parameter μ_{gct}, which corresponds to the "policy mood" of group g in country c at time t. In this formulation, we can therefore estimate, for example, the "policy moods" of *deputies* in *Argentina* in *2010* or of *citizens* in *Peru* in *2002*, provided of course that we have data for these groups. More generally, we can interpret a policy mood μ_{gct} as the expected value at time t of the ideal points of all individuals in group g in country c. Because the assumed distribution of ideal points is Normal, we can also interpret them as "medians" of ideal points, which is precisely the quantity of theoretical interest to us.

An additional advantage of basing a model of the public mood on item response theory microfoundations is that it allows estimation of a second parameter, namely, the *variance* of the distribution of ideal points, σ^2_{gct} in Equation 6.3. This second parameter plays an important role in McGann's approach because it captures the *spread* of the underlying distribution of the ideal points of individuals in the group. To convey intuitively why this

---

[5] That items Y_{gcqt} are "drawn from a common distribution" is equivalent to saying that Y_{gcqt} are assumed "exchangeable" (Jackman 2009, 39–40).

[6] The Beta distribution is sufficiently flexible that it can capture very different shapes of the probability density of numbers between 0 and 1. These different shapes obtain from different values of a and b.

parameter matters, consider the following situation: Compared to year t, the percentage of deputies that declare a "leftist" response to stimulus q in year $t+k$ increases markedly; simultaneously, a smaller number of "rightist" deputies become more radical (i.e., those that respond with a rightist answer report an even higher score for question q). In other words, the distribution of responses for stimulus q goes from unimodal and centrist to bimodal and relatively polarized, with a much larger mode on "leftist" responses. We should expect our estimate of the policy mood to veer "left," since that is the direction that a majority of legislators (including, by definition, the median legislator) are taking. However, as we noted earlier, Stimson's dyad-ratios algorithm could very well find a rightist turn in the legislators' policy mood despite the increase in leftist responses *precisely because of the increase in the rightist responses of a minority*. By estimating a separate spread parameter σ^2, McGann's model circumvents this possibility. With this measure of spread we can also obtain a sense of longitudinal variation in the ideological "heterogeneity" of Latin American political systems, an opportunity that we exploit elsewhere in this book (see Chapters 9 and 10).

The remaining parameters (α and λ^2) capture characteristics of the stimuli themselves; these are in fact the item parameters that we described previously in some detail. Parameter α_{qc} captures the "difficulty" of question q in country c, that is, it provides a general sense of how common it is to see pro-market responses to this item in a given country. Values of α_{qc} close to 0 correspond to items that divide respondents in the middle of the policy mood spectrum more or less evenly between pro-market and pro-state responses. Item q's "discrimination" ability is captured by parameter λ^2; as we explained before, values of λ^2_{qc} far from 0 suggest that item q is a relatively poor tracer of the underlying policy moods of all groups in country c.[7]

6.1.1 Adding Prior Information to the Model

In order to arrive at inferences about the quantities of interest in our model, especially about the policy moods μ, we need to be particularly clear about our *ex ante* beliefs, that is, we need to state explicitly our expectations about the likely distribution of these policy moods even before looking at data. This is especially important given that the model captured in Equations 6.3 and 6.4 is *not identified* by data. This means that there are actually an infinite number of values of α, λ^2, μ, and σ^2 that are consistent with the information furnished by data Y. To see why this would be the case, think about two legislatures, one leftist and one rightist, furnishing respectively very low and very high values of observed data Y. We could locate their positions on some arbitrary scale by picking any pair of values to represent that one is to the left of the other: -2 and 2 would work, but so would -1.5 and 2.5. This indeterminacy is known

---

[7] Note our switch from λ in Equation 6.1 to λ^2 in Equation 6.3, where the squared component obtains when we average over individual pro-market proclivities ζ. We again refer the reader to McGann (2013) for a technical discussion.

as the problem of *additive aliasing*: by adding 0.5 to our original −2:2 scale, we end up representing the exact same situation albeit with different numbers. Similarly, we could decide that negative values represent a "rightist" response and positive values a "leftist" response, so we could instead declare that −2 and 2 correspond to the positions of a "rightist" and of a "leftist" legislature. This indeterminacy is known as *multiplicative aliasing*: simply by multiplying by −1 we managed to represent the exact same situation but with different polarity. In order to obtain a single, workable set of parameter estimates, we need to impose a number of additional constraints. These constraints come from our *ex ante* assumptions – or prior beliefs – about the distribution of policy moods in Latin America.[8]

The first assumption that we make, our first belief if you will, is that average policy moods are Normally distributed. That is, in the absence of data, we would expect the median policy-maker and the median citizen to hold "centrist" views most of the time, which is a different way of saying that we expect "extremist" views to be relatively rare. To codify this expectation, we impose a standard normal prior on the policy mood parameters, that is, we assume $\mu_{gct} \sim \mathcal{N}(0, 1)$. In practice, using this prior as a constraint means that the policy moods that we estimate will be centered around 0, that most median policy moods across groups, countries, and years (a priori, about 64 percent of them, in fact) will be located between −1 and 1 and that only a handful of median policy moods (about 5 percent of them) may be larger than 2 or smaller than −2. This prior communicates that we think it would be very improbable to see policy moods beyond −3 or 3 (we expect only about 0.03 percent of all median policy moods would fall beyond these bounds). The assumption that median actors hold normally distributed preferences solves the problem of additive aliasing, and is also evidently feasible.[9]

6.1.2 Pooling Information Partially across Groups and Countries

Having solved the *additive aliasing* problem, we now explain how we address the *multiplicative aliasing* or *rotational invariance* problem, that is, the possibility of representing "rightist" legislatures and citizenries with either positive or negative numbers (we aim to represent "rightist" legislatures and citizenries

---

[8] For more on identification issues, we recommend Bafumi et al. (2005) and Johnson and Albert (1999).

[9] We also impose a specific distributional constraint on parameters σ^2, which capture within-group heterogeneity (where group, again, can be citizens or different policy-makers in a particular country-year). We stipulate that σ^2 can only take nonnegative values. A few additional technical details: parameters σ^2 have prior probability Gamma(2, 1). This particular distribution has expectation 2 and standard deviation $\sqrt{2}$. These priors have an important theoretical implication. Say that, from one year to the next, we observe that the fraction of individuals that provide a market response to a given item increases markedly. The prior that we use implies that we give *ex ante* similar weight (i) to the probability that the change reflects a shift in the policy mood and (ii) to the probability that the change reflects an increase in the heterogeneity of individual preferences.

with positive numbers and "leftist" legislatures and citizenries with negative numbers). To do so, we comment on modeling decisions that also determine how we combine information from different groups (citizens and policy-makers) and different countries to ensure that our policy mood estimates reflect, but are not unduly driven by, idiosyncratic country and group characteristics.

To motivate the discussion, consider the most obvious modeling option we could have taken, namely, to estimate the model described in Equations 6.3 and 6.4 on *separate* "country-group" samples: We could have estimated eighteen different models based on data from citizens in each of the countries we observe, plus eighteen different models based on data from policy-makers – in principle, we could even have estimated separate models for deputies, senators (where they exist), and presidents. We refer to this as a "no pooling" option. Had we followed this strategy, the policy mood scales across groups and countries would still be located on a scale with similar end points – after all, the policy moods would be identically identified by the common $\mathcal{N}(0, 1)$ prior distribution on μ that we stipulated before. Even then, there would still be no guarantee that the different stimuli would discriminate in similar ways across groups and countries. Any given stimulus – say, a question on whether government should provide unemployment benefits – may end up having very high discriminant power for citizens in Argentina but not for deputies in Mexico, which in fact means that we would not be placing citizens in Argentina and deputies in Mexico on the same scale.

Furthermore, in making inferences about policy moods and item parameters in group g in country c, this "no pooling" option would disregard *all* information from other groups or countries. We do not think this a reasonable strategy. The no-pooling option only makes sense if we believe that actors and countries in the region are so drastically different from each other that we stand nothing to gain by allowing information from policy-makers to make more precise inferences about the policy moods of citizens or that responses from citizens in Guatemala could not aid in measuring moods of citizens in Honduras. In other words, a no-pooling strategy overstates the degree of uniqueness across groups, countries, and time periods. This assumption does not seem plausible. Consider, for example, that knowledge that Peruvians embrace a turn to markets already provides a clue that nationals of other countries might behave similarly – unless, again, we are willing to state that Peruvians and all other citizenries in Latin America behave in a completely idiosyncratic fashion.[10]

---

[10] In preliminary work, we in fact estimated the policy moods of citizenries in eighteen independent models and discovered that the resulting policy moods were very similar across countries. Furthermore, we ascertained that the similarities were not produced by the types of questions contained in the AB and LB, which would be a reasonable concern because questions change from year to year, but not across countries within the same year. We concluded that there is in fact a strong regional similarity in country-specific citizen policy moods.

In contrast, consider the mirror strategy of fitting *one single model* where we pool together information from *all* groups in *all* countries and estimate a single set of item parameters α and λ^2. In this "complete pooling" scenario, the discriminant power of any given stimulus is assumed to be identical across groups and countries, regardless of whether we consider policy-makers or citizens and regardless of whether we look at actors in Brazil or in Guatemala. Clearly, this strategy depends on the assumption that identical positions on an underlying state–market divide get translated into identical stances on particular issues, hence on identical scores on survey stimuli throughout the region and across citizens and policy-makers. In other words, this modeling strategy completely ignores variation across groups, countries, and time periods. Thus, complete pooling also strains credulity, especially as we compare the opinions of policy-makers – whose business it is to develop clear positions on a number of issues and to package and advertise these positions in ideological bundles that they can "sell" to the electorate – with those of citizens, who are not always as willing to reflect on the ideological consistency of their own viewpoints.

We follow what we feel is an appropriate middle-of-the-road "partial pooling" modeling strategy in which our estimate of the policy mood of group g in country c at time t depends first and foremost on data for this subset but also "borrows strength" from information from other groups in other countries at different times.[11] The canonical way to achieve this is to combine information from all subsets in a principled way by imposing a so-called hierarchical structure on item parameters α and λ^2 that, again, represent the difficulty and discrimination characteristics of the various issues we consider. We first state what the hierarchical structure of these parameters looks like, we then comment on why we think imposing these particular structures is appropriate. We start with our prior views on λ^2, which we represent as follows:

$$\lambda^2_{qc} \sim \text{Gamma}(v_{\lambda_c} + v_{\lambda_q}, 2) \qquad (6.6)$$

$$v_{\lambda_c} \sim \text{Gamma}(2, 2)$$

$$v_{\lambda_q} \sim \text{Gamma}(2, 2)$$

To understand what this structure means, recall that we code all input data Y so that higher values correspond to larger proportions of citizens or policy-makers that register a pro-market response. By assuming that λ^2_{qc} follows a Gamma distribution, we force these parameters to take nonnegative values, that is, we stipulate that higher values of Y – values closer to 1 – correspond to a pro-market propensity among political actors. This assumption – that

---

[11] Huber and Gabel (2000) consider two of these options in an analysis of manifesto data and conclude that pooling across countries and years provides the most appropriate estimates of the left–right placements of parties, when compared against no pooling estimates; they do not consider partial pooling, however. See Jackman (2009, 308 ff) for a demonstration that the partial pooling estimator dominates the no pooling and complete pooling estimators in producing lower mean square error.

λ^2 follow a Gamma distribution – addresses the problem of multiplicative aliasing. Notice from the q and c subindexes that we estimate a separate λ^2 discrimination parameter for each item/country combination. The actual estimates $\widehat{\lambda}^2_{qc}$ are a compromise between two sources of information, which we label ν_{λ_c} (*nu*) and ν_{λ_q}. Consider ν_{λ_q} first: For every question q in our data set, we estimate a separate parameter ν_{λ_q} that captures the *average* discriminating power of stimulus q across all countries. We do the same for every country c, for which we estimate a separate parameter ν_{λ_c} that captures the *average* discriminating power of all stimuli within each country. Because these are probabilistic statements, we acknowledge the possibility that different items will have different discriminating powers across different countries. But the particular priors that we have selected – the "shape" and "scale" quantities within Gamma() – mean that these different discriminating power parameters will not be too far away from a common value.

An example may help us convey more intuitively what we mean. Say that we knew that the question on whether government should provide unemployment benefits tends to discriminate clearly among those that have pro-state views and those that have pro-market preferences, that is, items dealing with unemployment benefits are likely to have high discrimination power, which means that λ will likely be small. Say also that we learned simultaneously from responses to this question in a sample of Peruvian citizens that this particular item may not be a powerful predictor of the pro-market propensities of Peruvians. The hierarchical structure that we impose on the data allows for an estimate of $\lambda^2_{\text{employment, Peru}}$ that, based on data, will certainly be higher than the other λ^2 parameters corresponding to other items and countries but that will remain informed by our general prior knowledge that the employment question tends to be a good predictor of underlying propensities. The parameter $\lambda^2_{\text{employment, Peru}}$ will be "partially pooled" toward the mean of all λ^2 parameters; in other words, we could say that our estimate of $\lambda^2_{\text{employment, Peru}}$ "borrows strength" from the data that inform all other λ^2 parameters.

The prior distributions that we have assumed on λ^2 provide this partial pooling characteristic and guarantee that our estimates of these parameters are always positive, consistent with our coding of Y where higher values correspond to pro-market views. However, the prior distributions are still "wide" enough that they give us a chance to reassess whether the items should really be seen as positive "discriminants" and whether partial pooling is a plausible modeling assumption. In fact, the ex ante probability that we would observe a value of λ^2_{qc} larger than, say, 2 is about 1 in 10.[12] With these priors, we could still find that a particular stimulus λ^2_{qc} discriminates less powerfully in the direction of pro-market dispositions; the *observable clue* that this had happened

---

[12] Based on the assumptions we make about the prior distribution of λ^2_{qc}, its expected value is 1 and the mode of the prior distribution is 0.5.

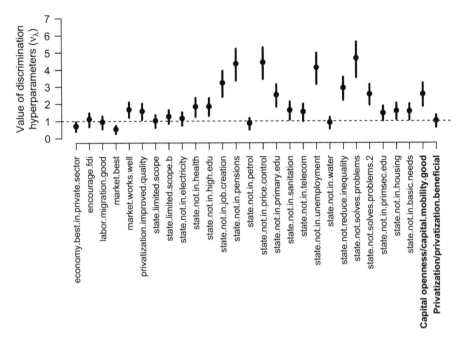

FIGURE 6.2. Posterior distribution of discrimination hyperparameters. The figure depicts the median and 50 percent highest posterior density interval of the posterior distribution of hyperparameters v_λ, which capture the partially pooled discrimination power of twenty-eight items across countries and years.

would be a *posterior* distribution $\widehat{\lambda}^2_{qc}$ extremely far from 0. This would signal that there really is no "linkage" (Hinich and Munger 1992) between issue q in country c and the state–market dimension. For example, Figure 6.2 shows the posterior distributions of v_{λ_q}, which captures the average discriminating power of each item q across all countries. It is obvious that, though some of them are larger than expected (and we expected them to hover around 1), they are all not very far from 0, which confirms that all of these items are positive discriminants that turn pro-market ideal points into pro-market aggregate responses.

However, some posterior distributions of *specific* values of $\widehat{\lambda}^2_{qc}$ are very far from 0. Figure 6.3 presents the cross-country distribution of the partially pooled discrimination parameters. In the plot, the light dots correspond to point estimates (means of the posterior distribution) of each *country-specific* discrimination parameter for each of the twenty-eight different items. In this set, the median discrimination parameter estimate is 2.39. The dark intervals capture the 25th–75th percentiles of the distribution of the point estimates. A dotted line at 1 corresponds to our prior expectation of the value of these parameters, and we have added a second dotted line at 5 to clearly distinguish the possibility that some errant country-specific parameters might hit that mark.

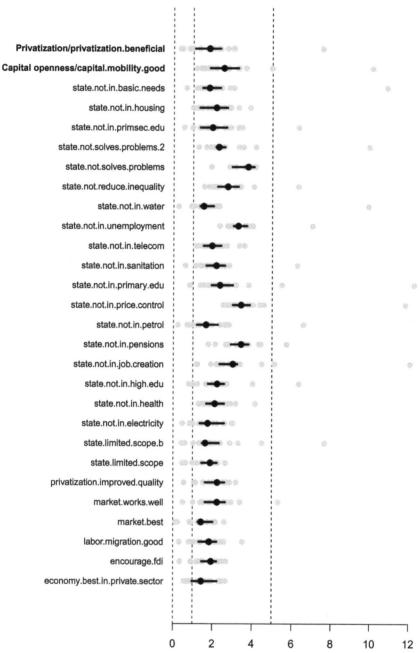

FIGURE 6.3. Posterior distribution of item discrimination parameters (λ_{qc}). The plot displays point estimates (means, in gray) of all country-specific discrimination parameters for twenty-eight items. The overlaid dark point and bar are the median and 25th–75th percentiles of the cross-country distribution of point estimates for each of the twenty-eight items.

Altogether, only a very small proportion of the country-specific discrimination parameters are larger than 5 (21 out of 503, or about 4.2 percent, which is a much larger than the 0.05 percent that we allowed for in our prior distributions). We infer that these correspond to items that lack discrimination in those particular countries.

Yet, the overwhelming majority of all items retain positive and small discrimination parameter estimates in all countries, which makes us feel at ease with using this particular restriction (a positive prior on item discrimination parameters) to guarantee that the diverse citizen and policy-maker policy moods that we need to estimate will have the correct polarity (i.e., that policy positions and attitudes will "load" on the latent policy mood scale "in the right direction," with higher scores corresponding to pro-market policies).

Aside from the discrimination parameters λ, we mentioned before that items are characterized by difficulty parameters α, which in a way capture how controversial an item is. Estimated values of α close to 0 correspond to items that divide a population with moderate preferences more or less along the middle. Values of α away from 0, both positive and negative, suggest that a larger number of individuals would provide the same response (when $\alpha < 0$, fewer individuals provide a pro-market response; see Figure 6.1).[13]

6.2 A PRINCIPLED INDEX OF PRO-MARKET PUBLIC POLICY

After showing how we identify the *policy mood* scale, our second task is to ensure that actual *policy orientations* – or the basket of economic policies adopted – are measured on that same scale. Just as with policy moods, our general policy orientation scale is a function of a number of policy items, which correspond to different economic policy areas. Table 5.1 in Chapter 5 displays the policy indicators that inform our policy estimates. As we explained in Chapter 5, we recoded all of these indicators to construct sets of ordered categories. For each policy, we consider four ordered categories: low, middle-low, middle-high, and high. In all cases, higher categories correspond to what we consider to be less state-oriented, more market-oriented policies.

As was the case with the policy moods, we start from the assumption that the items in Table 5.1 are observable measures of an underlying, unobservable policy dimension that we call pro-market *policy orientation*. The *policy*

---

[13] We comment briefly on priors for α, for which we also use a "nested" structure of the following form: $\alpha_{qc} \sim \mathcal{N}(v_{\alpha_c} + v\alpha_q, 10)$, $v_{\alpha_c} \sim \mathcal{N}(0, 10)$, $v_{\alpha_q} \sim \mathcal{N}(0, 10)$. As suggested by these equations, we place relatively informative priors for α_{qc} that vary around *common* country-specific values (v_{α_c}) and *common* question-specific values (v_{α_q}). These hyperparameters are in turn modeled as draws from Normal distributions with very narrow variances. These particular constraints serve no identification purposes, but they make sense given the scales we imposed for μ and λ^2 (Johnson and Albert 1999, ch. 6). Note that we use prior distributions for model parameters that vary from McGann's recommendations, but these differences do not introduce radical departures from his model.

orientation index we build is inspired by Morley, Machado, and Pettinato (1999) and Lora (2012), who construct average *structural reform policy* scores based on different additive indicators for a number of issue areas. However, we deviate from their efforts in some important respects. First, we extend Lora's (2012) data in terms of time coverage, updating some of the series that he originally considered up to the year 2014. The main result of this effort is that, whenever possible, we have added five more years of information for each of the eighteen countries in our study. However, as Table 5.1 shows, there are still a number of indicators that we are unable to update. In our measurement model, these indicators that we were unable to update generate a number of missing values from 2009 to 2014, adding to a smaller number of extant missing values elsewhere in Lora's data. Thus, as an improvement upon previous approaches, we treat empty cells as values missing-at-random upon conditioning on *observed* values of other indicators, thus incorporating all available information into our estimates of a policy dimension rather than resorting to list-wise deletion, which could possibly bias our estimates of *policy orientation* and would certainly reduce the number of country-years for which we could provide such estimates. To clarify, we do not carry out multiple imputation followed by model estimation; instead, each of these missing cells can be understood as a parameter for which we can provide a "guess" as a by-product of Bayesian model estimation.

Second, we embrace the notion that not all of the indicators that appear in Table 5.1 might be equally informative about the underlying *policy orientation* of a country. In fact, it seems patently obvious that not all pro-market policy movements convey the same amount of information about the underlying *policy orientation* of a country, which is the assumption that others make when they build additive indexes. To put it differently, some indicators reveal more information than others about a country's underlying *policy orientation* and we should therefore weight them differently.[14] A few of these policies could be very weak discriminants of the level to which a government's policies are state- or market-oriented. To see why, consider that some policies are by now so well established as appropriate to Latin American circumstances that governments of all ideological stripes adopt them without giving their implementation a second thought. For example, if both market- and state-fundamentalists were equally likely to adopt low tariffs, then learning that a new country implemented this particular policy is not likely to tell us much about the country's *policy orientation*, regardless of whatever we, as analysts, think about the market-orientation of that particular policy. Consequently,

---

[14] Escaith and Paunovic (2004) carry out a factor analysis scaling exercise and score the main principal factor as a policy index. This approach recognizes that not every item is equally informative about variation in the underlying policy orientation. At the same time, the factor analysis techniques that Escaith and Paunovic use rely on a number of distributional assumptions about the input indicators – that is, that these are continuous, unbounded, Normal variables – that are difficult to defend on empirical grounds.

just as we calculated item-specific discrimination parameters for citizen and politician policy moods, we allow here for the possibility that some of the policy indicators we consider may not really have much discriminating power. As was the case with item-specific discrimination parameters for policy moods, whether our policy items enjoy discriminating power or not is entirely an empirical question that we will be able to answer based on our estimates.

To obtain *policy orientation* scores, we estimate a graded-response model with the following functional form:

$$Y_{ctj} \sim \text{Categorical}(\pi_{ctj,1:4}) \tag{6.7}$$

$$\pi_{ctjk} = \begin{cases} P_{ctj1} & \text{if } k = 1 \\ P_{ctjk} - P_{ctj,k-1} & \text{if } k \in 2, \dots, 4 \end{cases} \tag{6.8}$$

$$P_{c,t,j,k} = \begin{cases} F\left(\frac{\theta_{ct}}{\eta_{jc}} - \kappa_{jk}\right) & \text{if } k \in 1, \dots, 3 \\ 1 & \text{if } k = 4 \end{cases} \tag{6.9}$$

In this model, c and t index observations at the country and year levels and j is a policy item index, with each policy item j taking values between 1 and 4 that correspond to different ordered categories (i.e., values 1–4 correspond to low, middle-low, middle-high, and high levels of the policy in question, and these values are set up so that higher numbers correspond to pro-market policies). Each outcome variable Y then corresponds to the value that policy j takes in country c at time t, and is modeled as having positive probability of being in the first to fourth categories. The chances that Y will take on values $1, \dots, 4$ are driven by the parameter vector π (*pi*), where the elements $\pi_1, \dots, \pi_4$ of this vector add up to one, as befits probability values. Probabilities π are calculated from a number of quantiles P_{ctjk}, which are themselves a function of policy orientation parameters θ_{ct} (*theta*), of three cut points κ_{jk} (*kappa*) for each policy item, and of item-specific discrimination parameters η_j (*eta*).[15] Parameters κ correspond to the cut points that determine whether a country with *policy orientation* θ will set policy at the lowest category (to the left of κ_1), the middle-low category (between κ_1 and κ_2), the middle-high category (between κ_2 and κ_3), or the high category (to the right of κ_3). We estimate all but one of these parameters (κ_1 is set to 0 for identification purposes). Parameters θ_{ct} correspond to the *policy orientation* of country c and time t and are the quantities of interest in our measurement model.

As was the case with McGann's model, the model specified in Equations 6.7 and 6.8 can only be identified upon adding a number of constraining assumptions. Without further constraints on θ, κ, and η, an infinite number of solutions exist that would fit the data equally well. Furthermore, even after placing appropriate constraints on θ, κ, and η to arrive at a unique solution,

---

[15] $F(\cdot)$ is the logistic cumulative distribution function, which makes this part of the specification an ordered logit model.

nothing guarantees that policy orientation parameters θ will be comparable to parameters μ, that is, to the policy moods of Section 6.1, which is the entire point of our enterprise. We thus require a number of additional assumptions to turn this into a profitable exercise.

We first place prior distributions on θ that are identical to the ones that we employed for parameters μ, that is, standard Normal distributions. This restriction implies that, a priori, we expect most policy orientations (and policy moods, as we explained before) to be more or less contained within a range bounded by -2 and 2. While this guarantees that the policy mood scale and the policy orientation scale will have similar "numbers," we have still not forced these similar numbers to have identical meaning. To do so, consider first the discrimination parameters η. To identify the direction of the policy orientation scale, we stipulate a Gamma prior distribution on each parameter η_j, which excludes the possibility that these parameters will take on negative values. This is the exact same assumption that we made before about the prior distribution of discrimination parameters λ^2. This guarantees that positive policy orientation scores can be interpreted as "pro-market" and negative scores as "pro-state," just as in the policy mood model the restriction on λ^2 helped us identify scores in a similar way. Based on our previous discussion about the benefits of "partial pooling," we also nest parameters η within countries and items, centering them around the sum of hyperparameters ν_{η_c} and ν_{η_q}. In short, we assume $\eta_j \sim \text{Gamma}(\nu_{\eta_c} + \nu_{\eta_q}, 2)$.[16]

Figure 6.4 shows the posterior distributions for parameters ν_{η_q}. All of the policy items are bounded away from zero; a few – *job termination cost, minimum wage*, or *social security tax* – provide relatively more information to help us discriminate among pro-market or pro-state policy orientations. In contrast, items like *average tariff, trade dispersion, financial transaction tax, hiring flexibility*, and *capital openness*/capital.mobility.good are slightly less powerful discriminants of the pro-market or pro-state policy orientation of governments. We conclude from inspection of the posterior distributions of these parameters as they appear in Figure 6.4 that imposing the assumption of nonnegative values achieves the purpose of eliminating rotational invariance in an unidentified model while remaining consistent with observed data.

The reader may have noted that two policies – *capital openness* and *privatization* – appear in Figure 6.4 linked to survey questions about policies named *capital.mobility.good* and *privatization.beneficial*. The paired mention of *capital openness/capital.mobility.good* and *privatization/privatization. beneficial* speaks directly to the linchpin of our strategy to place *policy moods* and *policy orientation* on a similar scale. While constraining η identifies the direction of the *policy orientation* scale, and while priors on θ and μ

---

[16] In turn, the prior distribution for ν_{η_c} and ν_{η_q} is Gamma(2, 2), just as we did for ν_{λ_c} and ν_{λ_q} in the equations following 6.6.

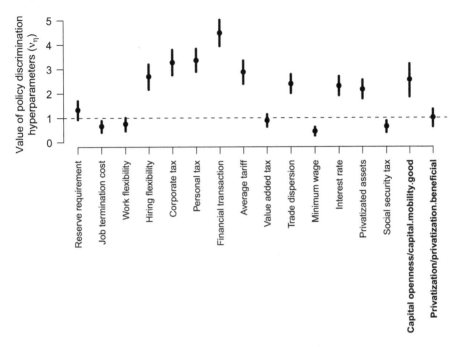

FIGURE 6.4. Posterior distribution of policy discrimination hyperparameters. The figure depicts the median and 50 percent highest posterior density interval of the posterior distribution of hyperparameters v_η, which capture the partially pooled discrimination power of sixteen policies across countries and years.

guarantee that *policy orientation* scores and *policy mood* scores are more or less commensurate, we still have not guaranteed that the thematic contents of these scales will be aligned. Even if the discrimination parameters of policies in the graded-response model (i.e., η) and the discrimination parameters of survey questions in the IRT model (i.e., λ^2) are all constrained to be positive, our estimates of these parameters may still be so different that the thematic content of policy orientations may be distinct from the thematic content of policy moods. This problem is made all the more grievous by the fact that the set of policies that we use to infer policy orientations and the set of survey questions that we use to infer policy moods are related to slightly different aspects of the economy. Among the policies that we use to capture policy orientations, for example, we count a number that have to do with regulation of labor markets, whereas we lack similar questions in our surveys of citizens and politicians. In contrast, the surveys include stimuli on the desirability that the state guarantees benefits to pensioners and the unemployed, but we only have a broad policy item – social security tax – that speaks to these matters.

In short, in the absence of identically worded items that can "bridge" the IRT and graded-response models, even the prior distributions that we have employed so far fail to deliver the common scale we require. We have thus embraced the strong assumption that the item discrimination parameters v_{η_q} and v_{λ_q} that correspond to *capital openness* and capital.mobility.good, on the one hand, and to *privatization* and privatization.beneficial, on the other, are one and the same quantities, that is, $v_{\eta_{\text{capital openness}}} = v_{\lambda_{\text{capital.mobility.good}}}$ and $v_{\eta_{\text{privatization}}} = v_{\lambda_{\text{privatization.beneficial}}}$. In practical terms, we simply changed the coding of these two policies (*capital openness* and *privatization*), considering them aggregate proportions instead of ordered categorical variables: we coded ordered categorical values of 1 and 2 as 0s and values of 3 and 4 as 1s.

With these items forced to act as common bridges between policy moods and policy orientations we ensure that *uncommon* item parameters for both the graded-response model and the IRT model will be scaled *in reference to* these two *common* item parameters. With all item parameters calibrated to the same yardstick, the contents of the policy mood and policy orientation scales are guaranteed to be thematically similar. As can be seen in both Figures 6.3 and 6.4, the item-specific hyperparameters for these two sets of common items – that is, *capital openness/capital.mobility.good* and *privatization/privatization.beneficial* – are identical across plots. More importantly, these parameters have middling-to-high discrimination power; the discrimination ability of "privatization/privatization.beneficial" is especially large.

Our identification strategy thus depends on bridging surveys, on the one hand, and a database on policy indicators, on the other, by imposing an assumption of identical meaning for two pairs of stimuli/policies. That is, there is only one set of discrimination parameters for each of these pairs of stimuli/policies; the discrimination parameters for *capital openness* and *privatization* are invariant across the model that includes *all the survey data* and the model that includes *all the policy indicators*. These discrimination parameters then guarantee that all other survey stimuli and all other policy indicators will have discrimination parameters that are scaled in accordance to the value taken by the discrimination parameters for *capital openness* and *privatization*, thus guaranteeing that *policy orientations* and *policy moods* are measured on the same scale. The crucial assumption is that survey responses about *capital openness* and *privatization* are commensurable with policies implemented in these areas. Once we make this assumption, the idea of using these stimuli/policies to "bridge" different scales is straightforward. In this regard, the use of similar techniques to "bridge" different scales is widespread in political science. For example, Saiegh (2015) "bridges" the positions of legislators and citizens in four Latin American countries by considering their placements of regional political figures, and Jessee (2009) "bridges" the positions of US senators and voters by requiring the latter to "vote" Aye or Nay on bills considered in the US Senate (see also, among many others, Bafumi and Herron 2010, Bailey 2007, Jessee 2010, 2012, Martin and Quinn 2002).

6.3 ASSESSING MODEL FIT

We work within a Bayesian inferential framework to estimate our unified IRT/graded-response model of policy moods and policy orientations. Complete Stan code for our model appears in Online Appendix D. In order to ensure that we appropriately sample from the posterior distribution of parameters in our model, we eschew the first 1,250 iterations of each of ten Markov chains. Inferences are based on 250 scans from each chain after apparent convergence. We assess convergence based on Gelman–Rubin's $\hat{R}$ statistic. Convergence details and code to replicate the model is available in our GitHub replication repository.

The attentive reader will worry that the combination of priors we have described may prove too constraining, preventing information contained in our data from changing our a priori beliefs about these parameters, and introducing so much extraneous information that our model might fail in the task of achieving good fit to the data. As a rejoinder, we discuss in this section the general fit of the model, which is relatively good. Because the model is complicated, we cannot provide a single statistic that summarizes how well the model reproduces relevant characteristics of the data. Instead, we decided to divide up the discussion to correspond to the different measurement levels that we have for the outcome variables in our analysis. Recall that the outcomes we inspect include: (i) aggregate percentages corresponding to the proportion of actors in a collective – citizens and policy-makers – that hold pro-market views, (ii) a dichotomous indicator corresponding to whether country c in year t has adopted policies consistent with high capital mobility (capital.mobility.good) and high levels of privatization (privatization.beneficial), and (iii) ordered categories for fourteen additional policies, any of which can take on integer values 1 through 4.

Consider first the aggregate percentages. Based on the posterior distribution of parameters in our model we can obtain complete predictive distributions for these percentages. For each aggregate percentage Y_{gcqt}, we calculate an 80 percent credible interval around the fitted value $\hat{Y}_{gcqt}$ (the mean of the posterior distribution), then ascertain the frequency with which observed values Y fall within said intervals. Overall, our predictive distributions contain the observed values Y 91.7 percent of the time. We see some variation in these statistics across different actors: 90.4 for citizens, 89.4 for presidents, 89.8 for legislators, and a whopping 97.6 for senators.[17]

These statistics can of course be misleading if our 80 percent credible intervals are simply so broad that they always contain observed values of Y. An alternative way to consider model fit is to estimate R^2 measures. When we

---

[17] One would be tempted to think of these as "coverage" statistics; they are not, since we are not constructing multiple confidence intervals based on different data samples and then counting how many of these contain the observed value of Y. If that were the case, we would expect observed values to be covered 80 percent of the time by an 80 percent credible interval.

TABLE 6.1. *Predictive success of the graded response component of the model of policy moods and policy orientations. The first row includes the average number of categorical values that our model predicts correctly, while the second row shows the predictive success of a "dumb" model that predicts all responses to be in a given category $k \in \{1, \ldots, 4\}$.*

	$k = 1$	$k = 2$	$k = 3$	$k = 4$
Average $\Pr(\hat{y} = k \mid y = k)$	0.68	0.58	0.69	0.77
Predictive success when all predictions are k	0.11	0.22	0.39	0.28

use the *median* of the posterior distribution of $\hat{Y}$ as our point estimate of Y, R^2 reaches about 0.66, indicating a correlation of about 0.8 between our model's predicted values and the observed aggregate percentages. Because the posterior distributions of $\hat{Y}$ are in the unit range, they tend to be skewed; however, even when we use *means* of $\hat{Y}$ as point estimates, we still estimate R^2 at 0.67.

The second set of outcomes corresponds to the two policies that we use to bridge the policy orientation and policy mood scales. Recall that these two policies are coded dichotomously, and that we use a logistic link function to tie outcomes to predictors. About 81 percent of the observed outcomes are 0, which means that merely considering modal prediction – that is, predicting all of these outcomes to be 0 – already sets a high bar for goodness of fit. Our model correctly predicts about 99 percent of all observations, which translates into an adjusted-count R^2 of 0.95. An alternative way to calculate a pseudo-R^2 measure for dichotomous models is to consider the predicted probability of observing 1 among observations that are in fact 1, and to subtract from this quantity the predicted probability of observing 1 among observations that are 0, that is, $\Pr(\hat{y} = 1 \mid y = 1) - \Pr(\hat{y} = 1 \mid y = 0)$. Based on our estimates, this statistic is 0.92 in our model (the average predicted probability that an observation will be 1 is 0.94 for observations coded 1 and 0.019 for observations coded 0).

Finally, we assess goodness of fit for the third set of outcomes, which are ordered categories, by considering first the average predicted probability that an observation will be in category k among observations that are in fact in category k. This information is related in Table 6.1, along with the predictive success that we would obtain for each category k if we simply predicted all observations to take on value k. As these statistics make clear, our predictive success for this third set of outcomes is more modest than for the set of dichotomous measures, but we still achieve a very reasonable fit to observed data. For example, were we use a null model that predicts that all observations take on value $k = 1$, we would succeed in correctly guessing 11 percent of these outcomes, but we would be wrong 89 percent of the time; our model, as can be seen in Table 6.1, correctly picks as $k = 1$ 68% of the observations that in fact take on that value, which means that 32 percent of the observations for which $k = 1$ are erroneously predicted as having a value of $k \in 2, 3, 4$.

TABLE 6.2. *Confusion matrix for ordered outcomes. The matrix shows the total number of correctly predicted categorical outcomes on the main diagonal; off the main diagonal, cell entries should be interpreted as bad predictions.*

Observed k	Predicted k			
	1	2	3	4
1	510	104	26	18
2	101	918	199	45
3	7	115	1,973	148
4	0	27	235	1,336

Perhaps a better way to look at the predictive capacity of the model for this third set of outcomes is to consider a confusion matrix, which appears in Table 6.2. Although we do see a nontrivial number of bad predictions (i.e., instances where our model predicts k but we observe something different), we note that the proportion of correctly predicted outcomes (those in the main diagonal) is 0.82. Notice as well that most errors in prediction result in predicted values of k that are within one category of the correct value; in other words, many of these errors are near misses.

We conclude that our model fits the data reasonably well. This is of course not a complete surprise. After all, our model is extremely flexible and has good fit precisely because it includes an inordinately large number of parameters. We make no apologies for this flexibility; this is, after all, the characteristic that guarantees that our estimates of *policy orientations* and *policy moods* are located on the same scale.

6.4 CHAPTER SUMMARY

As we close Part I of this book, which provides information about our measurement strategy for all components of the "stages" in the chain of representation, let us briefly summarize what our unified model achieves. We have endeavored in this chapter to show that our estimates of *policy moods* and of *policy orientation* do not only reflect information in our data faithfully, but also, and more importantly, that they are identified on a common scale. That is the important take-home point of this chapter. The basic assumption underlying our claim about a common scale is that two specific policies – *capital openness* and *privatization* – are so tightly mapped to two survey items – capital.mobility.good and privatization.beneficial – that we can estimate a single discrimination parameter for each of these pairs. This is the crucial identifying assumption that helps us "bridge" policy moods of citizens and politicians and actual policy orientations of the economic development strategies adopted. Armed with policy moods for a number of actors and with policy orientation scores, both of which vary across countries and throughout time, we are now better equipped to explore the questions of congruence and responsiveness that we first laid out in Chapter 1.

However, before we look at congruence and responsiveness across the stages of democratic representation, in Part II we discuss how the institutions that structure Latin American politics may help or hinder the possibility of a close correspondence between citizen and policy-makers' preferences, and between the preferences of policy-makers and the policy outcomes that they choose.

PART II

LINKAGES

7

Linkage 1: Electoral Systems

Our goal in this chapter is to make explicit our thinking about how electoral rules impact congruence – the extent to which voters' sincere preferences (see Chapter 3) are translated into the sincere preferences of politicians (see Chapter 4) – and to catalog the variation in those rules that we observe in Latin America. Electoral rules are used to select the individuals and parties who will consequently be in charge of making policy. Voters' ability to put into office elected representatives who share their policy preferences is undoubtedly a function of an enormous array of factors – among these the political sophistication of the average citizen, the forthrightness of those competing for office, and the extent to which voters and politicians share a vocabulary for talking about politics. We are interested in the role of election rules in this process of delegation. Electoral rules play a role in how many parties enter a race, where they locate themselves ideologically (on the state-to-market continuum), how voters coordinate on those offerings, and how their votes are translated into seats.

We reason that the incentives imposed by electoral rules produce variation in the likelihood that the median voter and the median politician will share a set of preferences, therefore producing differential levels of *one-to-one congruence*. Even more so, electoral rules produce variation in the likelihood that the distribution of preferences observed among citizens will be mirrored by the distribution of preferences among politicians in a particular branch or chamber, thus impacting *many-to-many congruence*. It follows then that electoral rules should also affect *many-to-one* congruence: the location of some pivotal policy-maker's preferences with respect to the distribution of citizens' preferences.

These variations in incentives are a function of the "strength" of the electoral system. "Strong" (restrictive or constraining) electoral systems constrain politicians to coordinate carefully around a few parties and voters to coordinate carefully around a few candidates if they want to translate their preferences into legislative seats. "Weak" (or permissive) electoral systems faithfully translate votes into seats even if elites offer many choices and voters distribute their support across them (Cox 1987). On the one hand, weak or permissive systems encourage voters to act on their sincere preferences, even when those preferences are not widely shared by other voters. As a result, these systems also encourage a wider array of elites to enter the fray. Strong or restrictive systems, on the other hand, encourage relatively greater coordination by entering elites and voting citizens. Citizens who anticipate that their most-preferred candidates will not be backed by a winning share of voters would have incentives to act strategically, looking for a viable choice not too far from their sincere preferences.

To be clear, we are not suggesting that entering candidates and parties or voting citizens can ever ignore strategic concerns entirely – even in the most permissive systems. Cox (1997) outlines the assumptions that must hold for strategic coordination by voters to obtain. First, we must assume that voters care primarily about the results of the election at hand (i.e., that they are short-term instrumentally rational). Their decision process must follow from the belief that, by electing the party or candidate making the proposals they most prefer, they will help assure that eventual policy outcomes are as close to their preferred ones as feasible. This assumption would not hold for a group of voters who, for example, are looking forward to postelection coalition formation. If they fear extremists in one direction will be elected in other districts, they might seek to counterbalance those districts by voting for extremists in the other direction in their own district, even if they sincerely prefer moderate candidates. Another assumption is that voters must have a shared sense of the electoral viability of parties or candidates. Without a clear sense of who stands a reasonable chance of winning, coordination is impossible. Voters may want to act strategically, but their efforts will still lead to wasted votes if they lack solid information about candidate viability. All that said, we reason that these assumptions hold most of the time for most voters. Under this reasoning, our claim is that, given sets of voters and potential candidates with equally heterogeneous preferences, those making decisions under constraining electoral rules will more often strategically deviate from their sincere preferences than those operating under more permissive rules.

In this chapter we discuss why the strength of electoral systems should have an impact on citizen-to-politician congruence and responsiveness. We then define the three specific electoral rules that determine a system's strength. Finally, we will describe how these rules vary across electoral systems employed to choose legislators and executives in Latin America.

7.1 CONGRUENCE, RESPONSIVENESS, AND THE STRENGTH OF ELECTORAL SYSTEMS

The starting point of most early studies of representation consisted of an elegant combination of two of the most insightful and influential works in the discipline: Duverger's (1959) intuitions about the mechanical and psychological consequences of electoral laws and Downs's (1957) spatial model of party competition. We refer to the combination of these two logics as the "reference model" of electoral representation.

In its most basic form, the reference model can be summarized as follows. Duverger (1959) reasoned that under more constraining (i.e., stronger) electoral laws – more specifically, those that allocate a single seat by plurality rule – something approaching a two-party system should emerge. Additional parties would prove unviable, and their leaders would merge into fewer parties or withdraw. If the elites proved too obtuse, the supporters of unviable parties would abandon them for the most proximate party they deemed viable. Downs (1957) then explained why those two viable parties should seek to position themselves near the median voter, given that support of the median was necessary to assure an accumulation of majority support. Thus, if this level of coordination on the part of entering elites and voting citizens could be achieved, constraining or restrictive electoral laws should be expected to lead to high one-to-one (i.e., median-to-median) congruence.

Based on this same logic, a representative assembly that results from a restrictive system is unlikely to reflect the distribution of voters around the median's position. If the assumptions outlined here hold, in strong or constraining systems voters with preferences to either side of the median voter will not find any viable candidates or parties offering to represent their interests. Instead, their greatest utility will result from picking the viable party located near the median that is closest to them. In the end, many-to-many congruence will be low, with representatives bunched in the middle and noncentrist voters feeling unrepresented.

In contrast, permissive electoral systems produce what Cox (1990) refers to as "centrifugal incentives." The consistently high proportionality between votes and seats that obtains in such systems means that parties will tend to spread themselves across the policy space or state-to-market continuum, building reputations for relatively explicit and narrow policy positions. This is, therefore, an ideal recipe for many-to-many congruence. The weaker or more permissive the system, the more likely it is that voters, no matter their preferred policies, will find a party nearby with those same preferences; moreover, virtually any party will have a much greater chance of being viable in a permissive system compared to a restrictive system.

In terms of one-to-one congruence between the median voter and the median politician, if parties are encouraged to array themselves across the spectrum (Austen-Smith and Banks 1988), the median voter should find a party nearby. Even if a party fails to stake out a position identical to the preferred policies of the median voter, the spread of parties across the spectrum means that the median voter should find a nearby option in either direction. Thus, permissive rules should produce good one-to-one congruence in addition to good many-to-many congruence.

To summarize, the reference model implies that weaker or more permissive systems will produce good congruence of all types, but especially many-to-many. Stronger or more constraining systems should excel at generating one-to-one correspondence but fail at producing many-to-many congruence.

Despite its elegance, the reference model's expectations are not entirely consistent with available evidence. While some have found no evidence of differences with respect to one-to-one congruence (see, for instance, Blais and Bodet 2006, Ferland 2016), others have found that permissive systems are discernibly better at producing even one-to-one congruence (see, for instance, McDonald and Budge 2005, Powell Jr. and Vanberg 2000). In order to reconcile seemingly contradictory evidence, the reference model needs a more nuanced theoretical development.

The deceivingly simple logic behind the reference model actually requires some pretty sophisticated, strategic behavior on the part of elites and voters, and the acceptance of a set of assumptions that might be difficult to justify – especially in the context of Latin America. A hiccup anywhere along the route can ruin one-to-one congruence without necessarily doing much to improve many-to-many congruence. First, in a constraining system, if any third (fourth, fifth, ..., etc.) party with polarizing views remains on offer and can attract the votes of even a relatively small group of voters, the chances of median-to-median congruence diminish dramatically (e.g., Kim, Powell Jr., and Fording 2010). A failure to "merge" by parties on one side of the median could allow a party somewhat distant from the median in the other direction to emerge victorious. Imagine, for instance, that the right-of-center electoral coalition in pre-reform Chile had fragmented: a united *Concertación* could have moved leftward, refusing to offer moderate policies, and still have generated sufficient support to win a majority of seats.

Even if all the strategic behaviors required to fulfill its predictions occur, the reference model relies on mechanisms that operate at the *district* level. In order for the reference model to produce correct predictions at the *national* level (where the vast majority of studies of congruence are conducted, including this one), variations across districts would have to cancel themselves out nearly perfectly (Powell Jr. and Vanberg 2000). With only one seat, or even a few seats, to hand out, any bias that slightly favors one viable party – perhaps due to gerrymandering or malapportionment – can result in a severe divergence between the national median preference and the preferences of the median policy-maker. Thus, although strong or restrictive rules *should* generate median-to-median congruence, they usually do so only if some fairly stringent contextual criteria are fulfilled. Similarly, while they *can* generate good many-to-many congruence, the right conditions must be present – for instance, if voter preferences are themselves homogeneous enough that a few similar parties can adequately capture the little diversity there is. This is plausible if the strength of the system itself "molds the political views of a rising generation [... in such a way that ...] voters' tastes become relatively homogeneous in the long run" (Downs 1957, 124–125).

By the same token, while more permissive systems can generate good overall congruence, they can also fail to do so if the right contextual conditions are missing. For instance, if no party locates itself at or near the median voter (or voters around the median fail to vote for those parties), the expected one-to-one congruence between the median citizen and the median policy-maker will fail to materialize. This can happen if, as is the case in presidential democracies, parties lack the centripetal incentives that stem from anticipating a government-formation stage (Blais and Bodet 2006).

If elites fail to coordinate in the sense that they stake out similar positions, the voters at the location that is overrepresented by party offerings may fail to coordinate in such a way that they win seats equivalent to their combined votes, thus hurting overall many-to-many congruence. This scenario seems most likely where permissiveness is very high and the party system consequently includes a large number of parties. In such scenarios, wasted votes could be enormous, and (somewhat counterintuitively) proportionality will decrease.[1] The oversupply of nearby options can, in extreme circumstances, produce even worse results in terms of many-to-many congruence than would be obtained in a less permissive system. Incidentally, this is the logic supporting the empirical finding of an electoral "sweet spot," which suggests that no difference should exist between the representational properties of very restrictive and slightly more permissive systems. In support of this logic, there is evidence of a nonlinear relationship between electoral system permissiveness and the quality of representation (Carey and Hix 2011).

In general, then, we want to stress two points. First, electoral systems can be complex, and understanding the incentives they put in place can be complicated. Thus, while the reference model is *the* reference model for good reason, we will not be surprised if we ultimately find that its predictions regarding congruence do not hold at all times and in every place. Second, there are reasons to believe that important *contextual* factors can affect the ability of entering elites and voting citizens to coordinate in precisely the way we would expect them to based purely on incentives set by electoral rules, a point we borrow from Powell Jr. (2013). For example, periods of fluctuating economic performance or party system flux may complicate efforts by elites and voters to behave strategically. Settling on one's own sincere preferences and anticipating the preferences of others is more challenging in some contexts than others.

Despite this, it is nevertheless possible to identify systematic connections between congruence and electoral systems. In Chapter 9, we will seek to account for appropriate contextual and issue-specific factors that moderate the effects of electoral rules on the possibility of representing preferences over a given issue, incorporating them into our analyses by using empirical models that are flexible enough to accommodate the sorts of conditional and nonlinear relationships they could potentially entail.

---

[1] This phenomenon, which was first clearly stated by Taagepera and Shugart (1989), is known as the "conservation of disproportionality."

7.2 COMPONENTS OF ELECTORAL SYSTEMS AND THEIR EFFECT ON STRENGTH

We focus on three rules that are part of every electoral system and determine their "strength." The characteristics of electoral systems on which we will focus are *district magnitude*, the *seat allocation formula*, and *electoral thresholds* – the latter being two different concepts depending on whether we are talking about legislative elections or presidential ones. As a summary indicator, in the tables in this chapter we will also include the electoral system family for each case. As will become clear, there are certainly commonalities that can be summarized by the family designation, but there is also a great deal of variation in magnitude, allocation formulas, and thresholds *within* many families. In this section, we will define each of these features of electoral systems, discuss at a conceptual level some of the values they can take, and suggest how we think those values affect one-to-one and many-to-many congruence. Subsequently we will catalog how these rules vary across elections for lower or only houses of national legislatures, across elections for upper houses (where they exist), and across elections for executives in Latin American countries during the period under study.

The amount of variation in the rules that affect the strength or weakness of electoral systems is quite astounding. Lower and only houses vary from one another across countries. Many chambers show variation over time with a frequency that we think many institutionalists will find surprising. The bicameral systems in the region vary widely in the extent to which the rules for selecting lower and upper houses impose divergent incentives on elites in terms of strategic entry and on voters in terms of strategic voting. District magnitude is held constant in the election of presidents (only one can be chosen); despite this constraint, the sets of rules for electing presidents show a good deal of variation as well.

7.2.1 District Magnitude

The most important electoral feature for which we must account is district magnitude. District magnitude is the number of seats awarded at the district level in a given election. It varies from a single seat to hundreds of seats (in some proportional representation (PR) tiers of mixed member systems or systems with nationwide, at-large districts). In purely mathematical terms, as district magnitude increases, the ability, if desired, to make more fine-grained allocations of seats across winners and between winners and losers increases. Given this mechanical effect, as district magnitude goes up, more parties will enter, reasoning that they are likely viable, and voters will have a better chance to vote sincerely, also reasoning that their choices are more likely to be viable. As we will show in the sections on lower and upper houses, district magnitude takes on what must be considered nearly the full range of practical values across our observations. As magnitude increases, the electoral system grows permissive or weak.

Because our policy moods for voters and politicians are captured at the national level, we also need to aggregate nationally the different components of an electoral system. In the case of district magnitude, we calculate weighted mean magnitudes for each legislative chamber, which we define as $\Sigma_d M_d^2 / \Sigma_d M_d$, with M_d corresponding to the magnitude of district d. Put another way, this is a weighted average of magnitudes, with weights determined by the share of assembly seats elected in each district. In several systems the simple mean magnitude and the weighted mean magnitude are identical, but in others they are dramatically different. We find the weighted mean magnitude to yield the most intuitive national-level measure of district magnitude given some unusual configurations. As one extreme example, take the case of the Colombian Senate. One nationwide district is used to select 100 members to the chamber. A second nationwide district is used to select two members that represent Colombia's indigenous population. In this case, mean magnitude would be 51. This figure does not reflect the institutional incentives of the vast majority of members. The weighted mean magnitude on the other hand is $(100 \times 100 + 2 \times 2)/102 = 98.07$. This figure is a more genuine reflection of the competitive environment that characterizes the selection of most of the chamber's members.

7.2.2 Seat Allocation Formula

The second feature for which we account is the seat allocation formula. The seat allocation formula is the precise mathematical prescription for translating votes into seats. Many of these formulas were exclusively developed to allot seats in multimember districts and could not be used meaningfully in single-member districts. Some of the PR formulas used in systems with multimember districts rely on quotas, while others rely on divisors. A *quota* is a number of votes that guarantees a party a seat in a particular district. In calculating the quota, the total number of votes cast in the district is the numerator, and the denominator is district magnitude plus some predetermined number (possibly even zero). The Hare quota, for example, is simply the number of votes over the number of seats to be awarded. A *divisor* system defines a series of numbers by which a party's vote total will be divided each time it obtains a seat. The quotients thus derived are then used to award seats, with the party with the largest quotient receiving the next available seat. Under the D'Hondt seat allocation formula the series of divisors used to create the quotients is simply 1, 2, 3, 4, … Under the Sainte-Laguë seat allocation formula the series of divisors used to create the quotients is 1, 3, 5, 7, … In terms of electoral system strength, it is common wisdom that these formulas are arranged from Hare to Sainte-Laguë to D'Hondt in terms of being most to least proportional.

There is one other, less common, seat allocation formula that has been applied in PR elections in a few Latin American countries. For at least part of the time under study, the upper chambers in Argentina, Bolivia, and Mexico used three member districts and awarded two seats to the plurality-winning party and one seat to the party that finished second – regardless of the exact distribution of votes across parties. Shugart refers to these systems as "limited nomination list plurality," because, even though three seats are to be awarded, no party nominates more than two candidates. Assuming that preference orderings over parties are similar across districts, this formula makes it likely that one party will control a majority or near majority of seats while still guaranteeing the presence of an opposition. We expect this to be the strongest or most restrictive formula of the PR cases we observe in Latin America.

The seat allocation formula for plurality/majority systems and for the single nontransferable vote (SNTV) system is likely to be least proportional of all. Seat allocation is simply by plurality. As we will detail later, two-round (TR) systems can require a "super-plurality" or a majority in order to win the seat while avoiding a second round. In SNTV systems, multiple seats are awarded by plurality, but voters only get one vote. In multiple nontransferable vote (MNTV) or block vote systems, multiple seats are awarded by plurality, and voters get as many votes as there are seats to be filled. While these systems are different from one another – varying in family and in magnitude, both relevant in determining the strength of the system – we expect them to require greater strategic behavior than any of the mixed or PR systems.

7.2.3 Legal Thresholds

The third characteristic of electoral systems that influences their weakness/ strength is the existence of any legal vote threshold that must be achieved in order to become eligible for a seat.[2] Legal thresholds are lower bounds on electoral shares that impede any candidate or party that fails to reach this floor from taking office. Thresholds can operate at either the district or the national level and they come in two types. In the most common type, a party that fails to obtain some predefined percentage of the vote in the district cannot participate in the allocation of seats. The second type, in a slight wrinkle, defines some percentage of a quota as the floor that must be cleared. As we noted earlier, quotas are created by dividing total votes cast by district magnitude (the number of seats to be allocated in a district) plus some modifier (including zero).

---

[2] The *effective* threshold is a concept developed by Lijphart (2012). All electoral systems *implicitly* impose thresholds determined by district magnitude. Lijphart uses "threshold of inclusion" to refer to the minimum percentage of the vote that can earn a party a seat under the most favorable distribution of votes. He calls the maximum percentage of the vote that a party could earn and still fail to obtain a seat under the least favorable distribution of votes across parties the " threshold of exclusion." The implicitly established "effective threshold" is a number somewhere in the range between these two values. Lijphart then works out that the best approximation across electoral systems of the midpoint between the thresholds of inclusion is $75\%/M + 1$, where M is the district magnitude. While this concept has meaning at the district level, it has no obvious correlate at the national level of aggregation.

In the TR systems used in many presidential races across the region, the term threshold comes into play in another sense. Note that in legislative races incentives for coordination *increase* as the legal threshold increases. In presidential races, the incentive to coordinate behind a very limited number of candidates *decreases* as the threshold to avoid a second round goes up. A candidate can win the seat and avoid a second round of voting by meeting some predefined percentage of the votes cast (and, occasionally, some margin of victory as well). The higher this threshold, the stronger the incentive for parties to field a candidate, and the stronger the incentive for voters to coordinate around relatively more candidates. Party elites and their supporters may estimate that they can be one of the two choices to make it through to the second round where the field will legally be constrained to two competitors. In a single round single-member district decided by plurality (SMDP) system, failing to come first means no seat. In a two-round (TR) system, failing to come in first place *in the first round* may mean no such thing. Obviously, the number of parties, elites or voters that anticipate that they can be among the top-two vote earners in a TR system is larger than the number of parties, elites, or voters that anticipate that they will be the single top vote earner in a one-round system. What is more, in TR systems parties may field a candidate and voters may remain loyal to that candidate even where they reason they will not be one of the parties competing in the second round. Parties eliminated in the first round can use any show of strength to bargain between rounds for concessions from the two remaining candidates in exchange for the party's endorsement and electoral support. Based on this logic for entering and remaining in a race in TR systems, we consider simple SMDP to be a relatively stronger or more restrictive system.

7.2.4 Aggregating the Components of Electoral Systems into Families

Political scientists typically consider electoral system families as a good summary indicator of an electoral system's strength. There are three broad family types and a leftover bin: plurality/majority, proportional, mixed, and "other" systems (Reilly, Ellis, and Reynolds 2005), and our Latin American cases run the gamut. In the descriptive tables that follow, we categorize the electoral systems we encounter by family. We note, however, that families are a rather crude indicator of strength; in fact, variations in strength are often greater within a family than across families.

As their name suggests, plurality/majority systems typically award seats in a district in a winner-take-all fashion, unless voters can cast more than one vote – which is not common – thereby allowing for as many winners as voters have votes. Given their tendency to reward the top vote-getter (or a few top vote-getters), we expect plurality/majority systems to be the strongest or most restrictive families, and therefore least likely to establish congruence between citizens' policy mood and politicians' policy mood. Proportional systems, on the other hand, have the potential to distribute seats across multiple winning parties. Thus, they should be most permissive, allowing for the most free expression of diverse, sincere preferences. Not surprisingly, we expect mixed systems – those with both a plurality tier and a proportional tier – to fall somewhere between the first two types of systems in terms of weakness/strength.

PR is the most commonly employed electoral family in legislative chambers across Latin America. However, as we will explain in detail, two upper legislative chambers employ plurality/majority rules – including SMDP and multimember districts decided under MNTV rules.[3] In addition, we are interested in the rules for executives; in the countries we observe they are all elected under what should be considered plurality/majority rules. However, we do make a distinction between single-round races for the presidency and those that allow for a second round should some threshold not be obtained by the top vote-getter in the first round. We reason that the need to obtain a threshold of votes greater than a mere plurality will encourage some voters to continue supporting their sincerely preferred candidate even when they estimate he or she will not clear the necessary threshold in an initial round. In the second round, the field will be narrowed to two candidates, and voters will be forced to settle for one of the remaining options, with a majority perhaps coalescing behind a candidate who finished second in the first round.

We also make a distinction between subtypes of mixed systems. Mixed-member electoral systems are composed of two tiers, one where seats are awarded by plurality – typically in single-member districts – and one where seats are awarded proportionally. In mixed-member *compensatory* systems, the votes cast in the PR tier are the only ones that figure in the allocation of seats across parties. Any shortfall or surplus of seats obtained in the plurality tier is compensated for with seats in the proportional tier, assuring that a party's share of seats is equivalent to its share of the proportional-tier vote. In mixed-member *parallel* systems, the two tiers, plurality and proportional, are unlinked. This lack of connection between the tiers, makes parallel systems, on average, stronger or less permissive than compensatory systems.

Finally, the residual "other" family includes one chamber that used what was ostensibly an SNTV system for a number of years. In Colombia's lower house, closed subparty lists competed against one another in multimember districts and voters were allowed to cast one vote at the subparty list level. It was extremely rare for any subparty list to elect more than one candidate, given the distribution of votes across lists for the same party, so the system functioned basically like a classic SNTV system (Pachón and Shugart 2010). Proportionality – at the party, not list, level – in an SNTV system is a function of two complex dynamics. First, decisions regarding how many candidates (in Colombia's case, lists) a party should put forward given the number of seats up for grabs and the party's likely level of support determine whether it has fielded

---

[3] Each voter gets as many votes as there are seats to be filled.

too few or too many candidates. The second and related dynamic is any effort to get supporters of the party to coordinate across the party's candidates/lists. If too many supporters coordinate on a particular subparty list, the list may earn more votes than it needs to capture a seat (but fewer than it needs to capture an additional seat), and those votes could have been better used by the party if they had gone to another one of its lists on the cusp of earning a seat.

7.3 COMBINATIONS OF ELECTORAL SYSTEM COMPONENTS

Having laid out the theoretically possible electoral rule options, let us turn now to national cases. We will provide our overview by player in the policy-making process – lower or only houses, then upper houses (if any), and finally executives.

7.3.1 Lower or Only Houses

In this section we describe variation in electoral rules for the lower houses of legislative assemblies in Latin America during the period for which we have data on citizens' preferences, politicians' preferences, and policy outcomes (roughly 1996–2014). In Table 7.1 we detail the institutional combinations of district magnitude, seat allocation formula, and legal thresholds that existed during the period under study. The "First year" column indicates the date that rules were adopted, and the "Last year" column indicates the last year in which they were employed (or 2014 if that institutional combination was still in force at that time). The "Electoral system family" column provides a summary categorization of systems. The entries are ordered by district magnitude, from lowest (strongest or most restrictive) to highest (weakest or most permissive).

The mean climbs not too steadily from a low of about 1.5 in Venezuela's version of a mixed-member parallel system through to Brazil's more than thirty members per district on average. The majority of cases have a mean district magnitude of fewer than ten, and only five cases have a mean number of members per district greater than fifteen. The existing literature, with which we fully concur, argues that the permissiveness of the system increases with magnitude.

The formulas employed for seat allocation also vary across the region. D'Hondt is employed in more than half the cases, with the Hare quota – the most permissive seat allocation formula – being the second-most frequent. Sainte-Laguë, which falls between Hare and D'Hondt in terms of permissiveness, is only employed once (in Bolivia). Plurality is the most constraining formula, and it is used only twice (in the dominant tier of Venezuela's and Mexico's mixed-member parallel systems).

In the vast majority of cases, nineteen of twenty-six, no legal thresholds were employed to bar parties from receiving seats based on their relative lack of support. Where they were employed, however, they ranged as high as

TABLE 7.1. *Electoral systems for lower houses. Electoral rules employed in Latin America to elect representatives to lower houses between 1996 and 2014. Electoral systems are ordered by increasing mean district magnitudes.*

Case	First year	Last year	Electoral system family	Mean district magnitude	Seat allocation formula	Legal threshold
Venezuela	2005	2010	Mixed-parallel	1.46	Plurality	0.00
Chile	1989	2013	PR	2.00	D'Hondt	0.00
Panama	1989	2014	PR	2.89	Hare quota	0.50[†]
Dominican Republic	2002	2010	PR	4.47	D'Hondt	0.00
Ecuador	1976	1996	PR	5.10	Hare quota	0.00
Ecuador	2009	2013	PR	6.65	D'Hondt	0.00
Colombia	2006	2014	PR	7.80	D'Hondt	0.50[†]
Colombia	1991	2002	Other (SNTV)	7.94	Hare quota	0.00
Venezuela	2000	2000	Mixed compensatory	8.06	D'Hondt	0.00
Paraguay	1993	2013	PR	8.27	D'Hondt	0.00
Guatemala	1970	1999	PR	8.41	D'Hondt	0.00
Ecuador	1998	2006	PR	8.63	D'Hondt	0.00
El Salvador	1985	2014	PR	9.99	Hare quota	0.00
Nicaragua	1996	2011	PR	10.67	Hare quota	0.00
Honduras	1985	2013	PR	11.72	Hare quota	0.00
Costa Rica	1970	2014	PR	11.87	Hare quota	0.50[†]
Dominican Republic	1982	1998	PR	12.26	D'Hondt	0.00
Guatemala	2003	2011	PR	12.81	D'Hondt	0.00
Peru	2001	2011	PR	13.23	D'Hondt	0.04
Venezuela	1993	1998	Mixed compensatory	13.28	D'Hondt	0.00
Argentina	1973	2013	PR	13.76	D'Hondt	0.03
Mexico	1997	2005	Mixed-parallel	16.60	Plurality	0.02
Bolivia	1993	1996	PR	17.22	Sainte-Laguë	0.00
Bolivia	1997	2014	Mixed compensatory	18.55	D'Hondt	0.03
Uruguay	1971	2014	PR	22.22	D'Hondt	0.00
Brazil	1990	2014	PR	31.15	Hare quota	0.00

[†]These thresholds are based on quotas and not on vote shares.

10 percent, posing a significant barrier to obtaining a seat in the legislature. In terms of broad electoral families, PR dominates lower houses in Latin America. As elsewhere in the world, the use of mixed-member systems was on the rise over the period under study. The extent to which mixed-member systems are

spread across the spectrum in terms of district magnitude indicates what a crude indicator of strength electoral system family alone would constitute.

By way of comparison, members of the House of Representatives, the lower house of the legislature in the United States, are chosen in an SMDP system. No lower or only house in Latin America has employed such a constraining or restrictive system to select its members during the period that we study. The use of SMDP in the United States Congress thus puts this country most out of step with the methods for selecting lower houses in the Americas.

7.3.2 Upper Houses

More than half the countries in the region have (or had during part of the time under study) upper chambers. During the last few decades, many countries with upper chambers have seen fit to tinker with how their members are chosen. Venezuela made the most dramatic change, eliminating its upper chamber entirely. Argentina went from indirect election of its Senate by state legislatures to direct election. Bolivia changed both the magnitude of its districts and the seat allocation formula for its upper chamber, making its electoral system more permissive by reforming both components to make the translation of votes into seats more proportional.

Finally, Brazil did not actually reform the election rules for its upper chamber, but it still warrants two different entries because the country alternates back and forth between two sets of rules. Each state elects three senators. When one-third of the chamber is renewed, each state elects one senator in an SMDP system. In alternate elections, when two-thirds of the chamber are renewed, each state elects two senators with each voter casting two votes and the seats decided by plurality. We refer to this as an MNTV system. Having $M = 1$ imposes stronger, more constraining incentives than $M = 2$.

Lijphart (1984, 2012) defined two features that characterize the variation in bicameral systems. The first key element is whether both chambers have equal constitutional powers (symmetry) rather than an upper chamber that is subordinate to the lower chamber (asymmetry). The powers of upper chambers in Latin America vary, but comparatively speaking they are relatively symmetrical with their lower chambers. Most pieces of legislation can have their origin in either chamber, and members of each chamber almost always have the right to amend bills with their origins in and approved by the other. We will return to the powers of legislative chambers in great detail in Chapter 8.

The second key element, of great interest to us here, is the way in which the upper chamber is elected relative to the lower chamber. If the upper chamber is designed to overrepresent minorities or geographic regions, for example, the preferences of members across chambers are likely to be incongruent rather than congruent. Looking at district magnitude, it is clear that upper chambers across the region fall into two groups relative to the largely population-based seat distributions of lower chambers. One group is intentionally dispropor-

TABLE 7.2. *Electoral systems for upper houses. Electoral rules employed in Latin America to elect senators to houses between 1996 and 2014. Electoral systems are ordered by increasing mean district magnitudes.*

Case	First year	Last year	Electoral system family	Mean district magnitude	Seat allocation formula	Legal threshold
Dominican Republic	1970	2010	Plurality	1.00	Plurality	0.00
Brazil	1982	2014	Plurality	1.00	Plurality	0.00
Brazil	1982	2014	MNTV	2.00	Plurality	0.00
Mexico	1997	2012	Mixed-parallel	2.00	Ltd. nomination	0.02
Chile	1989	2013	PR	2.00	D'Hondt	0.00
Venezuela	1973	1998	PR	2.26	D'Hondt	0.00
Argentina	2001	2014	PR	3.00	Ltd. nomination	0.00
Bolivia	1979	2005	PR	3.00	Ltd. nomination	0.00
Bolivia	2009	2014	PR	4.00	D'Hondt	0.00
Uruguay	1984	2014	PR	30.00	D'Hondt	0.00
Paraguay	1989	2013	PR	45.00	D'Hondt	0.00
Colombia	1991	2002	PR	98.08	Hare quota	0.00
Colombia	2006	2014	PR	98.08	D'Hondt	0.02
Argentina (appointed)	1973	1999	—	—	—	0.00

tional, seeking to represent geographic subunits equally, regardless of population. The other group, as we will detail later, is super-permissive. As a result, being symmetrical and sometimes incongruent, all upper chambers in the region have the powers to be politically relevant and some of them have electoral incentives that vary significantly from those of their lower counterparts.

In Table 7.2 we summarize the mean district magnitude, seat allocation formulas, and legal thresholds for the upper chambers of the region. As noted earlier, district magnitude is bifurcated as a function of the use of single, nationwide, at-large districts in Uruguay, Paraguay, and Colombia, making them significantly more permissive than the other upper chambers in the region. There are far fewer upper chambers than lower chambers, but there are nine upper houses with a district magnitude of four or fewer and only four lower houses with district magnitudes that low. Considering the United States Senate as a reference point, only the upper chamber in the Dominican Republic and the upper chamber in Brazil every other election chooses its members in the most constraining or restrictive SMDP system. (Admittedly, every US state is represented by two senators, but they are elected in separate races.)

D'Hondt is again the most frequent seat allocation formula employed. The Hare quota is used significantly less frequently in relative terms compared to its use in lower chambers. The highly constraining plurality and limited nomination (two seats to the winning party, one to the second-place party) formulas, on the other hand, are used much more frequently in upper than in lower houses. Given the use of small-M districts and seat allocation formulas that reward large parties (D'Hondt), most upper houses are characterized by relatively strong or constraining electoral rules. Somewhat counterintuitively, legal thresholds are not used to further strengthen the rules in most cases; in fact, legal thresholds are only used in Colombia and Mexico.

PR, again, dominates the region, but three other families make an appearance here or there. The family of upper houses alone would be a pretty good predictor of weakness or permissiveness. With the cases arranged roughly in order of district magnitude, the PR cases are, we expect, among the most permissive. Where constitution writers wanted particularly constraining electoral rules, they moved away from PR altogether, and, occasionally, even away from multimember districts entirely.

7.3.3 Executives

The absence of many alternative methods of electing a single executive probably contributes to the lack of time-serial variation in electoral rules to elect presidents during the period of our analysis – see Table 7.3. District magnitude is fixed at $M = 1$ and therefore plays no role in relative permissiveness across countries. In addition, variations in seat allocation formula and legal threshold are all closely correlated with one another. Recall that threshold in these races is the portion of the first-round votes needed to declare a winner without the need for a second round.

Three seat allocation formulas are employed in the region: plurality, super-plurality, and majority. The SMD system used in the United States is shared with five countries in the region, although no Latin American country imposes an anachronistic electoral college between the popular vote and the actual outcome during the period under study. TR systems dominate the region. The height of the bar that needs to be cleared in order to avoid a second round of balloting varies across systems. Most systems require a candidate to reach an absolute majority in the first round to avoid a runoff. However, three countries – Argentina, Costa Rica, and Nicaragua – allocate the executive by "super-plurality" (of various sizes) in the first round. As the number goes up, entering elites and voting citizens will reason that their chances of moving on to the second round are increasing. Thus, they will have more of an incentive to enter and vote sincerely.

7.4 A SIMULATION-BASED TAXONOMY OF ELECTORAL SYSTEMS

The wide array of combinations of electoral system components across the region makes it hard to derive case-specific expectations about something we might conceive of as *system-level* electoral strength. Although extant theoretical knowledge and empirical evidence allowed us to present expectations about

TABLE 7.3. *Electoral systems for presidents. Electoral rules employed in Latin America to elect presidents between 1996 and 2014. Electoral systems are ordered by increasing second-round threshold.*

Case	First year	Last year	Electoral system family	Mean district magnitude	Seat allocation formula	Second-round threshold
Honduras	1971	2013	Plurality	1	Plurality	0
Mexico	2000	2012	Plurality	1	Plurality	0
Panama	1989	2014	Plurality	1	Plurality	0
Paraguay	1989	2013	Plurality	1	Plurality	0
Venezuela	1973	2011	Plurality	1	Plurality	0
Costa Rica	1970	2014	TRS	1	Super-plurality	0.40
Nicaragua[†]	1996	2011	TRS	1	Super-plurality	0.40
Argentina[†]	1995	2011	TRS	1	Super-plurality	0.45
Bolivia	1979	2005	TR	1	Majority[‡]	0.50
Bolivia[†]	2009	2014	TRS	1	Majority	0.50
Brazil	1989	2014	TR	1	Majority	0.50
Chile	1989	2013	TR	1	Majority	0.50
Colombia	1994	2014	TR	1	Majority	0.50
Dominican Rep.	1996	2012	TR	1	Majority	0.50
Ecuador[†]	1979	2013	TR	1	Majority	0.50
El Salvador	1984	2014	TR	1	Majority	0.50
Guatemala	1985	2014	TR	1	Majority	0.50
Peru	1985	2011	TR	1	Majority	0.50
Uruguay	1994	2014	TR	1	Majority	0.50

[†]In Nicaragua (after 1999), Argentina (after 1994), Bolivia (after 2009), and Ecuador (after 1978), a presidential candidate can also win in the first round by having more than 40 percent of the votes and a 10 percent lead over second place (for Nicaragua, a 35 percent of votes and a 5 percent lead is needed).
[‡]The second-round runoff is conducted in congress, not through a popular vote.

the connection between each of the identified components of electoral systems and the system's strength, evaluating how the different components interact remains a challenge. What should we expect about a system that combines low average district magnitude (normally associated with strong or restrictive systems) with a Saint-Laguë seat allocation formula (associated with permissive systems)? More generally, are all components equally important in terms of their contributions to system-wide strength, or does one of them dominate the others?

Electoral systems are composite entities, and so any evaluation of their strength must perforce address the question of how their different components (with their own mechanical and psychological consequences for party/candidate entry and survival) interact to produce more or less permissiveness. Moreover, dealing with these potentially complex interactions between component-wise effects should avoid confusing the consequences of the institutions themselves and the more accidental, second-order consequences brought about by the way these institutions interface with specific political actors in particular cultural, economic, and historical contexts. With these considerations in mind, how can we aggregate the components that form each system in the region to produce a single, clear classification of countries with respect to their systems' strength? We argue that a simulation-based approach, paired with a model that can identify highly interactive relationships between components, can produce one such taxonomy of the electoral systems in our sample.

7.4.1 Simulating Elections

Electoral systems can be thought of as *algorithms* – a set of rules that process some given inputs (viz. voter preferences expressed as votes) and produce outputs (viz. seat assignments to parties or candidates) in systematic ways. Accordingly, it is possible to define a set of computer routines that combine expressed preferences with the electoral system components we discussed in the previous section (i.e., the seat allocation formula, district magnitude, etc.) to produce seat distributions across a set of competing parties. Using these routines allows us to evaluate an arbitrarily large number of elections held under different institutional arrangements without having to rely on the comparatively limited set of observed elections. More importantly, however, using a simulation approach allows us to avoid conflating institutional effects and their psychological consequences.

Indeed, the differences between true and expressed voter preferences (as well as strategic considerations in party entry) are second-order consequences that can potentially be confounded with the effects of electoral systems themselves if we were to use data from real elections. In other words, the endogenous relationships between rules, preferences, and entry decisions can distort the estimated relationship between electoral systems and proportionality, making it hard to use real data to explore this connection empirically.[4] In contrast, a simulation in which voters' true preference distributions are held constant under different electoral systems can address concerns of endogeneity, while allowing us to incorporate hard-to-measure phenomena like strategic voting and elite coordination failures.

Accordingly, we simulate election results by first drawing a set of voter preferences and party locations from a univariate Normal distribution, and then translate these preferences into votes using a simple spatial model of voting, whereby a voter is more likely to cast a vote for a party that is located close to

---

4 Of particular concern is the aforementioned "Law of Conservation of Disproportionality" – a little studied but potentially important source of endogeneity (see Cox 1997 for some empirical evidence supporting the existence of this mechanism).

her "ideal point" (i.e., the position she has given to represent her most preferred outcome) than for a party that is farther away from it. To capture the possibility of strategic decisions on the part of voters, we introduce a parameter governing the probability that a voter chooses her most preferred (i.e., the closest) party rather than her second-most preferred alternative, and allow scenarios to range from fully nonstrategic (in which the probability of voting sincerely for the closest alternative is equal to 1) to somewhat strategic (in which said probability is reduced to 0.5). In this way, our classification of existing electoral systems on a scale of permissiveness will average over scenarios in which voters choose sincerely, and scenarios in which we allow the second-order consequences of electoral rules to have some effect on voter behavior.

Once votes are "cast," we translate these votes into seats for competing parties using plausible combinations of the electoral system components we have discussed, and computing measures of disproportionality using the resulting party-level vote-shares and seat-shares.[5] To do so, we codify different electoral systems into computer routines that take votes as inputs and return a distribution of seats across competing parties. For example, consider a system that uses the Hare quota seat allocation formula with a district magnitude of $M = 10$ and a legal threshold of 5 percent of the valid votes. Algorithm 1, which presents these steps in pseudo-code, captures the relevant algorithm for translating a vector of party-level votes into a vector of party-level seats.

Coding these electoral systems as computer routines allows us to obtain measures of disproportionality under a large number of scenarios defined by combinations of electoral system components.[6] Finally, and to further allow for differences induced by coordination failures and/or strategic entry decisions, we also allow these scenarios to vary with respect to the number of parties that compete. In all, we consider over 14,000 scenarios defined by differences in district magnitude, legal threshold, and seat-allocation formula, as well as probability of voting for one's most-preferred party and the number of competing parties. We repeat this process 1,000 times, each with a different sample of voter preferences and party locations, and proceed to evaluate the average strength of the system under each set of conditions. We now discuss how we evaluate the potentially complex relationships between all these components and electoral system strength, as well as how we operationalize the strength of a given system.

---

[5] By 'plausible' we mean combinations of components that are either observed or that could be expected to occur in reality, precluding for instance systems in which PR formulas are used along with single-member districts, or in which the number of votes afforded to each voter is greater than the district's magnitude.

[6] We use R 3.4.1 and C++ (via Rcpp) to conduct our simulations.

Algorithm 1: Electoral system with a Hare allocation formula, a legal threshold of $\tau = 0.05$ and a magnitude of $M = 10$.

---

1 function Hare $(V, M = 10, \tau = 0.05)$;
   Input : Integer vector of votes V, magnitude M, and threshold τ
   Output: Seat vector S
2 *total.votes* $\leftarrow$ sum of V;
3 *quota* $\leftarrow$ *total.votes*$/M$;
4 *remaining.seats* $\leftarrow M$;
5 **for** $i \leftarrow 1$ *to length of* V **do**
6   **if** $V[i]/total.votes \geq \tau$ **then**
7       $S[i] \leftarrow$ integer division $V[i]/quota$;
8   *remainders*$[i] \leftarrow$ modulo of $V[i]/quota$;
9   *remaining.seats* $\leftarrow$ *remaining.seats* $- S[i]$;
10   **else**
11       $S[i] \leftarrow 0$;
12   *remainders*$[i] \leftarrow 0$;
13   **end**
14 **end**
15 **while** *remaining.seats* > 0 **do**
16    $j \leftarrow$ which maximum *remainders*;
17    $S[i] \leftarrow S[j] + 1$;
18   *remaining.seats* $\leftarrow$ *remaining.seats* $- 1$;
19   *remainders*$[j] \leftarrow 0$;
20 **end**
21 **return** S;

7.4.2 Analyzing Results from Simulation Runs

Single-tree models attempt to find combinations of predictor variable values such that the outcome of interest is more or less homogeneous among observations that take on those predictor value profiles. Thus, given a set of predictors (such as electoral system components) and an outcome (such as electoral system strength), a Classification and Regression Tree (CART) model will produce a set of binary splitting rules that ultimately sorts all possible combinations of the predictors into distinct groups characterized by sharing similar outcome values and defined by specific combinations of predictor variable values. In our case, this amounts to a data-driven algorithm to produce an outcome-based taxonomy of electoral rules based on their effects on system-wide strength.

Like standard regression models, CART models can accommodate both continuous (e.g., legal electoral threshold) and categorical predictors (e.g., electoral system family). Unlike standard models, however, tree-based approaches do not rely on any assumptions of linearity in the relationship between predictors and electoral system strength, accommodating both nonlinearities and conditional (i.e., interactive) effects if the data support them. In addition, tree-based models can perform a type of variable selection unavailable to linear models. At each splitting point, CART selects the variable and value pair that reduce prediction errors the most, thus providing a natural measure of variable importance in the process of building a model of its outcome. As a result, CART is an ideal modeling technique for exploring the relationship between individual electoral system components and their combined strength as a system.

For our purposes, the set of predictors is thus the set of electoral rule components just discussed, with one exception. Because of the proportionality-enhancing properties of mixed-system compensatory systems, we classify them along with their pure PR counterparts. Similarly, as we discussed earlier, mixed-member-parallel systems effectively operate as two independent tiers on the same party system, and we therefore group them along with the less permissive plurality/majority counterparts (at least for the purposes of pre-dicting electoral system strength). Our set of predictors thus includes electoral system family (taking a value of "PR," "Plurality/majority," or "Other"), mean district magnitude (taking on values between 1 and 98), seat allo-cation formula (including "Plurality," "Super-plurality," "D'Hondt," "Hare," "Sainte-Laguë," "Ltd. nomination," and "Majority") and legal threshold (rang-ing from 0 to 50 percent of the vote). All of these correspond to real-existing rules used to elect representatives, senators, and presidents in Latin America.

Measuring the outcome (i.e., the strength of the electoral system) requires us to operationalize the degree of permissiveness induced by rules and their strategic effects. One possible avenue would measure the raw (or, better yet, the effective) number of parties in a system. At first sight, a measure like the effective number of parties (Laakso and Taagepera 1979) has the advantage of being an unambiguous way of capturing the idea that more permissive systems should result, *ceteris paribus*, in a greater number of relevant actors in the political system. The problem with such an approach, however, is that the effective number of parties (and other closely related measures) is the result of both the electoral system strength *and* social pressures to reflect heterogeneous preferences (Clark and Golder 2006, Amorim Neto and Cox 1997): as we discussed earlier, even highly permissive systems can result in few actors if there is not enough demand for parties/candidates representing many different policy and/or ideological positions. In other words, the effective number of parties captures one possible consequence of electoral system strength, rather than strength itself.

Accordingly, we focus on *proportionality* as a measure of electoral system strength. Proportionality, measured using Gallagher's scaled Euclidean distance between seat-shares and vote-shares,[7] captures the degree to which a system allows strategically expressed preferences to be reflected by the allocation of seats across competing parties *after* parties have made their strategic entry decisions, and thus *after* social and cultural preferences have exerted their pressure on party entry. Hence, for a set of expressed preferences over a given slate of alternatives, more proportional systems correspond to what we have been referring to as weak, or permissive, systems.

7.4.3 Results

After completing all simulations, we average our results over those dimensions that are *not* strictly institutional: the number of parties competing, the degree of voter sophistication, and the distribution of both voters and parties along our single ideological dimension. This results in a set of roughly 5,000 scenarios that differ only with respect to their electoral system components, along with the average level of disproportionality they produce under otherwise equal conditions. We then analyze these data using a cross-validated CART model to produce the taxonomy of electoral systems depicted in Figure 7.1.[8] The full classification of different systems can be achieved by effectively "dropping" a given system from the top of the tree in Galton board-like fashion, determining whether to go left or right at each branch depending on whether the splitting condition is met or not (respectively). For instance, a case like the Colombian Senate after the 2003 electoral reform – a system characterized by the use of a D'Hondt formula, a legal threshold of 0.02 of valid votes cast, and districts with an average magnitude of 98.08 – would first go left at the top of the tree, then left again at the second fork down, then left again at the third fork down, and finally right at the last branch. Any system, understood as a combination of components, can be similarly classified into one of six groups – the terminal nodes of the regression tree.

The results are illuminating, and generally in line with the expectations we outlined earlier in the chapter. The first split in the regression tree divides seat

---

[7] More specifically, Gallagher's measure of disproportionality is given by $\sqrt{0.5 \sum_i (v_i - s_i)^2}$, where v_i and s_i correspond to party i's vote- and seat-shares, respectively.

[8] As we briefly mentioned in Chapter 2, tree-based methods require a systematic way of defining tuning parameters. In the case of CART, we need to define a complexity parameter (which determines the minimum amount of prediction error reduction required to induce a new binary split) and the minimum number of observations in the induced terminal node required for a split to happen (which prevents having a terminal node for a very small number of observations, therefore limiting the possibility of overfitting). We use a fifteen fold cross-validation approach (which entails splitting the data into fifteen mutually exclusive subsets, fitting the model using each of the fifteen parts as a test set for the model estimated with the remaining observations, and choosing the parameters that reduce the mean test-set prediction errors) to select good values for these tuning parameters.

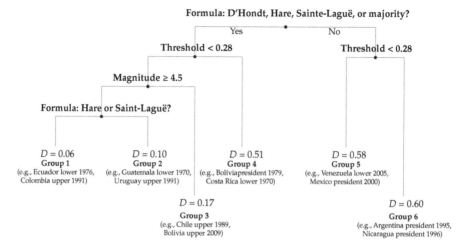

FIGURE 7.1. Taxonomy of electoral systems. The figure shows a classification tree for electoral systems, based on the level of disproportionality induced by different combinations of electoral system components. Nodes in the tree are formed by splitting condition (viz. a splitting variable and values that determine the split). Left branches indicate the path in which the splitting condition is met; right branches indicate the path along which the splitting condition is not met. Lower values in the terminal node signify less disproportionality D (i.e., more permissive systems).

allocation formulas almost perfectly into proportional and nonproportional systems. On the left branch, the model quickly distinguishes between majoritarian and strictly proportional rules, and terminal nodes under the strictly proportional rules, on the far left of the tree, correspond to scenarios that produce noticeably lower levels of disproportionality – thus institutionalizing clearly more permissive systems. Among PR systems (and, importantly, regardless of legal thresholds or allocation formulas), those with district magnitudes less than 4.5 are singled out as having relatively high levels of disproportionality, and we only see the distinction between formulas gaining traction among districts with a large number of seats to be awarded. Finally, among nonproportional systems, the CART distinguishes between limited nomination, majority, and any plurality systems, classifying them in that order. Systems with plurality and super-plurality allocation formulas (which include SNTV and MNTV systems) appear to be the most disproportional.

This exercise allows us to reduce the complexity of electoral system variation along three dimensions to a simple set of six categories, defined in terms of the dimension that is most relevant to the issue of representation as correspondence of preferences, namely, strength. These distinctions are more fine-grained than simply lumping cases into one of three families of electoral systems (majoritarian, PR, and mixed), identifying key differences in components within and across those families. In future chapters, therefore, we will use this six-way classification scheme of different electoral systems in order to predict the degree of congruence between citizen preferences and policy-maker preferences, once again relying on a tree-based model to allow for potential interactions between these types of electoral rules and more contextual conditions that could potentially modify the effects of institutions on representation. In Table 7.4 we order our policy-makers – lower or only houses, upper houses, and presidents – according to the strength of the electoral systems used to select them. The panels of the table correspond to the end nodes (or electoral system groups) in the tree in Figure 7.1, with policy-makers chosen under the most permissive or weakest rules (left side of the tree) at the top of the table and those chosen under the most restrictive or strongest rules (the right of the tree) at the bottom.

Not surprisingly, while the relationship is not perfect, lower houses tend to be elected under the most permissive rules, upper houses under somewhat stronger rules, and presidents under the most restrictive rules. For example, rules for electing presidents are contained within the three most restrictive categories identified in Figure 7.1. Conversely, fewer than a half-dozen lower houses are elected under similarly strong or restrictive rules. Rules for electing upper houses are the most widely dispersed across the dimension of electoral system strength, although only one instance (Colombia's Senate from 1991 to 2002) is among the most permissive rules, and none are chosen under the most restrictive rules.

7.5 ELECTORAL INCENTIVES IN LATIN AMERICA'S SEPARATION OF POWERS SYSTEMS

In separation of powers systems the concurrence of two or three actors is required to pass policy. From some perspectives, the ways in which these actors represent the preferences of citizens do not seem amenable to comparison, but, in fact, a limited number of institutional rules embodied in electoral systems capture the incentives that determine whether members of the lower or only house, members of the upper house (if there is one), and presidents are likely to congruently reflect the preferences of citizens. Looking at electoral rules like district magnitude, seat allocation formula, and thresholds, we can provide a complete characterization of the incentives that citizens have to coalesce around different parties and candidates.

In theory, each of these actors or policy-makers – lower or only house, members of the upper house (if there is one), and presidents – will play an important role in the policy-making process (PMP). We reason that the institutional incentives for congruence that guide each one of them will ultimately impact whether they reflect citizens' preferences for more state or more market. Given that all actors play a role in the PMP, the values taken by magnitude,

TABLE 7.4. *Electoral system strength. Six-way classification of all electoral systems used in Latin America to elect lower houses, upper houses, and executives.*

Case	First year	Last year	Electoral system family	Mean district magnitude	Seat allocation formula	Legal threshold
GROUP 1: Weakest or most permissive systems						
LOWER						
Ecuador	1976	1996	PR	5.10	Hare quota	o
El Salvador	1985	2015	PR	9.99	Hare quota	o
Nicaragua	1996	2011	PR	10.67	Hare quota	o
Honduras	1985	2013	PR	11.72	Hare quota	o
Bolivia	1993	1996	PR	17.22	Sainte-Laguë,	o
Brazil	1990	2014	PR	31.15	Hare quota	o
Colombia	1991	2002	SNTV	7.94	Hare quota	o
UPPER						
Colombia	1991	2002	PR	98.08	Hare quota	o
GROUP 2						
LOWER						
Ecuador	2009	2013	PR	6.65	D'Hondt	o
Venezuela	2000	2000	Mixed compensatory	8.06	D'Hondt	o
Paraguay	1993	2013	PR	8.27	D'Hondt	o
Guatemala	1970	1999	PR	8.41	D'Hondt	o
Ecuador	1998	2006	PR	8.63	D'Hondt	o
Dominican Republic	1982	1998	PR	12.26	D'Hondt	o
Guatemala	2003	2011	PR	12.81	D'Hondt	o
Peru	2001	2011	PR	13.23	D'Hondt	0.04
Venezuela	1993	1998	Mixed compensatory	13.28	D'Hondt	o
Argentina	1973	2013	PR	13.76	D'Hondt	0.03
Bolivia	1997	2014	Mixed compensatory	18.55	D'Hondt	0.03
Uruguay	1971	2014	PR	22.22	D'Hondt	o
UPPER						
Uruguay	1984	2014	PR	30.00	D'Hondt	o
Paraguay	1989	2013	PR	45.00	D'Hondt	o
Colombia	2006	2014	PR	98.08	D'Hondt	0.02
GROUP 3						
LOWER						
Chile	1989	2013	PR	2.00	D'Hondt	o
Dominican Republic	2002	2010	PR	4.47	D'Hondt	o
UPPER						
Chile	1989	2013	PR	2.00	D'Hondt	o
Venezuela	1973	1998	PR	2.26	D'Hondt	o
Bolivia	2009	2014	PR	4.00	D'Hondt	o
GROUP 4						
LOWER						
Panama	1989	2014	PR	2.89	Hare quota	0.50
Colombia	2006	2014	PR	7.80	D'Hondt	0.50
Costa Rica	1970	2014	PR	11.87	Hare quota	0.50

TABLE 7.4. *(continued)*

Case	First year	Last year	Electoral system family	Mean district magnitude	Seat allocation formula	Legal threshold
PRESIDENT						
Bolivia	1979	2005	TR	1.00	Majority	0.50
Bolivia	2009	2014	TR	1.00	Majority	0.50
Brazil	1989	2014	TR	1.00	Majority	0.50
Chile	1989	2013	TR	1.00	Majority	0.50
Colombia	1994	2014	TR	1.00	Majority	0.50
Dominican Republic	1996	2012	TR	1.00	Majority	0.50
Ecuador	1979	2013	TR	1.00	Majority	0.50
El Salvador	1984	2014	TR	1.00	Majority	0.50
Guatemala	1985	2015	TR	1.00	Majority	0.50
Peru	1985	2011	TR	1.00	Majority	0.50
Uruguay	1994	2014	TR	1.00	Majority	0.50
GROUP 5						
LOWER						
Venezuela	2005	2010	Mixed-parallel	1.46	Plurality	0
Mexico	1997	2005	Mixed-parallel	16.60	Plurality	0.02
UPPER						
Dominican Republic	1970	2010	Plurality	1.00	Plurality	0
Brazil	1982	2014	MNTV	2.00	Plurality	0
Mexico	1997	2012	Mixed-parallel	2.00	Limited nomination	0.02
Argentina	2001	2015	PR	3.00	Limited nomination	0
Bolivia	1979	2005	PR	3.00	Limited nomination	0
PRESIDENT						
Honduras	1971	2013	Plurality	1.00	Plurality	0
Mexico	2000	2012	Plurality	1.00	Plurality	0
Panama	1989	2014	Plurality	1.00	Plurality	0
Paraguay	1989	2013	Plurality	1.00	Plurality	0
Venezuela	1973	2011	Plurality	1.00	Plurality	0
GROUP 6: Strongest or most restrictive systems						
PRESIDENT						
Costa Rica	1970	2014	TR	1.00	Super-plurality	0.40
Nicaragua	1996	2011	TR	1.00	Super-plurality	0.40
Argentina	1995	2011	TR	1.00	Super-plurality	0.45

formula, and threshold *within a given national setting* may be far more varied than any one of our previous three tables would suggest.

7.6 CHAPTER SUMMARY

Until now, we have primarily compared the rules for electing lower or only houses to one another, the rules for electing upper houses (where they exist) to one another, and rules for electing presidents to one another. In Table 7.4, we

TABLE 7.5. *The strength of electoral systems for selecting sets of policy-makers*

Policy-maker	Country	First year	Last year	Electoral system strength
Lower	Argentina	1973	2013	2
Upper	Argentina	2001	2015	5
President	Argentina	1995	2011	6
Lower	Bolivia	1993	1996	1
Upper	Bolivia	1979	2005	5
President	Bolivia	1979	2005	4
Lower	Bolivia	1997	2014	2
Upper	Bolivia	2009	2014	3
President	Bolivia	2009	2014	4
Lower	Brazil	1990	2014	1
Upper	Brazil	1982	2014	5
President	Brazil	1989	2014	4
Lower	Chile	1989	2013	3
Upper	Chile	1989	2013	3
President	Chile	1989	2013	4
Lower	Colombia	1991	2002	1
Upper	Colombia	1991	2002	1
President	Colombia	1994	2014	4
Lower	Colombia	2006	2014	4
Upper	Colombia	2006	2014	2
Lower	Costa Rica	1970	2014	4
President	Costa Rica	1970	2014	6
Lower	Dominican Republic	1982	1998	2
Upper	Dominican Republic	1970	2010	5
President	Dominican Republic	1996	2012	4
Lower	Dominican Republic	2002	2010	3
Lower	Ecuador	1976	1996	1
President	Ecuador	1979	2013	4
Lower	Ecuador	1998	2006	2
Lower	Ecuador	2009	2013	2
Lower	Guatemala	1970	1999	2
President	Guatemala	1985	2015	4
Lower	Guatemala	2003	2011	2
Lower	Honduras	1985	2013	1
President	Honduras	1971	2013	5
Lower	Mexico	1997	2005	5
Upper	Mexico	1997	2012	5
President	Mexico	2000	2012	5
Lower	Nicaragua	1996	2011	1
President	Nicaragua	1996	2011	6
Lower	Panama	1989	2014	4
President	Panama	1989	2014	5
Lower	Paraguay	1993	2013	2
Upper	Paraguay	1989	2013	2

TABLE 7.5. *(continued)*

Policy-maker	Country	First year	Last year	Electoral system strength
President	Paraguay	1989	2013	5
Lower	El Salvador	1985	2015	1
President	El Salvador	1984	2014	4
Lower	Peru	2001	2011	2
President	Peru	1985	2011	4
Lower	Uruguay	1971	2014	2
Upper	Uruguay	1984	2014	4
President	Uruguay	1994	2014	4
Lower	Venezuela	1993	1998	2
Upper	Venezuela	1973	1998	4
President	Venezuela	1973	2011	5
Upper	Venezuela	1973	1998	3
Lower	Venezuela	2000	2000	2
Lower	Venezuela	2005	2010	5

Note: Starting year corresponds to first year after a rule change or 1970, whichever is earlier.

suggested that there is a continuum of electoral system strength and that, while policy-makers are roughly grouped from lower house electoral systems at the more permissive end and systems for electing presidents at the other end, there are important deviations from this linear pattern. We reorder the data presented in Table 7.4 in Table 7.5 in order to capture the rules that have characterized each PMP. In other words, we bring together the rules used to elect policy-makers by country over time. This seems an appropriate task to accomplish before turning our focus to the institutional powers each of these actors has at its disposal during the PMP.

If the congruence between voters' preferences and policy-makers' preferences is a function of electoral system strength, countries where all policy-makers are elected through equally weak/permissive or equally strong/constraining rules should have the greatest prospect for *consistent* congruence (or incongruence) between voters and each player in the PMP. In countries where one policy-maker is elected under a particularly permissive set of rules and another is elected under a particularly constraining set of rules, in contrast, it may be that one policy-maker ends up being significantly more congruent with voters than the other. As we will argue in the next chapter, the institutional powers with which each actor is endowed will determine whose preferences prevail during the process of crafting policy – those of the congruent actor or those of the incongruent one.

Only Mexico has used rules of equal strength when choosing all of its policy-making bodies or branches. In every other case, the rules vary in strength across policy-makers within a case, sometimes quite dramatically. Nicaragua stands out for the very permissive or weak rules used to choose its only legislative chamber combined with its very restrictive or strong rules for selecting the president, staking out both ends of the spectrum identified in our electoral-strength tree exercise. Several of the bicameral examples are characterized by rules that guarantee that no two policy-makers are selected under rules of equal strength, seemingly complicating the calculus of voters and assuring that policy-makers will disagree about who represents "the will of the people."

To sum up, voters have two and sometimes three elected agents in separation of powers systems: the lower or only house, sometimes an upper house, and a president. The rules governing the election of each agent vary not only across countries, but also within them. In this chapter we looked at the rules for each agent individually, describing the relative strength of the rules used to select them, and then concluded by thinking about electoral *systems* based on all of the choices voters had to make in a given country at a given time. In the next chapter we take up how the rules governing the PMP bring those agents, with their varying sets of preferences, together to determine policy outcomes.

8

Linkage 2: Policy-Making Processes (PMP)

While it seems straightforward to suggest that policy-makers' preferences should be reflected in the policies a nation ends up pursuing, the powers of politicians – executives and legislators – to act on their preferences vary from country to country. In separation of powers (presidential) systems, some of which are bicameral, the existence of multiple veto players suggests that the ultimate location of the policies put in place would have to be acceptable to all of them (relative to the status quo). Predictions about exactly where this location would be in a one-dimensional policy space become trickier, especially predictions we can systematically test empirically.

Not only do we face systems that vary in terms of the number of legislative chambers, we also face wide variation in terms of the constitutionally allocated (or otherwise formally assigned) powers of the various players as well. For example, some presidents can issue decrees with the force of law while others are prohibited from doing so. Some legislatures have effective committee systems while others lack this level of institutional development. There is widespread cross-national variation in terms of policy-making powers, but we also observe some time-serial changes in the form of constitutional reforms and/or revisions to cameral procedures.

In Chapter 10 we will look for one-to-one congruence and responsiveness between pivotal politicians – median members of a chamber and/or the president – and policy orientation captured on the state-to-market continuum. We will also test for many-to-one congruence and responsiveness, looking at where the policy orientation falls within the distribution of politicians' preferences. Not surprisingly, we expect one-to-one congruence and/or responsiveness between policy and the median member of congress to be greatest in systems where the legislative branch possesses relatively more power in the PMP. We expect one-to-one congruence and/or responsiveness between policy and the president to be greatest in systems where the executive branch possesses relatively more power in the PMP. If we think of the many in many-to-one congruence as pivotal players across branches – the lower house median, the upper house (where there is one), and the president – we expect congruence and responsiveness to be greatest where the branches are relatively evenly matched in terms of powers during the PMP.

The number of dimensions along which policy-making powers vary is large enough that we cannot meaningfully include all of these indicators as predictors of congruence and responsiveness in multivariate models. Furthermore, these dimensions do not lend themselves easily to the construction of an additive index. However, there appear to be certain "affinities" in how these different policy-making powers are bundled across the cases that we inspect. Consequently, we carry out a clustering exercise in order to group actors with similar powers.

We proceed as follows. First we will list the policy-making powers of legislators that directly or indirectly empower them during the process of hammering out policy. We present a clustering exercise that groups legislative chambers with similar powers, distinguishing carefully between chambers in bicameral systems. The variety of ways in which chambers are empowered is extensive, including groupings where legislators seem to lack basic policy-making tools. We then do something similar for executives. A clustering algorithm ends up distinguishing among presidents who appear to have the power to move the policy status quo unilaterally, those that are empowered to dictate which issues will rise to the top of the country's political agenda, and those that lack either of these sets of powers. We conclude, as we did with electoral systems, by returning to the country level of analysis to examine the powers of the constellation of actors that characterize each case. We show the combination of policy-making powers that characterize each of the actually observed country-cases, adopting more-or-less intuitive shorthand labels for each constellation of powers.

8.1 THE PMP IN SEPARATION OF POWERS SYSTEMS

Madison's logic behind separating powers across branches was that the actors involved in policy-making would have to mutually consent to a change. In its simplest form, a separation of powers system might include two actors – a legislative assembly and an executive – who have ideal points that in large part reflect the distinct configurations of voters who brought them to power through separate electoral systems. Institutionally, the system could be made more complex by adding a second legislative chamber chosen through a third set of electoral arrangements, including configurations of districts and rules for turning votes into seats, and therefore a distinct aggregation of votes and voters. Policy change would be made more difficult by the addition of this third actor who must concur with the president and the lower chamber that some policy proposal is superior to the existing status quo.

While this simple depiction of separation of powers systems – in their unicameral and bicameral forms – is accurate to a point, it does not begin to account for the myriad ways in which policy-making systems can be designed to advantage one actor over another in the process of trying to reach (or avoid) agreement on where policy should be located. Some institutional designs appear intended to pit actor against actor on relatively even terms, while others seem to clearly tip the balance of power toward one or the other (Mainwaring and Shugart 1997, Morgenstern and Nacif 2002). Let us quickly review the ways in which policy-making institutions can vary in ways that influence our simple story of mutual consent to policy change before describing how those institutions vary across our cases.

Some constitutional provisions go so far as to eliminate the need for consent from one or more actors before policy can be changed. For example, in some countries the legislature can amend the constitution without the participation of other elected or unelected bodies. This is a particularly powerful tool in unicameral systems, giving one elected assembly the power to redefine the fundamentals of how the political system works, including most of the other institutional provisions listed later. A less fundamental but perhaps more flexible and precise tool is the decree authority granted to several presidents throughout the region, that is, the power to unilaterally change the policy status quo to their preferred positions. Sometimes the power is limited to particular policy areas. Other times, this power is constrained by the need to obtain post-decree congressional authorization. In some instances, the decree lapses after some interval unless it is reauthorized by congress, while in others it remains the law of the land unless it is purposefully voted down by the legislature. Finally, some constitutions allow presidents to submit bills to popular referenda, bypassing the legislatures' opportunity to amend or reject the proposal.

Legislatures are not unitary, rational actors with a single preferred policy across their members. Any provision that raises the bar for the extent of collective action required to signal consent – in other words, any provision that requires some kind of qualified or super-majority – decreases the ability of the branch to identify policy outcomes preferred to the current status quo. These kinds of decision-making rules empower relatively extreme members, allowing them to prevent or slow down the body's more moderate members from moving policy. Conversely, any process that calls for only a plurality or a simple-majority of members to agree on a new policy increases the variety of outcomes that those members would find preferable to the status quo or to another policy-maker's proposal. More specifically, in the face of executive opposition in the form of a veto, some legislatures can override that objection with the same majority that put the proposal on the president's desk in the first place. Other constitutions ask for greater levels of consensus, requiring some form of super-majority before the legislature can overcome the president's efforts to protect the policy status quo.

The ability to set the policy-making agenda can be a powerful tool for shaping outcomes. In Latin America, executives can directly introduce legislation and, in some cases, presidents have the ability to designate a bill as "urgent," forcing it to the top of the legislature's agenda. Similarly, some constitutions allow the president to call special sessions of congress and while doing so to lay out the agenda for the special session. Again, this power does not dictate a particular outcome, but it does allow the president to select for consideration policies on which he or she believes a preferred outcome is most likely. Finally, the right to propose policy in certain policy areas is reserved for the executive in some of the systems that we study. In other words, the president has negative agenda control in these areas. If he or she does not introduce legislation in the reserved area, the policy status quo in that area is protected.

Several features of the PMP can impact the ability of players to assess where a policy, including the status quo, is located on the state-to-market continuum and which policy they prefer over another. We mentioned the ability to declare a proposal urgent. Limiting the time the legislature has to consider and modify a policy proposal can limit its ability to achieve a preferred outcome. In some cases, presidents can use partial observations or overrides to enact only certain parts of a policy adopted by the legislature. Where these powers do not exist or are easy to override, it is more likely that the legislature can craft policy that actually ends up being located at its preferred point. When the executive has the power to selectively implement legislation, the policy that the legislature votes on may not be the policy that is ultimately pursued. In addition, legislatures can build internal institutions that enhance their ability to assess executive proposals and to craft their own. Strong committees, an adequate staff, or the right to question executive branch officials, for example, empower legislatures when it comes to crafting policy.

Finally, powers related to the budget are essential components of the PMP given that adequate government spending is necessary to guarantee that a policy will produce its intended impact. In many countries, legislators have the right to increase government spending in pursuit of their policy goals, while in others, their ability to do so is limited. In some instances the executive's power to veto legislation extends to the budget itself. The size of the majority the legislature has to assemble to overcome such a veto varies across cases, impacting the ability of the president to impede the legislature's pursuit of its priorities.

In sum, separation of powers systems feature the need to obtain the consent of multiple actors in order to enact policy change. That said, the potential for variation in the powers that characterize the PMP across cases is enormous. Legislatures may have some of many powers designed to help them wrestle the best possible policy outcome from an ideologically distant president. Likewise, constitutional founders and reformers have deviced many different ways of granting executives influence over the PMP. As we will see later, in some instances it would appear that policy-making institutions are clearly stacked in favor of one branch or the other. In other cases, the institutional powers seem more balanced.

8.2 POLICY-MAKING POWERS: LEGISLATORS

We are interested in the institutional characteristics of legislatures that might help translate the preferences of legislators into policy – especially since legislators' preferences may not be congruent with those of another, more-or-less powerful actor, the president (see Section 8.3). Our sources for these characteristics of legislatures are Negretto's Comparative Index of Legislative Powers (Negretto 2014) and the Varieties of Democracy Project (Coppedge et al. 2017, Pemstein et al. 2017). In Table 8.1 we list the individual characteristics we believe empower legislatures to make policy to the liking of their members. The table provides the data source for each variable, a description of the institutional characteristic to which it corresponds, and the values it can take.

Note that the table is made up of three panels. The first panel contains five powers or characteristics that our sources attributed to the legislature as a whole, meaning that in bicameral systems they apply to both lower and upper houses. The second panel adds three additional powers, which our sources attribute to the only house in unicameral systems or the lower house in bicameral systems. The third panel contains two more powers that characterize only the upper house in bicameral systems.

Given the nature of our powers – applicable to the legislature as a whole or applicable only to a specific chamber – we adopted a two-stage clustering process (Online Appendix E provides a detailed description of this exercise). In the first stage we clustered all legislative chambers, resulting in three distinct sets. The set to which a chamber is assigned becomes a cameral characteristic to be considered in the second round of clustering. The initial set assignment is considered along with a number of additional characteristics that are lower or upper specific. For only and lower houses, the initial assignment is clustered with the three powers in the second panel of Table 8.1. Similarly, for upper houses, the cluster assigned in the first stage is considered along with the two powers in the third panel of Table 8.1.

The powers coded for the legislature as a whole include its ability to amend the constitution. Where the legislature has the power to amend the constitution without the participation of other actors, legislators can, among other things, fundamentally remake the PMP itself. As we mentioned briefly already, some legislatures face no restrictions in terms of adding expenditures to the budget while making other policies, but other legislatures are flatly prohibited from doing so. The ability to formally question members of the executive branch is an important information-gathering tool that some legislatures possess for learning what the executive branch intends with its proposals (and actions) and what the executive estimates the impact of the legislature's proposals will be. Especially with intricate economic policies, executive branch appointees and

TABLE 8.1. *Legislators' policy-making powers. Sources and description of powers available to Latin American legislatures.*

Variable	Description	Value = 0	Value = 1	Value = 2	Value = 3
Legislature amends constitutions (amend) *Source:* Coppedge et al. (2017), Pemstein et al. (2017)	By law, can the legislature (including both chambers of the legislature) change the constitution without the involvement of any other body?	No	Yes	—	—
Budget spending (budgetspending) *Source:* Negretto (2014)	Whether congress can increase spending	Congress cannot increase spending	Congress can increase spending	—	—
Legislature questions officials in practice (question) *Source:* Coppedge et al. (2017), Pemstein et al. (2017)	In practice, does the legislature routinely question executive branch officials?	Never or very rarely	Yes – routinely	—	—
Partial observations (partialobsoverride) *Source:* Negretto (2014)	Are partial vetoes allowed, if so, how are they overridden?	No override	Partial observations subject to qualified majority override	Partial observations subject to simple majority override	No partial observations
Veto override (vetooverride) *Source:* Negretto (2014)	Veto override threshold	No override	Veto subject to qualified majority override	Veto subject to simple majority	No veto
Lower chamber introduces bills (introdbillslo) *Source:* Coppedge et al. (2017), Pemstein et al. (2017)	By law, does the lower (or unicameral) chamber of the legislature have the ability to introduce bills in all policy jurisdictions?	No	Yes	—	—
Lower chamber committees (committeeslo) *Source:* Coppedge et al. (2017), Pemstein et al. (2017)	Does the lower (or unicameral) chamber of the legislature have a functioning committee system?	No	Yes, but only special (not permanent) committees	Yes, there are permanent committees, but they are not very significant in affecting the course of policy	Yes, there are permanent committees that have strong influence on the course of policy-making
Lower chamber staff (stafflo) *Source:* Coppedge et al. (2017), Pemstein et al. (2017)	Does each member of the lower (or unicameral) chamber of the legislature have at least one staff member with policy expertise?	No	Yes	—	—
Upper chamber introduces bills (introdbillsup) *Source:* Coppedge et al. (2017), Pemstein et al. (2017)	By law, does the upper chamber of the legislature have the ability to introduce bills in all policy jurisdictions?	No	Yes	—	—
Veto upper (vetoupper) *Source:* Negretto (2014)	Number of chambers intervening in veto override and voting procedure	Veto: one chamber	Veto: two chambers voting together	Veto: two chambers voting separately	No veto

bureaucrats may have superior knowledge regarding the likely performance of policy choices. The remaining powers attributed to legislatures across the region relate to the ease with which they can overcome a recalcitrant president. It is possible to face a president with no veto authority, whole or partial. At the other extreme, in theory, a relatively weak legislature would face a president with the ability to issue partial observations that are impossible to override.

Pemstein et al. (2017) and Coppedge et al. (2017) also coded powers that could be attributed to the lower chambers in bicameral systems (and to the only chamber in unicameral systems). These chambers vary in terms of their ability to introduce legislation, the quality of the staff they have at their disposal for help drafting policy, and the strength of the committee system they have for revising legislation as it moves along the legislative process. For upper chambers, Pemstein et al. (2017) and Coppedge et al. (2017) code whether they have the unfettered right to introduce legislation along with the role that they play in overriding presidential vetoes. In both cases – lower/only and upper – our clustering exercise identified three groups of chambers.[1]

8.2.1 Lower or Only Houses

Table 8.2 shows the clusters identified for lower/only house legislative powers. The panel labels are our effort to capture the key characteristics shared by most cases in each cluster. The chambers in the topmost cluster have many tools at their disposal for crafting their preferred economic policies, including usually the right to introduce legislation, staff to help draft it, and committees capable of shaping its content. They face a president with a partial veto, albeit one that is relatively easy to override. However, only in a few chambers in this group do legislators have the right to increase spending without compensating with cuts elsewhere. Where they can – in Nicaragua and Paraguay – we might consider these legislatures with the greatest chance of seeing their preferences reflected in economic policy. As a point of reference, it seems likely that the US House of Representatives would fall among this group of chambers.

The second panel comprises chambers that can introduce their own bills but lack staff to aid in drafting and evaluating bills. Legislatures in this group do not face partial vetoes, but they do face package vetoes that are burdensome to override. They do, however, share the ability to increase spending. Finally, the cases in the third panel are legislative chambers that lack tools necessary to be highly effective at drafting and adopting legislation reflective of the preferences of their members. In particular, most of them look like they could be effectively stymied by a president exercising his or her right to veto anything they could originally adopt.

---

[1] See Online Appendix E for a detailed reporting of the clustering results.

TABLE 8.2. *Lower chambers' policy-making powers. Distribution of policy-making powers of lower or only chambers across Latin America.*

Country	Years	Constrained only by the budget							
		Amend	Spend	Question	Partial veto	Override	Introduce	Committees	Staff
Bolivia	2010–2015	0	0	1	2	3	1	2	1
Brazil	1989–2015	1	0	1	2	2	0	3	1
Colombia	1992–2015	1	0	1	2	2	1	3	1
Nicaragua	1990–2006	1	1	1	2	2	1	3	1
Nicaragua	2007–2015	1	1	0	2	2	1	3	1
Paraguay	1993–2015	0	1	1	2	2	1	2	1
Peru	1980–1991	1	0	1	2	2	1	3	1
Peru	1992–2000	1	0	0	2	2	1	3	1
Peru	2001–2015	1	0	1	2	2	1	3	1
Venezuela	1970–1998	0	0	1	2	2	1	3	1
Venezuela	1999–2002	0	0	0	2	2	1	2	1
Venezuela	2003–2015	0	0	0	2	2	1	2	1

Country	Years	Constrained except by the budget							
		Amend	Spend	Question	Partial veto	Override	Introduce	Committees	Staff
Bolivia	1979–1981	1	1	0	3	1	1	2	0
Bolivia	1982–1994	1	1	1	3	1	1	2	1
Bolivia	1995–2005	1	1	1	3	1	1	2	1
Bolivia	2006–2009	0	1	1	3	1	1	2	1
Dominican Republic	1970–1999	1	1	0	3	1	1	2	0
Dominican Republic	2000–2015	1	1	0	3	1	1	2	0

TABLE 8.2. *(continued)*

Country	Years	Amend	Spend	Question	Partial veto	Override	Introduce	Committees	Staff
					Constrained except by the budget				
Guatemala	1970–1985	1	1	0	3	1	1	2	0
Guatemala	1986–2015	1	1	1	3	1	1	3	0
Honduras	1970–2015	1	1	0	3	1	1	2	0
Mexico	1970–1987	0	1	0	3	1	1	2	0
Mexico	1988–1999	0	1	0	3	1	1	2	1
Mexico	2000–2015	0	1	1	3	1	1	3	1
					Very limited powers				
Argentina	1983–2015	0	1	1	1	1	1	3	1
Brazil	1983–1988	0	0	0	1	1	0	2	1
Chile	1970–1974	0	1	0	1	1	1	3	0
Chile	1990–2015	0	0	1	1	1	1	3	1
Colombia	1970–1991	1	0	0	2	1	1	3	0
Costa Rica	1970–2015	0	1	1	1	1	1	2	1
Ecuador	1979–1998	1	1	1	1	0	0	2	1
Ecuador	1999–2006	1	0	1	1	0	0	2	1
Ecuador	2007–2015	1	0	0	1	0	0	2	1
Salvador	1984–2015	1	0	0	2	1	1	2	0
Nicaragua	1985–1989	1	0	0	2	1	1	3	0
Panama	1989–2015	1	0	1	1	1	1	3	1
Paraguay	1989–1992	0	1	0	2	1	1	2	1
Uruguay	1985–1997	0	0	1	2	1	0	3	1
Uruguay	1998–2015	0	0	1	1	1	0	3	1

8.2.2 Upper Houses

As noted already, our clustering exercise also identified three groups of upper chambers based on data on policy-making powers. While the mix of upper-chamber powers on which we have data is not identical to that for lower houses, the three clusters of upper houses roughly break down along similar lines. In the topmost panel of Table 8.3 are chambers that possess many tools, but mostly share an inability to increase spending. While they typically cannot mess with the budget, they have the right to question members of the executive branch, and most of them can act on information gleaned by introducing legislation on any subject matter of interest. They typically face presidents with a veto that is relatively easy to override, and the upper chamber is guaranteed a formal role in that process. The second cluster comprises upper chambers that lack one or more of the tools possessed by the cases in the first panel, *but* they do share the right to increase spending when pursuing their goals. They do not face partial vetoes, but the package vetoes they face are difficult to override. Few of the chambers in this cluster have an unfettered right to initiate legislation. Had we included the United States among our cases, it seems likely that the Senate would have fallen in this cluster. Finally, the last panel of Table 8.3 lists the upper chambers that would seem least likely to draft and adopt legislation reflecting the preferences of their members. Again, as with the least well-equipped lower or only chambers, these chambers lack some of the powers that would allow them to pursue their goals, particularly to overcome a president who was seeking to thwart legislative interests.

As this section has made clear, the ability of legislators to effectively craft economic policy reflecting their preferences varies dramatically across countries. In some instances, the median member in one chamber may have to contend with the policy goals of the median member of another chamber – a chamber with a similar constitutionally defined role in the PMP but with potentially incongruent desires in terms of the balance between state and market. Even beyond whether a system is unicameral or bicameral, we see plenty of variation in the policy-making powers with which chambers are endowed. However, noticeably rare are chambers that have all the tools necessary to draft their preferred policies, to overcome a recalcitrant president, and to alter the budget if need be. Almost all of the legislatures in the region lack some possible weapon with which a fully armed legislature could have, at least in theory, been endowed. Many of the legislatures in the region seem rather poorly equipped to achieve any congruence between their preferences over economic policy and the policy that is actually drafted and adopted.

8.3 POLICY-MAKING POWERS: PRESIDENTS

We use the remaining components of Negretto's Comparative Index of Legislative Powers to capture the policy-making institutions that determine how presidents' preferences get turned into policy outcomes (Negretto 2014). For details on the coding see Table 8.4. All else equal, we reason that a gain in

TABLE 8.3. *Upper chambers' policy-making powers. Distribution of policy-making powers of upper chambers across Latin America.*

Country	Years	Amend	Spend	Question	Partial veto	Override	Introduce	Override role
					Constrained only by the budget			
Bolivia	2010–2015	0	0	1	2	3	1	0
Brazil	1989–2015	1	0	1	2	2	0	1
Colombia	1992–2015	1	0	1	2	2	1	2
Paraguay	1993–2015	0	1	1	2	2	0	2
Peru	1980–1991	1	0	1	2	2	1	2
Venezuela	1970–1998	0	0	1	2	2	1	1
					Constrained except by the budget			
Dominican Republic	2000–2015	1	1	0	3	1	1	2
Mexico	1970–1987	0	1	0	3	1	0	2
Mexico	1988–1999	0	1	0	3	1	0	2
Mexico	2000–2015	0	1	1	3	1	0	2
					Very limited powers			
Argentina	1983–2015	0	1	1	1	1	1	2
Brazil	1983–1988	0	0	0	1	1	0	1
Chile	1970–1974	0	1	0	1	1	1	2
Chile	1990–2015	0	0	1	1	1	1	2
Colombia	1970–1991	1	0	0	2	1	1	2
Paraguay	1989–1992	0	1	0	2	1	0	2
Uruguay	1985–1997	0	0	1	2	1	1	1
Uruguay	1998–2015	0	0	1	1	1	1	2

TABLE 8.4. *Presidents' policy-making powers. Distribution of policy-making powers of presidents across Latin America. (Source: Negretto 2014).*

Variable	Description	Value = 0	Value = 1	Value = 2	Value = 3
			Proactive		
Decree content (decreecont)	Constitutional decree authority and content limitations	No explicit decree authority	Decree authority subject to content limitations	No content limits on decree authority	—
Decree outcome (decreeout)	Constitutional decree authority and reversionary outcome	No explicit decree authority	Decree lapses in the absence of congressional approval	Decree stands in the absence of congressional approval	—
Referendum (referendum)	Presidential authority to submit a bill to referendum	No presidential authority to submit a bill to referendum	Presidential authority subject to congressional authorization	Unilateral authority to call a referendum but the outcome is nonbinding	Unilateral authority and outcome binding
Urgency bills (urgencybills)	Urgency bills and reversionary outcome	No urgency bills	Power to submit urgency bills but proposal lapses in the absence of congressional approval	Power to submit urgency bills and proposal becomes law if congress does not approve in a constitutionally defined period	—
Sessions (sessions)	Whether the president can convene congress for extraordinary sessions	No power exists	Power exists	—	—
Budget outcome (budgetoutcome)	Whether the presidential proposal is the reversionary outcome in the absence of approval	Decree does not stand	Decree stands	—	—
			Reactive		
Partial promulgation (promulgation)	Whether the president can promulgate the non-observed parts of a bill	No partial promulgation	Partial promulgation	—	—
Reserved area (reservedareas)	Whether president has exclusive initiative on important financial or economic legislation	No power exists	Power exists	—	—
Budget veto (budgetveto)	Whether the president can veto the budget bill	No budget veto	Budget veto	—	—

powers for the president makes it more likely that policy will be more congruent with his or her preferences and less congruent with legislative medians, to the extent their preferences differ from one another. Likewise, powerful presidents with unique preferences make many-to-one congruence between the members of the legislature and the policy enacted less likely.

We subdivide powers into proactive ones and reactive ones (Mainwaring and Shugart 1997). Proactive powers aid the president in changing the location of the policy status quo, and reactive powers aid him or her in resisting any unwanted attempt by the legislature to change the location of policy. Proactive powers include aspects of presidential decree authority, influence over the legislature's agenda, the possibility of bypassing the legislature altogether, and reversionary outcomes when the legislature proves recalcitrant. Reactive powers include the ability to prevent the legislature from taking up discussion of some types of legislation, the ability to selectively act on policy decisions taken by the legislature, and the ability to reject decisions taken by the legislature. We will proceed through each power in a little more detail.

8.3.1 Proactive Powers

An obvious predictor of whether policy will reflect the president's preferences is whether the constitution provides the executive with decree authority. Beyond the mere existence of decree authority, Negretto also codes whether there are any limitations to the content of decrees, noting whether some substantive issue areas remain solely in the domain of the legislature (decree.content). He also notes whether a decree will stand or whether it expires without congressional approval (decree.outcome). Distinct from "every day" decree authority, he also notes whether presidents' assume decree authority in states of emergency (residual.decree).

Presidents have several other ways of trying to move the status quo. Some constitutions allow presidents to force their priorities to the top of the legislature's agenda by designating a bill as urgent. There is huge variation in what happens if congress does not act on urgent bills (urgency.bills). Similarly, in some instances, if the legislature fails to pass a budget, the president's proposed budget becomes the law of the land (budget.outcome). Some presidents in the region have the ability to call special sessions of congress and to define what subject matters will be considered (sessions). Finally, in terms of proactive powers, some constitutions allow presidents to appeal directly to the population via a referendum, while others require congressional consent for the referendum and still others make no provision for a referendum (referendum.2).

As Table 8.5 makes clear, our cases display a great deal of variation in terms of proactive powers. Not only is there cross-national variation within a single country, but in some cases there is significant time-serial variation. Several presidents have only the ability to convoke special sessions. Conversely, during

TABLE 8.5. *Presidents' proactive powers. Full coding of the ability of Latin American presidents to move the policy status quo.*

Country	Years	Decree content	Decree outcome	Call referendum	Declare bills urgent	Schedule sessions	Budget outcome
Argentina	1957–1993	0	0	0	0	1	0
Costa Rica	1949–2015	0	0	0	0	1	0
Dominican Republic	1966–2015	0	0	0	0	1	0
El Salvador	1962–2015	0	0	0	0	1	0
Guatemala	1965–2015	0	0	0	0	1	0
Honduras	1965–2015	0	0	0	0	1	0
Mexico	1917–2015	0	0	0	0	1	0
Nicaragua	1995–2015	0	0	0	0	1	0
Peru	1933–1978	0	0	0	0	1	0
Venezuela	1961–1998	0	0	0	0	1	0
Bolivia	1967–2015	0	0	0	0	1	1
Ecuador	1967–1978	0	0	0	0	1	1
Panama	1972–2015	0	0	0	0	1	1
Venezuela	1999–2015	0	0	1	1	1	0
Chile	1970–2015	0	0	0	1	1	1
Nicaragua	1974–1986	0	0	0	1	1	1
Peru	1979–1992	0	0	0	1	1	1
Paraguay	1992–2015	0	0	0	2	1	0
Uruguay	1967–2015	0	0	0	2	1	0
Ecuador	1979–1982	0	0	2	0	1	0
Ecuador	2008–2015	0	0	1	2	1	1
Brazil	1983–1997	0	0	2	2	1	0
Brazil	2001–2015	1	1	0	1	1	0
Ecuador	1998–2007	0	0	2	2	1	1
Argentina	1994–2015	1	2	1	0	1	0
Brazil	1988–2000	2	1	0	1	1	0
Colombia	1968–2015	1	2	0	1	1	1
Peru	1993–2015	1	2	0	1	1	1
Brazil	1967–1987	1	2	0	2	1	1
Paraguay	1967–1991	2	1	0	2	1	1
Nicaragua	1987–1994	1	2	0	0	0	0

part of the time under study, presidents in Brazil and Paraguay had the ability to move, at least temporarily, any policy via a presidential decree, and the ability to force their bills to the top of the legislative agenda.

As a point of reference, presidents in the United States do not fare well in terms of constitutionally allocated proactive powers. While they can issue executive orders and those orders have at times had significant policy impact, this ability does not compare with the decree powers we observe across Latin America. Likewise, in terms of setting the agenda, US presidents cannot put a referendum before the American people, nor can they demand that congress drop its other business and consider a bill that the president deems urgent. Presidents in the United States can convene congress under extraordinary circumstances, although this power is rarely used. The budget reversion point in case of interbranch stalemate is a government shutdown, which does not clearly give one branch an advantage over the other.

8.3.2 Reactive Powers

Reactive powers are designed to increase or decrease the president's power to protect the status quo. Some constitutions set aside areas of legislation that can only have their origins in the executive branch (reserved.areas). As a result, if a president refuses to propose, the legislature is forbidden from considering any changes to existing policy. In policy areas where the legislature is not prohibited from initiating a change to policy, some presidents can promulgate parts of a bill with which they agree, while vetoing the portions they find objectionable relative to the status quo (promulgation). Finally, some presidents are given the authority to veto the budget, even if it initially had its origins in the executive branch itself. Thus, when these presidents object to changes to their proposals that are introduced by the legislature, they have the ability to make the legislature reconsider.

We provide the coding of reactive powers for our cases in Table 8.6. Again we see both cross-national and time-serial variation. In a half-dozen countries, legislatures have widespread power to change the status quo and their presidents have little ability to combat such moves. In only three cases were presidents given the full repertoire of reactive powers.

Again, presidents in the United States are, by these measures, relatively weak. They lack any of the reactive powers listed here, putting them squarely among the cases in the top portion of Table 8.6.

8.3.3 Proactive and Reactive Powers Combined

As with the powers of legislators, we used a clustering exercise to help identify patterns in the allocation of powers across cases.[2] Again, the exercise identified

---

[2] See Online Appendix E for a detailed reporting of the clustering results.

TABLE 8.6. *Presidents' reactive powers. Full coding of the ability of Latin American presidents to defend the policy status quo.*

Country	Years	Partial promulgation	Reserved areas	Veto budget
Costa Rica	1949–2015	0	0	0
Ecuador	1967–1997	0	0	0
Honduras	1965–2015	0	0	0
Mexico	1917–2015	0	0	0
Paraguay	1967–2015	0	0	0
Peru	1933–1978	0	0	0
Argentina	1957–1993	0	0	1
Dominican Republic	1966–2015	0	0	1
El Salvador	1962–2015	0	0	1
Guatemala	1965–2015	0	0	1
Nicaragua	1974–1986	0	1	0
Nicaragua	1987–2015	0	0	1
Panama	1972–2015	0	0	1
Peru	1979–2015	0	0	1
Venezuela	1961–2015	0	0	1
Argentina	1994–2015	1	0	1
Bolivia	1967–2015	0	1	1
Brazil	1988–2015	0	1	1
Chile	1990–2015	0	1	1
Colombia	1968–2015	0	1	1
Brazil	1967–1987	1	1	1
Ecuador	1998–2015	1	1	1
Uruguay	1967–2015	1	1	1

three groups of cases with similar sets of powers. We detail those clusters in Table 8.7. The clusters have fairly straightforward interpretations. In the first panel are cases where the president has the power to unilaterally change the policy status quo with the use of his or her decree authority. We refer to these executives as potentially proactive (Mainwaring and Shugart 1997). The second panel contains cases where the president cannot unilaterally change the policy status quo, but can, via declaring a bill urgent, force the legislature to focus on his or her agenda. The last and largest group of presidents have neither of these powers. We call these weak presidents. Again, just as a point of comparison, had we included the US presidency in our analysis the office would likely appear in the lowest panel of Table 8.7.

The fact that most observers would not consider presidents in the United States to be politically weak highlights the fact that we are focusing on formal, legislative powers here. All of these presidents, even the formally weak ones, have a host of informal powers that they can use during the PMP. Presidents everywhere command the media's attention and can use it in an

TABLE 8.7. *Legislative powers of the president. Distribution of policy-making powers of presidents across Latin America.*

Country	Year	Decree authority	Decree outcome	Referendum	Urgency bills	Call sessions	Budget outcome	Partial promulgation	Reserved area	Budget veto
Proactive presidents										
Argentina	1994–2015	1	2	1	0	1	0	1	0	1
Brazil	1967–1987	1	2	0	2	1	1	1	1	1
Brazil	1988–2000	2	1	0	1	1	0	0	1	1
Brazil	2001–2015	1	1	0	1	1	0	0	1	1
Colombia	1968–2015	1	2	0	1	1	1	0	1	1
Nicaragua	1987–1994	1	2	0	0	0	0	0	0	1
Paraguay	1967–1991	2	1	0	2	1	1	0	0	0
Peru	1993–2015	1	2	0	1	1	1	0	0	1
Agenda-setting presidents										
Chile	1970–2015	0	0	0	1	1	1	0	1	1
Ecuador	1983–1997	0	0	2	2	1	0	0	0	0
Ecuador	1998–2007	0	0	2	2	1	1	1	1	1
Ecuador	2008–2015	0	0	1	2	1	1	1	1	1
Nicaragua	1974–1986	0	0	0	1	1	1	0	1	1
Paraguay	1992–2015	0	0	0	2	1	0	0	0	0
Uruguay	1967–2015	0	0	0	2	1	0	1	1	1
Weak presidents										
Argentina	1957–1993	0	0	0	0	1	0	0	0	1
Bolivia	1967–2015	0	0	0	0	1	1	0	1	1
Costa Rica	1949–2015	0	0	0	0	1	0	0	0	0
Dominican Republic	1966–2015	0	0	0	0	1	1	0	0	1
Ecuador	1967–1978	0	0	0	0	1	1	0	0	0
Ecuador	1979–1982	0	0	2	0	1	0	0	0	0
Salvador	1962–2015	0	0	0	0	1	0	0	0	1
Guatemala	1965–2015	0	0	0	0	1	0	0	0	1
Honduras	1965–2015	0	0	0	0	1	0	0	0	0
Mexico	1917–2015	0	0	0	0	1	0	0	0	1
Nicaragua	1995–2015	0	0	0	0	1	0	0	0	1
Panama	1972–2015	0	0	0	0	1	1	0	0	1
Peru	1933–1978	0	0	0	0	1	1	0	0	0
Peru	1979–1992	0	0	0	1	1	1	0	0	1
Venezuela	1961–1998	0	0	0	0	1	0	0	0	1
Venezuela	1999–2015	0	0	1	0	1	0	0	0	1

effort to set the agenda (sometimes called "going public"). Presidents have national constituencies, something legislators might be able to claim in only a very limited number of cases, and they can endeavor to convince members of congress, publicly and privately, that supporting their preferences is akin to supporting the country as a whole (the power of persuasion). As heads of state, presidents have an advantage in the conduct of foreign policy, and agreements between executives across countries, even if nonbinding, can have an impact on the legislative process at home. Finally, presidents may use their bureaucracies to make some policy options seem more effective and practical than other options. Pronouncements by cabinet members responsible for enormous bureaucratic entities often serve to influence legislative debate. We have no way of systematically capturing any variation in informal powers across Latin American presidents, and we will assume that most if not all presidents can take advantage of them – making them constants across our cases. Even more idiosyncratic than informal powers, we make no effort to account for individual characteristics like intelligence, charm, speaking ability, or other features unique to individuals holding the presidential office.

In the next section, we turn our attention to a comprehensive view of the PMP, looking simultaneously at the powers of legislators *and* presidents in the combinations that we observe across the region.

8.4 PMPS IN SEPARATION OF POWERS SYSTEMS

As with electoral systems, we have worked our way through PMPs one dimension or factor at a time, making note of how that individual factor has varied across countries and, not infrequently, over time within countries. In this last section, we will focus on how these factors combine to create PMPs in a given country at a given time.

Recall that we identified three clusters of legislative chambers based on their abilities to draft legislation with the potential to reflect the preferences of the chamber's members and on their authority to increase budget deficits if they felt this was justified. While our clustering exercise indicated that chambers fell into one of three groups, it is important to note that we allowed for the fact that some of our cases have a single house while others have two. That said, in all of our bicameral cases, the lower and upper houses ended up in the same cluster, as will become clear later.[3] In other words, there is very little asymmetry in powers across chambers in the bicameral systems of Latin America (García Montero 2009).

We also identified three clusters of presidents based on their roles in the PMP. We looked at both the proactive powers – those used to change the policy

---

[3] This may be in part due to the fact that our sources contributed many characteristics to "the legislature" as a whole. The five characteristics (three for lower and two for upper) that were unique to a specific chamber did not lead to vastly different roles in the PMP.

status quo – and reactive powers – those used to protect the policy status quo – that have been identified in previous works as distinguishing among executives (Mainwaring and Shugart 1997, Morgenstern and Nacif 2002). Variations in proactive powers ended up defining these clusters – those who could act unilaterally, those who could dominate the legislature's agenda, and those who could do neither. This difference with the existing literature – our finding that reactive powers are not really key to discerning among "presidential types" – is not as substantively important as it might seem at first. Recall that *veto override* is a power that we attributed to legislative chambers. Most previous work has sought to classify executives, not to classify PMPs by also taking seriously the powers of legislative chambers. In our distinction, the reactive powers of the president included the right to *avoid* initiating legislation in a particular substantive area, the right to only partially promulgate legislation approved by congress, and the right to reject the budget. Our clustering exercise downplayed distinctions along these lines and focused on differences in proactive powers.

Thus, across legislatures and executives, we started with a long list of individual powers related to their roles in the PMP. For each actor, we attempted to aggregate those individual powers into meaningful groups. When we examine the combined clusters actually observed in our cases, we find thirteen different patterns, which we depict in Figure 8.1. The number in the center of each pie is the number of times that each particular combination of powers was observed among our cases. In Online Appendix E, Table E.1, we report which country-years are characterized by each pie.

The shading of the pie slices indicates our sense of strength, with lighter colors reflecting greater powers. The order in which the pies are presented – reading from left to right and top to bottom – reflects first cases where the legislature seems like it might have the upper hand in the PMP, transitioning to cases where there might be relative parity across the branches, and ending with cases where we might expect executives to dominate the decision of whether economic policy should be characterized by a great deal of state intervention or by a relatively free market.

Moderately strong legislatures – those with limited policy-drafting tools but with the authority to spend – that confront moderately strong presidents – those with the ability to determine the legislature's agenda – are the rarest combination, as they occur in only one instance (Paraguay 1993–2015). In every other instance, the constitutional framers and the designers of cameral procedures tended to show relative favor to one branch over the other. Powerful legislatures – those with extensive policy-drafting tools except the authority to increase spending – *always* face the relatively weakest presidents (the Dominican Republic, Mexico, Guatemala, and Bolivia during most of the period under study). Put another way, we never see an instance where a legislature with a full array of policy-making powers confronts a president with the power to unilaterally change the location of the policy status quo. Perhaps those in charge of designing institutions strongly feared the type of "zig-zag"

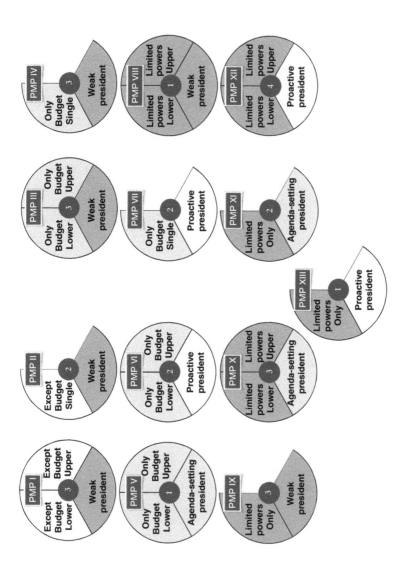

FIGURE 8.1. Policy-making processes. The pies depict the different combinations of powers across the three branches of government with policy-making prerogatives, forming thirteen different PMPs. Shading of the pie pieces indicates our sense of strength, with lighter colors reflecting greater powers. Pies are ordered (and labeled from I to XIII) from more legislature-centric PMPs to more executive-favoring PMPs. Values in the middle of each pie indicate the number of cases of each PMP in our sample. PMP, policy-making process.

policy volatility that might ensue from two powerful branches confronting one another in separation of powers systems that by definition have fixed terms.

In the plurality of our cases (fourteen of thirty), the legislature was endowed with limited policy-making tools. Oddly enough, in a plurality of cases (fifteen of thirty) the president was endowed with limited policy-making tools. A relatively weak legislature and a relatively weak executive together characterized four of our cases – Argentina (before 1994), Costa Rica, El Salvador, and Panama. The extant literature might lead one to believe that the region is dominated by all-powerful executives overwhelming underpowered legislative branches. In terms of the policy-making powers we observe, this combination characterized only five countries, and even then not for the entire period under study in any given case (Argentina 1994–2015, Brazil 1983–1988, Colombia 1970–1991, Paraguay 1989–1992, and Nicaragua 1987–1992).

8.5 CHAPTER SUMMARY

To sum up, institutional variation is not lacking in Latin America's separation of powers systems when it comes to endowing legislatures and presidents with policy-making powers. We only witness lack of variation in terms of symmetry across chambers within bicameral systems. Founders never established two chambers and then gave one a significantly different role in the PMP than the other. Beyond that limitation, founders have designed an impressive array of PMPs across the region. In Chapter 10 we will determine whether the design of the PMP has an impact on congruence and responsiveness between policymakers (both legislators and executives) and the policies they put in place.

PART III

TESTING THE CHAIN OF REPRESENTATION

9

From Citizens to Policy-Makers

Although based on probabilistic measurement and classification models, our efforts in Parts I and II of this book have been primarily descriptive in nature. In those parts we offered a comprehensive look at the preferences of citizens and politicians and the institutional arrangements linking them to one another that have framed Latin America's policy-making experience for the last quarter century. This thorough descriptive exercise has provided us with all the pieces required to answer our main motivating question, namely, what are the institutional conditions under which high-quality representation – congruence and responsiveness – occurs in separation-of-powers systems? In this chapter we take the first step toward producing an answer, and focus on linking the first two stages in the chain of representation using more inferential approaches.

To do so, we map the market moods of citizens to those of the policy-makers they choose, and evaluate both how close the two are (i.e., how congruent they are) and the extent to which shifts in one result in shifts in the other (i.e., how responsive policy-makers' moods are) – all as a function of the electoral institutions in place in each country. Our modeling strategy, which we will adopt for later chapters as well, involves use of hierarchical models, allowing random intercepts and slopes to vary by the electoral system groups identified in Chapter 7.

Before we can begin our estimation exercise, however, there are a couple of operationalization issues we need to resolve. Accordingly, the chapter begins with discussion of how *year-to-year* measures of market moods are obtained for citizens and policy-makers – and particularly how different assumptions about policy-makers' attention to changes in citizen moods can result in different ways of interpolating their moods during the years between elections. In addition to imputing years for which no survey instrument was deployed, this exercise will help us match the correct set of citizen moods to the policy-maker moods in any given year. We then discuss the different ways in which "congruence" and "responsiveness" can be understood and measured, and offer a simulation-based baseline against which observed values of our proposed measures can be compared in order to characterize the levels of congruence in the region. The chapter then focuses on the results of our congruence and responsiveness models. We find that congruence and responsiveness vary systematically depending on the strength of electoral institutions, but not always in ways that are consistent with the reference model that we described in Chapter 7. In particular, we find that both relatively strong and relatively weak electoral systems are capable of producing high levels of congruence, at least among legislatures. In contrast, "middling" levels of electoral strength seem to lead to a disjuncture between the preferences of voters and their elected representatives. Regarding responsiveness, we find that Latin American presidents very commonly fail not only to react to the preferences of their constituents, but often appear to actually contradict them.

9.1 CONSTANT OR EVOLVING MOODS

As we discussed in Chapters 3 and 4, data are not uniformly available for citizens and policy-makers. In addition, we have more data points for the former than for the latter, as politicians are normally surveyed only once per term, while citizens in each country are typically – but not always – surveyed annually. These data availability issues raise two empirical concerns. First, should we interpolate citizen and policy-maker moods in those intervening years for which no observations are available? Second, how do we pair-up citizen and policy-maker moods whenever they are available?

Beyond these practical issues, however, the lack of year-by-year policy mood observations for all relevant actors raises a more interesting substantive question about the nature of mood evolution. Are policy moods generally "sticky" – that is, stable over time – or do they follow time-evolving trends? In other words, do policy makers remain committed throughout their fixed terms to the positions that got them elected to office, or are they constantly revising those positions in order to respond to perceived changes in the moods of their constituents? Many theoretical accounts of representation require answers to these questions in order to be viable explanations of the democratic process. For example, so called "mandate" and "accountability" conceptions of representation – where citizens elect policy-makers with a clear vision of what positions they should espouse in office – make assumptions about the stability of preferences of both citizens and policy-makers over time (Manin, Przeworski, and Stokes 1999). Similarly, the ideas of "authorized representation" (Powell Jr. 2000) and "dynamic representation" (Stimson, Mackuen, and Erikson 1995) imply the possibility of actively evolving preferences between elections.

One of the simplest assumptions we can make about citizen moods is that they display some degree of smoothness over time: moods at time t

are some smooth non-linear function of moods adjacent in time, with data points carrying exponentially less information about a given point as we move away from it. This assumption allows preferences to show different degrees of temporal stability, assuming only that (aggregate) citizen moods do not display radical swings. When applied within countries, an interpolation exercise based on this smoothness assumption (more specifically, on a cubic spline fit to the policy moods as a function of time) generally leaves the observed moments (i.e., the mean and variance) of the mood distributions unaltered, increasing potential match candidates for politicians' policy moods with little overall impact on the general characteristics of the data.

The issue is less straightforward when we consider policy-makers, as there are generally two assumptions we could make about the nature of their preferences between elections. On the one hand, we could assume those preferences remain constant for the duration of their terms. This is the view most consistent with the "mandate model" of good representation. Furthermore, the assumption is reasonable, given how strange it would be to pose, for example, that Rafael Caldera, anticipating Hugo Chávez's rise to power, would progressively adjust his policy mood in the direction of a less market-oriented economy. The assumption of constant preferences would also be consistent with the notion that congruent representation occurs by "replacement," whereby voters cast "bad" policy-makers – those who no longer reflect their evolving preferences – out of office in order to bring into office policy-makers who promise to reflect their current preferences.

If, on the other hand, congruence is to occur by "adaptation" (or, as others have called it, "rational anticipation") another interpolation strategy is in order. Adaptation suggests that current incumbents foresee potential retribution from voters at the next election if they fall out of step with evolving public opinion, and they are, therefore, quick to change their positions during the course of a term in order to steadily maintain or even improve congruence (Erikson, MacKuen, and Stimson 2002, Stimson, Mackuen, and Erikson 1995). The latter mechanism is more consistent with an alternative, equally plausible recipe for interpolating missing data, which would make interpolated observations for missing years some compromise between a previous observation and a subsequent one. As adjudicating between these alternative assumptions is a priori impossible (and is beyond the scope of our work), we simply choose to interpolate policy-maker preferences using both (i) a constant model consistent with "replacement" and (ii) a cubic spline model – the same we use to interpolate citizen moods – consistent with "evolving preferences."

Once interpolation has taken place, the data alignment issue becomes a lot easier to solve. While different assumptions about the dynamics of representation can lead to different and potentially complex interdependence between citizen and policy-maker moods, we choose to keep matters simple by aligning policy-maker preferences at time t with citizen preferences at time $t-1$ – data points that are, thanks to our interpolation exercise, generally available for most time periods in our original range. Having resolved these data issues, we now turn to the concepts of congruence and responsiveness.

9.2 WHAT IS CONGRUENCE? WHAT IS RESPONSIVENESS?

While simple in principle, the concept of *congruence* – the alignment of preference or sentiment between two sets of actors – is notorious for having a wide variety of operational meanings. For one, the actors among whom congruence is to be measured are themselves fluid notions. Can we focus on a single representative of an entire class of actors, or should we take all individual members into account? And once this matter is settled, the related questions of how to measure discrepancies between relevant actors must also be addressed. If single representative actors are enough to characterize congruence and representativeness, is a simple absolute difference between their preferred outcomes adequate? If multiple actors need to be taken into account, how do we summarize differences in the distributions of their policy moods?

In turn, policy-maker preferences may be constrained in ways that citizen preferences are not, and this could generate a divergence that makes it hard for the two to coincide perfectly. These additional constraints can come from a variety of sources – from additional expert information that citizens are not privy to, to pressures from party elites, to simple path dependence in policy definition. Under such constraints, policy-makers face different incentives and different choice sets, potentially discouraging them from adopting positions corresponding to those of their constituents. We would still like to know whether changes in citizen moods are generally met by at least somewhat similar changes in the preferences of policy-makers. In other words, if there is a pro-market change in the policy mood of citizens, do we subsequently see pro-market preferences among policy-makers? This type of temporal covariance is what we call *responsiveness*, and, just as we need to answer the questions on how to operationalize congruence, addressing the matter of how to measure responsiveness is a prerequisite to evaluating the expectations derived from Chapter 7.

9.2.1 Measuring Congruence

In studies of the quality of representation, the most common answer to the issue of *which* actors are relevant is derived from the spatial model of voting. The median actor – the one located at the position that minimizes the distance between himself or herself and every other preference among actors of the same type – takes precedence among alternatives. As a result, it is convenient to think of congruence between citizens and politicians in terms of how far apart the median policy-maker(s) and median citizen are. Because by staking out the location of the median citizen a policy-maker can manage to minimize the sum of her distance to all citizens in the body-politic, comparing the location of policy-makers to this traditional standard is reasonable from a normative perspective. Even this seemingly straightforward comparison is made more complex in separation of powers systems. No single set of policy-makers can lay claim to being decisive across chambers or branches. Therefore, we first focus on the proximity of the median citizen to the median of the lower or only house, the median of the upper house, and the president. Accordingly, we adopt a simple measure of one-to-one correspondence that ranges between 0 (no congruence) and 1 (perfect congruence) and is given by[1]:

$$\frac{1}{1 + |\text{Median citizen} - \text{Median policy-maker}|}$$

While this is where we will start, the appealing simplicity of this measure is nevertheless problematic on at least two important accounts (Achen 1978, Andeweg 2011, Blais and Bodet 2006, Lupu, Selios, and Warner 2017). First, its focus on the median voter fails to capture the fact that, if citizen preferences are very heterogeneous, comparing policy-makers' positions to the position of a single citizen could prove misleading: measures of central tendency are only good summaries when variation is not too high. Second, the median voter is not an especially meaningful actor in settings in which PR and multiple parties are at least part of the equation of how votes get translated into seats, as important centrifugal forces can be expected to make the center a less relevant portion of the preference space. Of course, in contexts in which preference aggregation occurs via plurality or majority rules (e.g., in single-member districts or during ordinary legislative affairs), the median voter remains an actor of substantive interest – not only because he or she holds the most "representative" location, but also because the median voter is a necessary member of any ideologically connected majority coalition and her preferences are therefore most likely to be enacted as policy (Downs 1957).

Consequently, in addition to the one-to-one (or median-to-median) measure we rely on two alternative measures of congruence that take into account the amount of dispersion around median locations. The first incorporates heterogeneity of citizen preferences by calculating the relative dispersion around the citizen median as a fraction of dispersion around median policy-makers in each branch:

$$\frac{\sum_i (\text{Mood}_i - \text{Median citizen})^2}{\sum_i (\text{Mood}_i - \text{Median policy-maker})^2},$$

which captures the degree to which *average* distance is increased by having a representative located at the policy-maker branch median rather than at

---

[1] Technically, although this measure can attain a value of 1 when congruence is perfect, it can only approach a value on zero in the limit, as the difference between median citizen and median policy-maker tends to infinity.

the citizen median or, equivalently, the accuracy with which individual citizen moods are "predicted" by median policy-maker locations.[2] The measure is bounded between 0 and 1, which correspond to no and perfect congruence, respectively.

Although relying on median policy-makers is less problematic than using median citizens (given the majoritarian, binary aggregation mechanisms normally used to reach decisions during the PMP), the study of congruence would be incomplete if we did not consider the possibility that the entire distribution of policy-makers' preferences may match the full distribution of citizen moods. This notion, which is more consistent with "consensual" (or "proportional") visions of democracy and the bargaining they entail, suggests the need for all types of citizen preferences to be reflected in policy-making bodies (and, ultimately, in enacted policies themselves). As a result, measuring correspondence between *full distributions* becomes relevant. To do so, we use a distribution-to-distribution distance measure based on the Kolmogorov–Smirnov test statistic, which computes the complement of the maximum distance between cumulative distributions across mood values:

$$1 - \sup_{x} |F_{\text{citizen}}(x) - F_{\text{policy-maker}}(x)|$$

where $F.(x) = \frac{1}{N}\sum_{i} \mathbf{I}(Mood_i \leq x)$ is the empirical distribution function of actor moods. Like our many-to-one congruence measure, this distribution-to-distribution measure is also bounded between 0 (no congruence) and 1 (perfect congruence).

Both distribution-based measures of congruence rely on individual-level preference observations, and yet our measurement model outputs *aggregate* moods and indicators of dispersion around them. To address this apparent shortcoming, we use $n = 1,500$ draws from the posterior distributions of citizen and policy-maker policy moods to calculate our distribution-based congruence measures. While this strategy could obscure important differences when studying congruence at low levels of aggregation (e.g., the voting precinct), our focus on the national level should assuage concerns related to small-sample sizes. In addition, all computations are conducted by pairing policy-makers' moods at time t with those of citizens at time $t - 1$, as discussed in the previous section.

9.2.2 A Simulation-Based Benchmark of Congruence Levels

What do normal levels of congruence look like? Although all our measures have finite bounds, observing a score in the middle of the range (or anywhere else, for that matter) does not tell us whether these values are, in any practical sense,

---

[2] This functional form, which is similar to what Golder and Stramski (2010) call *many-to-one congruence*, more clearly reveals the connection between congruence and the standard R^2 measure of linear fit to a set of predictions (which, in this case, are constant and given by the median policy-maker location).

"average". In other words, making general claims about the extent to which congruence is "high" or "low" in the region is impossible without access to a yardstick that allows for meaningful comparisons. More specifically, relative assessments of the kind we would like to use to characterize the region's congruence levels require a plausible *distribution* of congruence values.

Although we could use the observed congruence levels in our sample as a plausible reference distribution, this would not allow us to say anything about the relative congruence levels across the region as a whole. In turn, collecting the amount of information needed to obtain comparable congruence measures in countries outside of our set of cases would require data collection efforts that are beyond the scope of our project. Accordingly, a more viable approach consists of *simulating* elections under a wide variety of citizen moods, policy-maker moods, and electoral institutions – a set of conditions that far exceeds those observed in our sample – and then computing congruence levels between hypothetical citizens and elected hypothetical policy-makers using the three measures we discussed earlier. Considering values of congruence across all of these different electoral conditions can provide us with the kind of distribution we need in order to evaluate whether congruence levels in the region are high or low during the period we study.

To do so, we rely on the simulations we used to generate a taxonomy of electoral systems in Chapter 7. As before, our simulation exercise begins by sampling a set of voters', legislators', and presidents' moods from normal distributions. To increase the validity of our results, we define the mean and standard deviations of these distributions using the corresponding typical mean and standard deviation parameters estimated by the model in Chapter 6. Once we have a set of hypothetical voter moods and a set of positions taken by hypothetical legislative and presidential candidates, we proceed by simulating 1,000 elections of legislators and presidents under a wide variety of institutional arrangements – always assuming that voters assess alternatives spatially.

Specifically, we consider elections under D'Hondt, Hare, Sainte-Laguë, limited nomination, plurality and majority formulas, as well as district magnitudes ranging from 1 to 120 and electoral thresholds ranging from 1 percent to 5 percent. We also allow for differences in the extent to which voters are willing to vote for their second-most preferred alternative, using a probability parameter that ranges from "always vote for the closest alternative" (sincere voting) to "tossing a coin between the most and second most preferred alternatives" (vote strategically with probability 0.5). In total, our simulation exercise comprises 64,800 different institutional arrangements. After drawing a set of elected policy-makers under each set of institutional arrangements,[3] we compute our measures of median-to-median, distribution-to-median, and, where applicable, distribution-to-distribution measures of congruence for each

---

[3] We use plausible institutional arrangements for each office; thus, we do not use proportional rules, for example, to elect executives.

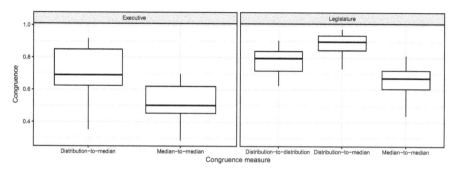

FIGURE 9.1. Simulated congruence, citizen to policy-makers. The boxplots depict the distribution of citizen-congruence levels across *simulated* elections under different institutional arrangements (see main text for more details). The left panel depicts congruence between simulated citizens and executives. The right panel depicts congruence between citizens and legislators. Each boxplot corresponds to a different measure of congruence.

election outcome. The averages across the 1,000 replications for each electoral scenario are depicted in Figure 9.1, which shows variation across these different scenarios using boxplots for each of the congruence measures and each branch.

Overall, we find that congruence between citizens and executives (left panel of Figure 9.1) can be expected to be lower than the corresponding congruence type between citizens and legislators (right panel of Figure 9.1). On average (i.e., across simulated elections under different electoral systems), distribution-to-median congruence with respect to presidents is 0.69, compared to an average of 0.9 for legislators. Similarly, median-to-median congruence with respect to presidents is typically about 0.5, while the same type of congruence is generally about 0.66 when considering legislators. However, as evidenced by the wider interquartile boxes of the boxplots on the left, we should generally expect more variability in citizen-to-executive congruence vis-à-vis citizen-to-legislator congruence across electoral systems. Finally, typical levels of distribution-to-distribution congruence across electoral system types oscillate between 0.7 and 0.85, with a median of 0.79.

For our sample, actually-observed congruence levels are depicted in Figure 9.2. Overall, our data shows many of the same trends evidenced by the simulation exercise: executives tend to have lower levels of congruence with respect to citizens, and there is more variability in the congruence levels of executives vis-à-vis *legislatures* – at least when it comes to distribution-to-median measures, which in turn tend to have higher values than median-to-median measures. Our data also show very few differences in terms of interpolation strategies for constant or evolving moods, except perhaps for small differences in all measures involving the distribution of voters, which tend to be lower on average when using a constant interpolation strategy.

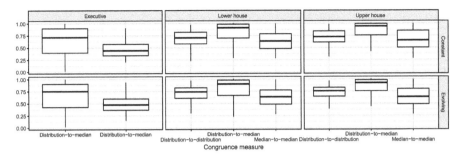

FIGURE 9.2. Observed congruence, citizen to policy-makers. Distribution of congruence levels across *observed* elections in our sample. Panels are organized with branches along columns (from executive on the left, to lower house in the middle, and upper house on the right) and yearly interpolation strategy along rows (with constant interpolations in the top row, and evolving interpolations in the bottom row). The boxplots in each panel correspond to different congruence measures.

9.2.3 Measuring Responsiveness

Although generally taken to mean the degree to which policy-makers react to changes in citizen preferences so as to better reflect those preferences, the literature on democratic representation has used the term "responsiveness" in somewhat fluid ways (Manin, Przeworski, and Stokes 1999). While in some cases it is used in a broad sense, almost interchangeably with "democratic representation" (e.g., Dahl 1989, Powell Jr. 2004), in others it can refer to the more narrow evaluation of the expected change in seat shares as a result of changes in the share of votes (e.g., McGhee 2014, Powell Jr. 2000). In the absence of actual preference data, seats and votes have served as a proxy in the representation literature – explaining why "responsiveness" has often been taken to be a characteristic of the so-called seats-votes curve (e.g., Gelman and King 1990, Linzer 2012). As we discussed earlier, the issues with using vote and seat data as proxies for preferences is that they conflate the strategic and mechanical effects of electoral systems.

With access to more direct data on preferences over time, however, better operational definitions of responsiveness become available. Stimson (1999) and Soroka and Wlezien (2010), for instance, use the term to refer to a *dynamic* characteristic of democratic representation, whereby preferences of policy-makers *change* in the same direction that voters' preferences move. Our measurement efforts provide us with the kind of time-specific data needed to compute these changes, so we adopt this dynamic approach to measuring responsiveness. More specifically, for each year in our data set we compute

$$\delta_i = I(\text{sign}(\delta_{\text{citizen}, \, t-1}) \times \text{sign}(\delta_{\text{policy-maker}, \, t}) > 0)$$

where $\delta_{., t}$ is the difference in actor moods from time $t-1$ to t (positive if mood is more pro-market in time t than at time $t-1$, negative otherwise), sign($\cdot$) is equal to −1 if its argument is negative, 1 if its argument is positive, and 0 otherwise, and $I(\cdot)$ is the indicator function (equal to 1 if its argument is true, and 0 otherwise). The resulting binary responsiveness measure is therefore equal to 1 (whenever both changes occur in the same direction) or to 0 (whenever changes occur in different directions, or if at least of the two moods stays constant). By using a binary measure (rather than a continuous difference in changes, for instance), we avoid the issues that would ensue if changes in policy-maker moods were larger in magnitude, on average, than those of citizens (or vice versa), and we are thus better able to distinguish between congruence and responsiveness without conflating the two.

9.2.4 A Simulation-Based Benchmark of Responsiveness Levels

To generate a benchmark of "normal" responsiveness levels that is not specific to our sample, we once again rely on a simulation exercise. In fact, the same data generated in the simulation used to produce a distribution of plausible congruence values can help us establish a reference mode for responsiveness. For each of our simulated elections (which occur under different electoral settings), we simply evaluate our proposed congruence measure, and use the average across elections held under the same set of rules as a proxy for the probability that policy-makers will be responsive to citizens' changing preferences. Since each of the 1,000 elections are independent, voters in our simulation are not backward-looking: they do not "punish the rascals" by voting them out of office. As a result, the simulation benchmark is likely to show more variance in responsiveness than we would expect in the real world, which is why we choose this unusually large number (viz. 1,000) of simulated elections under each institutional arrangement. Figure 9.3 depicts the distribution of these probabilities across a variety of electoral systems.

As indicated by the nearly identical distributions, the simulations suggest that we should not see a discernible difference in the levels of responsiveness of

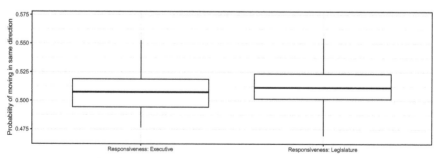

FIGURE 9.3. Simulated responsiveness, citizen to policy-makers. The boxplots depict the distribution of responsiveness levels across *simulated* elections under different institutional arrangements, with respect to executives (left boxplot) and legislatures (right boxplot).

presidents and legislatures to changes in citizen preferences. They also suggest that, on average, the probability that policy-makers' moods move in the same direction as citizen moods is little over 0.5. The result, which is largely a function of how much more heterogeneity in voter moods we can expect to see vis-à-vis policy-makers, helps us contextualize the seemingly low levels of responsiveness in our own sample. Among executives, the percentage of observed elections that result in movements in the same direction as citizen mood changes is 39 percent, which is only slightly lower than the 41 percent of lower house elections that did the same. Among the three branches, upper houses appear to be the most responsive in our sample with about 44 percent of changes in average moods occurring in the same direction as changes in citizen preferences.

We are now in a position to get to the heart of this chapter's question: under what linkage conditions can we expect to see congruence and responsiveness in Latin America's separation-of-powers systems? To answer this, we estimate a set of flexible regression models, and discuss their implications in the next section.

9.3 CONGRUENCE AND RESPONSIVENESS BETWEEN CITIZENS AND POLICY-MAKERS

In Chapter 7 we created a taxonomy of electoral systems based on simulated election outcomes. They allowed us to categorize on a single dimension – electoral system strength – cases that vary along many different details of actual electoral rules. The numbers assigned to the six "terminal nodes" of the regression tree that our classification created are thus meant to convey the degree to which the system is permissive or constraining – with lower numbers corresponding to weaker, more permissive, institutional arrays. Recall that "strong" systems encourage a heterogeneous population to strategically seek out proximate *but* viable candidates while "weak" systems exert less pressure of this sort. When we assign these six categories of systems to the three branches they are used to elect, we end up with twelve different national electoral system combinations.

To evaluate whether average levels of congruence differ significantly across electoral rules, we rely on a generic mixed-effects linear model with random intercepts by each of the electoral system groups we identified in Chapter 7. We define models for each of our three measures of congruence and for each of our two interpolation strategies, for a total of six models.

Our models of median-to-median congruence also account for estimated levels of citizen mood heterogeneity to ensure electoral system comparisons occur in contexts in which coordination problems are similarly difficult to solve. Furthermore, as we indicated earlier, it is important to control for the dispersion of preferences among the electorate if median-to-median differences are to be adequately used as measures of congruence (rather as confounded indicators of the polarization levels among those being represented, Achen 1978). We also include a fixed effect by branch, with "executive" as the baseline category (to accommodate the possibility that executives and legislatures have discernibly different levels of congruence, as evidenced in the simulation benchmark exercise), as well as controls for the mood of the party of the median legislator and the party of the executive – to account for the "market friendliness" of relevant partisan actors.[4] As we discussed in Chapter 8, policy-making institutions can render some *partisan* players the relevant actors in terms of representation, and as a result we would like to hold partisan conditions constant to the extent possible.[5]

As they stand, these generic multilevel models allow for almost any relationship between electoral system strength and congruence, as our discrete measure of the former (which splits constraint/permissiveness into six different categories, corresponding to our electoral system groups) can accommodate even the most irregular relationships between the two. The expectations we laid out in Chapter 7, however, are much smoother in nature: strength and congruence have clear patterns of association that do not require "wiggly" functions to be represented. We capture these prior expectations by including the electoral group as a linear and square term in the set of predictors – an approach that effectively pools the random intercepts toward a smooth, single-peaked curve, but allows for more irregular relationships if the data support them (Gelman and Hill 2007, Ghitza and Gelman 2013). If the data do not support more complex relationships between electoral system strength and congruence (beyond the concave or convex smooth relationship allowed by the continuous terms), then the models should produce estimates of variance approaching zero (i.e., $\widehat{\sigma}_2 \approx 0$).

Table 9.1 shows the results of estimating the generic mixed-effects linear model using both the constant and the evolving interpolations of policy-maker preferences for each of three measures of congruence. On average, the models account for about 14 percent of total variation in the different congruence measures, with data-level R^2 values ranging from 0.08 (in the case of distribution-to-distribution congruence using an evolving interpolation) to 0.23 (in the case of median-to-median congruence using a smooth interpolation). Much of the variation in our data appears to occur *within*

---

[4] Recall that our measurement model produced *aggregate* market moods. To produce these party-level mood measures, therefore, we rely on the A–M model discussed in Chapter 4, which helps us produce party-level moods.

[5] In Online Appendix F we present these and all other models in the book with a series of controls for economic performance (viz. moving averages for inflation, GDP growth, and unemployment levels). The substantive conclusions to be drawn from those models are the same that we report here, with some patterns becoming even more pronounced (viz. the U-shape results we discuss next are apparent across all types of congruence measures). Unsurprisingly, including these predictors also improves the fit of the models. We chose to report the more parsimonious models, however, as these economic performance indicators are not expected to confound the relationship between institutional arrangements and either congruence or responsiveness levels.

TABLE 9.1. *Regression of citizen congruence on electoral system groups. Multilevel linear regression of different congruence measures, with random intercepts by country and branch/electoral system group combinations, using different interpolation strategies for policy-maker moods.*

	Dependent variable					
	Median-to-median		Distribution-to-median		Distribution-to-distribution	
	Evolving	Constant	Evolving	Constant	Evolving	Constant
Intercept	0.54*	0.49*	0.57*	0.60*	0.62*	0.63*
	(0.06)	(0.05)	(0.07)	(0.07)	(0.06)	(0.10)
Citizen heterogeneity	0.02*	0.03*				
	(0.01)	(0.01)				
Market friendliness of executive party	−0.12*	−0.20*	−0.22*	−0.28*	−0.21*	−0.25*
	(0.07)	(0.07)	(0.09)	(0.09)	(0.06)	(0.06)
Market friendliness of median lower house party	0.06	0.03	0.03	−0.11	−0.03	−0.06
	(0.08)	(0.08)	(0.11)	(0.11)	(0.07)	(0.07)
Electoral system group	−0.05	−0.06*	0.03	0.00	−0.00	−0.02
	(0.03)	(0.03)	(0.04)	(0.04)	(0.03)	(0.06)
Electoral system group^2	0.01*	0.01*	−0.00	−0.00	0.00	0.00
	(0.00)	(0.00)	(0.01)	(0.01)	(0.00)	(0.01)
Fixed effect: Lower house	0.13*	0.17*	0.18*	0.20*	0.07*	0.06*
	(0.03)	(0.02)	(0.03)	(0.03)	(0.02)	(0.02)
Fixed effect: Upper house	0.14*	0.18*	0.19*	0.21*	0.09*	0.08*
	(0.02)	(0.02)	(0.03)	(0.03)	(0.02)	(0.02)
Var. group	0.00	0.00	0.00	0.00	0.00	0.00
Var. residual	0.04	0.03	0.06	0.06	0.02	0.02
BIC	−155.32	−196.41	85.90	98.51	−381.77	−379.65
R^2	0.13	0.23	0.12	0.18	0.08	0.12
N	512	512	512	512	512	512

*$p < 0.1$

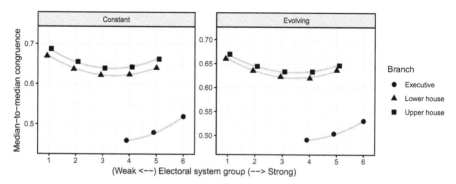

FIGURE 9.4. Predicted median-to-median citizen-to-politician congruence by electoral system group. The panels show predicted distance between median citizen and median policy-maker moods (for executives, lower houses, and upper houses) as a function of electoral system strength (as indicated by electoral system group). The left and right panels present results from models using constant and evolving yearly interpolation strategies, respectively.

electoral system groups (rather than across them), as indicated by the fact that there appears to be little difference across groups after we account for their smooth trends with the linear and quadratic terms in the main equation.

Figure 9.4 presents the predicted median-to-median congruence levels by branch for each of our electoral system groups and each of the interpolation strategies of policy-maker moods. The two interpolation strategies produce nearly indistinguishable results. Median-to-president congruence (circles) is lower than median-to-median congruence for either representatives (triangles) or senators (squares). Among presidents, those elected under some of the stronger rules are predicted to have higher levels of congruence with the median citizen. In other words, being bound by restrictive electoral incentives appears to encourage viable presidential candidates to somewhat better represent the median citizen, in accordance with the reference model. The Argentinean and Costa Rican executives (elected under a TR system and a super-plurality formula) exemplify this kind of relationship well, as they both display citizen congruence levels that score in the top quartile across policy-makers. When it comes to the polarizing choice of choosing a president, having less restrictive rules is not conducive to eliciting alternatives that are close to the median voter.

In contrast to presidents, when we consider legislative branches, we find some of the highest levels of median citizen-to-median legislator levels of congruence in the most permissive systems used to elect deputies and senators (i.e., those classified as 1s and 2s). These are systems with high district magnitudes and highly proportional electoral formulas, like Hare. However, a U-shaped relationship between electoral system strength and congruence is apparent for both houses, with the least congruent systems being those classified in group 3 – PR systems with low thresholds *and* low district magnitudes – and congruence increasing again as we move toward the less permissive systems classified in group 5 – majoritarian systems with low magnitude. The model would thus suggest that a change like the one moving Colombia's lower house from group 1 (as given by the highly proportional system defined in the 1991 constitutional reform) to group 4 (where it landed after a move to using the D'Hondt formula with high thresholds) would result in *worse* representational outcomes – at least in terms of congruence between citizen preferences and the preferences of deputies. We find this to be the case in our data, with a drop from 0.94 to 0.52 in the years immediately prior and immediately following the reform.

The same general pattern holds regardless of our assumptions about how policy-maker moods evolve. It is important to remember, when thinking about differences in the findings for executives and legislators, that the districts used to elect them are very different. Specifically, the latter tend to be much smaller in size and population. As a result, it is not surprising to find different challenges to coordination – with ensuing consequences in terms of representation – across these settings, which in turn affects the relationship between strength and congruence in these branches.

When we turn our attention to other types of congruence, we again find a large discrepancy between executive and legislative representation. Figure 9.5,

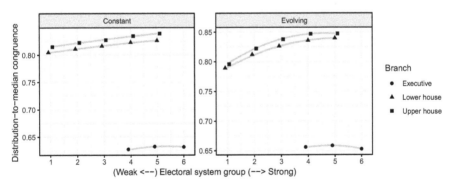

FIGURE 9.5. Predicted distribution-to-median citizen congruence from citizens to politicians by electoral system group. The panels show predicted congruence between citizen and policy-maker moods, taking into account the dispersion of citizen moods. Congruence is predicted as a function of electoral system strength (as indicated by electoral system group) for presidents, lower houses, and upper houses. The left and right panels present results from models using constant and evolving yearly interpolation strategies, respectively.

for instance, depicts predicted levels of distribution-to-median congruence for executives (circles), lower houses (triangles), and upper houses (squares), under each of the mood interpolation strategies for all of these policy-makers. While both kinds of legislators are predicted to display high levels of congruence, presidents display much lower (although still typical, given simulated results) levels. More interestingly, these levels of citizen-to-executive congruence appear to be far less sensitive to the rules under which executives are elected than median-to-median congruence appeared to be, as evidenced by the relatively flat smoothing curves connecting predicted executive congruence levels in Figure 9.5. This, however, is not surprising: although weaker rules used to elect executives can make it easier for a wider variety of positions to be viable, only a single position can be represented ultimately, thus making it harder for that one position to reflect the distribution of moods in the electorate.

For legislatures, electoral system strength can alter the composition of the entire body (by increasing not only the variety of viable positions, but also the distribution of actual elected officials), which directly affects the mood of its median actor. As a result, the strength of electoral systems does appear to have a discernible effect on this many-to-one type of congruence – particularly when we allow moods to evolve smoothly during years between elections. For lower and upper houses, we find that distribution-to-median congruence increases as electoral rules used to choose them get stronger – consistent with the reference model. This suggests that rules that make it important to coordinate on a few viable alternatives can make the median legislator more representative of the overall population of citizens.

Do these kinds of rules also make it possible for the entire distribution of legislators to reflect the variety of positions among citizens? Recall that we can also evaluate the degree to which the distribution of citizen preferences overlaps with the preference distributions of members of lower and upper houses. When we evaluate how this overlap varies as a function of electoral rules (with results depicted in Figure 9.6), a pattern echoing that of median-to-median congruence emerges: both weak and strong electoral systems produce comparatively good levels of congruence, as evidenced by the fact that predicted congruence levels for lower (depicted, once again, as triangles) and upper houses (depicted as squares) are discernibly higher in electoral system groups 1 and 6 than they are for group 3.

Thus, it appears that the reference model discussed in Chapter 7 is only partially correct, as we had anticipated then. More constraining systems produce good one-to-one and many-to-one congruence, and highly permissive systems do comparably well using those same congruence measures, as the reference model would predict. However, our results also suggest that constraining systems can also produce good *distribution-to-distribution* congruence – an outcome that is unexpected under the reference model and that prior studies

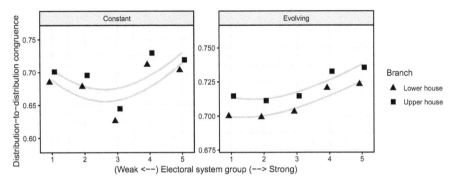

FIGURE 9.6. Predicted distribution-to-distribution congruence by electoral system group. The panels show predicted congruence between citizen and policy-maker moods, taking into account the dispersion of both citizen moods and of policy-maker moods (thus, no predictions are made for executives). Congruence is predicted as a function of electoral system strength (as indicated by electoral system group). The left and right panels present results from models using constant and evolving yearly interpolation strategies, respectively.

(e.g., Powell Jr. 2000) have found to be inconsistent with available evidence. Both prior work and the reference model coincide in connecting weaker systems with better distribution-to-distribution congruence, and stronger systems with worse distribution-to-distribution congruence. Our findings squarely contradict these results. A good example of this pattern is given by the Senate in the Dominican Republic, which is elected under restrictive plurality rules in SMD districts and which consistently scores above average in terms of distribution-to-distribution congruence – reaching a high score of 0.92 in 2010 (about 1.7 standard deviations above the observed mean) out of a theoretical maximum of 1.

As we discussed in Chapter 7, this effect can be the result of conservation-of-disproportionality dynamics in highly permissive systems: as permissiveness increases, smaller parties with little chance of winning enter the race, and votes wasted on them increase the distortion of seat-vote translations and, consequently, render the degree of distribution-to-distribution congruence between policy-makers and citizens similar to those observed under more restrictive rules. Similarly, the result can be explained by considering citizen mood heterogeneity as a function of electoral system permissiveness: if voters adjust their preferences as a strategic response to restrictive electoral rules, then homogeneous policy-makers produced by strong systems will have an easier time reflecting the entire distribution of citizen preferences. In essence, variation in the distribution of preferences collapses, and distribution-to-distribution measures become less distinguishable from median-to-median measures. Some evidence in support of this idea is given in Figure 9.7, which depicts the

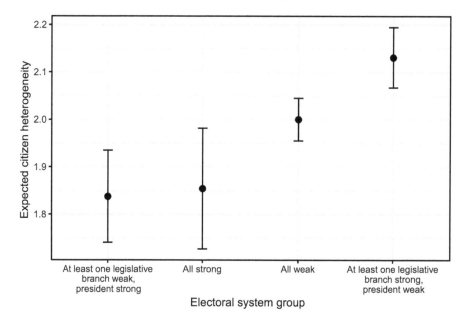

FIGURE 9.7. Predicted citizen heterogeneity by electoral system group. The figure shows predicted levels of heterogeneity in citizen moods as a function of electoral system group combinations across policy-makers.

predicted levels of citizen mood heterogeneity by combinations of electoral system rules.[6] As anticipated, stronger rules seem to be associated with more homogeneous citizen preferences over how market oriented the economy should be.

9.3.1 Responsiveness as a Function of Electoral Institutions

Our next goal is to define a model of the binary outcomes resulting from our operational definition of dynamic responsiveness, which is equal to '1' when a median policy-maker's mood changes in the same direction as the mood of the median citizen in the time period immediately before, and is '0' otherwise. We are interested in evaluating whether the probability that such concomitant changes will occur is a function of electoral system strength, with a prior belief that the relationship will be smooth and monotonic, as discussed in Chapter 7. As before, however, we define a model that can accommodate more nuanced relationships between electoral strength, on the one hand, and responsiveness, on the other, if the data support them.

---

[6] In Figure 9.7, a "strong" system for electing presidents is one classified in group 6 – that is, under plurality rules with high thresholds. A "strong" system for electing senators or representatives is one classified in groups 4 or 5.

More specifically, we allow these probabilities to vary by electoral system group, while assuming that all such effects are drawn from a common distribution and that they are pulled, a priori, toward a smooth (potentially quadratic) relationship. This kind of "bet on smoothness" allows us to precisely estimate effects, even for electoral system constellations that are not very common, by "borrowing" information from effects estimated using groupings with more observations in them. In addition, we include a fixed effect by branch, and control for the mood of the executive's party and the median (lower house) legislative party to account for the role of parties in representation. Given the binary nature of our outcome of interest, we define a mixed-effects binomial logit model that incorporates these predictors and random intercepts.

As our definition of responsiveness is equal to '0' when either citizen or policy-maker moods stay the same, we need to be careful not to artificially deflate our measures when using the constant interpolation of policy-maker. Accordingly, we restrict our attention to the first observation after an election has taken place when considering this type of interpolation, while maintaining all interelection observations when adopting the evolving interpolation strategy. This decision explains the drastic drop in observations reported in Table 9.2, which includes the maximum likelihood estimates of parameters in our responsiveness model.

Overall, models assuming either interpolation strategy do a good job of capturing variation in the observed responsiveness levels. A common measure of model fit with binary outcomes, the area under the receiver-operating characteristic curve (AUC-ROC) allows us to evaluate predictive gains over a random classifier (i.e., a model that simply guesses, with equal probability, whether an observation is responsive or not), which has an AUC-ROC score of 0.5 by construction. Our models show AUC-ROC scores of 0.56 and 0.73 – notable improvements over the random classifier, particularly when we assume moods of policy-makers stay constant between election years.

Regardless of whether we assume evolving or constant moods, we find that the relationship between electoral system strength and responsiveness is fully captured by the smoothing terms in the main regression equation, as evidenced by the fact that there is no discernible random variation around the smooth mean. In fact, most of the variation is captured by the linear term. This is most easily seen in Figure 9.8, which depicts the predicted probability that policy-maker moods and citizen moods move in lock-step by mood interpolation strategy and branch, as a function of electoral system group.

In contrast to our congruence results, the relationship between electoral system strength seems to be squarely consistent with the reference model. Figure 9.8 shows that, as electoral systems become stronger, the probability that politicians' moods will move in the same direction as citizens' moods increases. When we focus on terms right after an election (i.e., when we assume policy-maker moods are constant throughout a term in office), the effects of electoral system strength can be quite substantial: whereas the probability that elected

TABLE 9.2. *Policy-maker responsiveness to citizens, by electoral system group. Multilevel binomial logistic regression of mood change in same direction for policy-makers and citizens. Random intercepts and slopes by electoral system group.*

	Dependent variable (binary): Change in same direction?	
	Evolving	Constant
Intercept	−1.27*	−2.57*
	(0.43)	(0.92)
Market friendliness of	−0.45	−0.11
executive party	(0.80)	(1.72)
Market friendliness of	1.18	5.37*
median lower house party	(0.93)	(2.11)
Electoral system group	0.18*	0.42*
	(0.09)	(0.18)
Lower house	0.52*	1.86*
	(0.28)	(0.64)
Upper house	0.41	1.62*
	(0.28)	(0.73)
BIC	667.44	182.03
AUC-ROC	0.56	0.73
Log likelihood	−312.21	−74.11
N	467.00	125.00
SD group	0.00	0.00

*$p < 0.1$

policy-makers move in the same direction of citizens can be as low as 0.32 when weak or permissive rules are used, it can be close to 0.8 (for lower houses) under stronger, more constraining rules. And, while the magnitude of the effect is lower under the assumption that moods vary smoothly over time (right panel of Figure 9.8), the same pattern is evident then.

The model also suggests that, consistent with the results on congruence, responsiveness can be expected to be lower among presidents than among legislators, with predicted probabilities generally below 0.5 of showing movement in the same direction as citizens. This is equivalent to saying that presidents appear generally less likely to move in lock-step with citizens than if they were being chosen at random to occupy any point on the state-market dimension. In fact, presidents may appear to be *anti*-responsive. This conclusion would resonate with findings reported by Stokes (2001), who found that several presidents in the region were "mandate switchers" during the 1990s – portraying themselves as preferring one set of economic policies while on the campaign trail, but then pursuing the exact opposite economic strategy once elected.

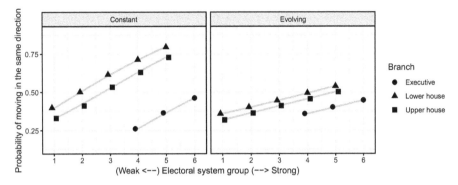

FIGURE 9.8. Predicted probability of responsiveness of policy-makers to citizen mood by electoral system strength. The panels show predicted probability that policy-maker moods move in the same direction as citizen moods (i.e., responsiveness). Responsiveness is predicted as a function of electoral system strength (as indicated by electoral system group) for presidents, lower houses, and upper houses. The left and right panels present results from models using constant and evolving yearly interpolation strategies, respectively.

We do not entirely embrace this interpretation. We mentioned early in the book (see fn. 1, Chapter 1) that the indicator we chose to capture responsiveness had the advantage of simplicity, but would require careful interpretation. For example, a negative responsiveness score could mean two different things. First, if the median citizen and the president are already far apart from each other, such "anti-responsive" movements could actually increase congruence as the president moves closer to representing the actual policy stances of the citizenry. A second form of "anti-responsive" movements are instances when presidents are actually taking up positions further away from citizens than they previously had held. This kind of "anti-responsive" move is clearly problematic, as it signals a potential breakdown in representation.

To understand whether anti-responsive movements by the president fall under the former or latter category, we calculate the proportion of instances in which such movements – times when voters and the president seem to be moving in opposite directions – actually lead to an increase in congruence. On average, anti-responsive moves that increase congruence happen 55 percent of the time. In contrast, instances that we could really characterize as failures of representation – that is, when the president moves away from citizens and decreases congruence — happen less than 25 percent of the time. This is not a rate to be easily dismissed, but it is much less dire than considering all instances of not moving in sync as failed representation.

Interestingly, while the mood of the president's party does not appear to affect responsiveness levels, the mood of the median legislative party does (and then only when we assume moods of policy-makers stay constant over the course of their terms). In this case, as the median legislative party becomes more pro-market, responsiveness is predicted to increase markedly. This is likely the result of the higher level of congruence observed between legislators and citizens.

9.4 CHAPTER SUMMARY

The congruence and responsiveness models we have estimated paint a relatively homogeneous picture of representation in the region: although the quality of representation, as measured by the levels of both congruence and respon-siveness, appears to be generally high during the period of study, there are systematic differences across institutional arrangements. These differences tend to be consistent across dimensions of the representation space: for legislatures, permissive systems tend to show high levels of both congruence and responsive-ness, and the same is true for the strongest, restrictive constellations of electoral rules – a tendency that results in a U-shape relationship between electoral system strength and quality of representation. Executives, in turn, appear to be most congruent when they are elected under the least permissive rules, a pattern that results in a linear relationship between strength and congruence of all types.

Our results suggest that countries like Costa Rica, Nicaragua, and Argentina (after the reform that allowed direct election of senators) – which use clearly strong or clearly weak rules to elect legislatures, along with strong rules to elect presidents – should have the highest levels of congruence. In our sample, these countries have congruence levels (averaged across branches) that can be as much as 12 percent higher than in countries like Ecuador, where mid-strength rules are used to elect legislatures, and relatively weak rules are used to elect presidents.

While not fully consistent with the reference model, our results emphasize the idea that there are different paths to achieving high levels of congruence – particularly where multiple actors can be elected under potentially different rules. While strong electoral systems send a clear signal – coordinate strategi-cally with great care or be punished electorally – so do weak systems – it is probably safe to vote your sincere preferences (with somewhat less concern for viability) because the hurdles to obtaining office are lower. When there are strong electoral institutions in place, voters apparently tend to recognize the need to coordinate, and elites are more likely to position themselves at the median citizen preference. This results in the high levels of median-to-median congruence we observe.

In turn, when electoral rules are weakest, voters recognize that no one needs to coalesce, and viable candidates (at least in lower houses) from across the spectrum – including at the median – get elected (since most alternatives are viable). When the electoral incentives are moderately strong, everyone knows that some (but not all) voters need to coalesce, and some (but not many) candidates are viable. However, actors appear to err in assessing who is who – waiting for someone else to compromise and unable to coordinate on viable candidates. In other words, systems "in between" may leave both entering candidates and voting citizens at a loss: they know some level of coordination is probably important, but the signal is not strong enough to provoke sufficient convergence on viable alternatives. As for presidents, we find little congruence between their preferences and those of citizens, and even some evidence that could be interpreted *prima facie* as consistent with gross anti-responsiveness. We have argued that this interpretation is not quite correct, as many such instances of presumed anti-responsiveness actually correspond to executives that "move closer" to the median citizen when the distance between them had been relatively large.

Our results also offer new insights to the well-studied trade-off between accountability and representativeness, whereby representational gains of weaker systems are eventually offset by their consequences in terms of fragmentation of bodies in charge of producing policies (Carey and Hix 2011). The electoral "sweet-spot," where both representativeness and accountability are maximized, is predicated on the idea that electoral system strength has a nonmonotonic relationship with representation. We show that, in fact, the strongest systems can be just as good at producing congruent representatives as their more permissive counterparts – although probably through different mechanisms. Whereas weaker systems are able to accommodate a wider variety of perspectives, stronger systems are likely to shape voters' preferences in ways that reduce their heterogeneity, making it easier for less diverse policy-makers to represent voters. This appears to be particularly true for presidents, who are elected under the strongest rules possible.

In the next chapter we shift our attention to the second linkage in the chain of democratic representation, using similar empirical strategies to study the degree of congruence and responsiveness between *policy orientations* and the policy moods of policy-makers.

10

From Policy-Makers to Policies

While it seems straightforward to suggest that policy-makers' preferences will be reflected in the policies they adopt, in reality there are several complexities for which we must account. In separation of powers (presidential) systems, the existence of multiple veto players whose institutional powers vary from country to country suggests that the ultimate location of the policies put in place might end up being the result of compromise among branches. It also suggests that, even when the preferences held by one branch or chamber change, perhaps even dramatically, finding a new policy that all involved prefer to the status quo may prove impossible.

As we saw in Chapter 8, Latin American systems vary not only in terms of the number of their legislative chambers, but also in terms of the constitutionally allocated (or otherwise formally allocated) powers of the various policy-makers as well. For example, some presidents can issue decrees with the force of law, while others are prohibited from doing so. Some legislatures can override a presidential veto with a simple majority vote in a single chamber while others need to mount a super-majority override in two chambers. The widespread variation we see in policy-making powers is primarily cross-national, but we also observe several time-serial changes in the form of constitutional reforms and/or revisions to cameral procedures.

One of the most valuable results of our measurement exercise is the possibility of placing policies on the same space as policy-makers' preferences. In this chapter, we exploit this ability by first evaluating the degree to which estimated policy orientations coincide with legislators' and executives' policy moods, and how this congruence varies as a function of the policy-making processes (PMPs) identified in Chapter 8. Overall, we find that the extent to which policies conform to the preferences of policy-makers depends heavily on how legislature-empowering or executive-empowering PMPs are. More specifically, we find that PMPs that empower executives result in levels of congruence that are more likely to make both presidents and median legislators better off. Such executive-empowering PMPs, however, also detract from measures of congruence that focus on the distribution of preferences among legislators. In fact, we find that this type of congruence is highest when PMPs balance the powers given to each branch. Those same balanced PMPs result in higher levels of responsiveness of policy to changes in policy-maker moods (when we assume that those moods remain constant over the course of policy-makers' terms in office).

But before we present these results in more detail, we take a brief detour to discuss issues of data alignment that are particular to this portion of the chain of representation. Although our measurement model provides us with yearly policy orientation scores, we again face the issue of how to assign preferences to policy-makers throughout the duration of their term in office. As before, we adopt an agnostic approach and conduct all analyses using two different interpolation strategies: one that assumes policy-maker moods remain constant for the duration of a term, and another that assumes such moods evolve smoothly over time – an approach we implement by using a generalized additive model of country-branch moods as a function of year. These strategies reflect different beliefs about the nature of representation, with constant preferences more closely capturing the idea that policy-makers operate under the mandate that brought them into office. In turn, allowing policy-maker preferences to evolve over time is consistent with a more dynamic notion of representation, in which incumbent policy-makers adjust their moods gradually. Having done the interpolation, we align the policy orientation of a given year with policy-maker moods from the immediately prior year.

In addition to this alignment exercise – and based on the fact that we found lower and upper chamber moods to be not only very highly correlated, but also similarly congruent and responsive to citizen moods across different electoral institution arrangements – we collapse the moods of these two sets of actors by simply taking their average (we work with the mood of the members of the only legislative chamber in unicameral systems). Since our measurement model also captures the heterogeneity of policy preferences or moods in lower and upper chambers, we take the pooled estimate of the branch-specific heterogeneities as the overall degree of diversity of preferences in the legislative branch.[1] This will produce a more parsimonious set of results, while avoiding the type of degeneracy that could result from having such highly colinear variables on the right-hand side of our models.

We now focus our attention on evaluating whether PMPs affect levels of congruence and responsiveness between policy-makers and policies. To this end, we begin with a discussion of measurement and operationalization, and proceed with a presentation of the results of our statistical analysis.

---

[1] Specifically, we use $\sqrt{\frac{1}{2}(\text{Heterogeneity}_L^2 + \text{Heterogeneity}_U^2)}$ as our pooled estimate of heterogeneity.

10.1 CONGRUENCE AND RESPONSIVENESS BETWEEN POLICY-MAKERS AND POLICY

In Chapters 7 and 9 we discussed the importance of considering different types of congruence in order to capture various features of democratic representation. Back then, we drew a distinction between one-to-one measures of congruence that focus on representative actors (e.g., the median citizen and the median legislator), and measures that take into consideration the heterogeneity of preferences among actors when evaluating how close their positions are. When considering the closeness of policy-maker preferences and the orientation of policies, many of the same challenges arise: should we focus on a few pivotal players in the PMP, or should we account for the variety of preferences represented in the collective bodies, like legislatures? And do the measures developed for capturing the degree of congruence between citizen and policy-makers make sense when considering the quality of congruence between the latter and the policies they adopt? We address these issues next.

In turn, responsiveness has generally been studied in the context of citizens to policy-makers (as we did in the previous chapter) or in the context of citizens to policy directly (as we will tackle in the next chapter). However, the chain of representation encourages us to discuss the extent to which policies move in directions preferred by policy-makers themselves. Accordingly, we will also discuss how to best operationalize responsiveness in this new context. In both cases, we also present benchmarks that help us determine what to expect in terms of overall levels of congruence and responsiveness in the region.

10.1.1 Measuring Policy-Makers to Policy Congruence

Previously, we argued that the role of the median voter is less clearly central to understanding decision outcomes in multiparty, proportional systems. However, most standard legislative decision-making procedures, including votes on the final passage of bills, involve the type of plurality selection among binary alternatives (the status quo vs. the new policy proposed) that is expected to turn the median member into a pivotal actor.[2] In turn, executives in separation-of-powers systems are more easily conceived of as unitary actors than their collective counterparts in parliamentary systems, especially given the latter's tendency to be formed by a *coalition* of parties. Together, these facts would seem sufficient to justify studying the factors that affect congruence levels between

---

[2] Exceptions often include constitutional amendments and the consideration of legislation in certain reserved substantive areas – what are sometimes termed "organic" laws. We capture relevant variation along this dimension in our classification of PMPs; see Chapter 8 for more details. While the individual that is pivotal in this kind of legislation may no longer be the median, he or she is still characterized by a single policy mood, as opposed to the distribution of moods that characterizes the chamber as a whole.

the median legislator and policy, on the one hand, and between the president and policy, on the other.

As we discussed in Chapter 8, one of the distinctive features of separation-of-powers systems like those in Latin America is that policy is the result of often complex exchanges between independently elected branches. Accordingly, evaluating these compromise policy outcomes in their separate relationships to each branch makes very little sense. A better approach to measuring this type of one-to-one congruence would take into consideration the role played by *both* pivotal actors in the production of policy orientations, and how successful their negotiations are at producing outcomes close to their own preferences. Such an alternative approach is offered by the spatial model of policy-making in systems where the concurrence of several actors is needed in order to pass policy (i.e., in settings where all policy-makers enjoy a veto over policy change) in the form of the *winset* (Tsebelis 2002). In these settings, the winset includes the set of policy proposals that could potentially replace a status quo policy without making any policy-maker "worse off" in terms of spatial utility.

Figure 10.1 shows two winset intervals, along one dimension, corresponding to economic orientations at time $t - 1$ (P_{t-1}) that lie inside (top panel) and outside (bottom panel) of the interval defined by the positions (i.e., the policy moods) of the executive (E) and the legislature (L). In the former case, a new policy at time t cannot move in any direction without making one of the two policy-makers worse off (and therefore prone to veto policy change), and so the "winset" of P_{t-1} is in this case empty; no improvement is possible in this scenario. In the latter case, a new policy at time t can be enacted anywhere in the interval defined by the status quo policy and its mirror image over the mood of the closest policy-maker (L in our example), and such a policy would make both policy-makers better off. In a single dimension, and with only two

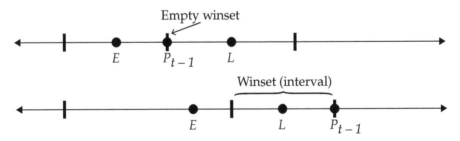

FIGURE 10.1. Winset illustration. The figure illustrates the notion of a winset under two different scenarios: an inner status quo policy (top), and an outer status quo policy (bottom). E is the policy mood of the executive, L the policy mood of the median legislator, and P_{t-1} the status quo. The dash marks capture the intervals that contain policies that both executive and median legislator prefer to the status quo. Their intersection determines the winset regions.

policy-makers, these two scenarios exhaust the possible types of observable winsets (Crisp, Desposato, and Kanthak 2009).

Armed with the concept of a winset, and exploiting the unique feature of our measurement model that allows us to place policies and policy-makers on the same space, we define a binary measure of congruence (which we call, unimaginatively enough, *winset congruence*). This new measure evaluates whether the policy orientation at time t lies inside the winset defined by policy-maker moods and policies at time $t - 1$. A value of 1 indicates the policy is inside the winset of the status quo policy at $t - 1$, and is therefore congruent in the sense that the policy at t made both policy-makers better off.

The measure has several desirable properties – including of course that it is defined as a function of the positions of *both* the executive and the median legislator – but it also makes it harder for changes of status quo policies that already reflect a viable compromise between the two branches – that are, for instance, already in between the moods of these two actors – to be coded as increases in congruence; for such improvements on a viable compromise to qualify as increases in congruence, we would still need to see change in at least one actor's policy mood such that both policy-makers appear to be closer together. This measure also helps us tie our empirical discussion of the quality of representation in the region to the long-standing theoretical tradition often used to understand separation-of-powers policy-making that relies on the spatial model.

As was the case with the measures of congruence in the previous stage of the chain of representation, it is important to establish a benchmark in order to make claims about the overall level of congruence in the region during the time of our study. To do so, we once again rely on a simulation study. The details of the simulation were explained in Chapters 7 and 9, but, as a reminder, its goal is to consider a variety of institutional and preference scenarios for both citizens and policy-makers in order to generate a more general perspective on what "normal" congruence levels look like. The synthetic nature of the exercise allows us to consider a much wider set of conditions under which congruence can be evaluated than the necessarily limited set of institutional arrangements and moods available in our sample.

Specifically, we simulate 1,000 policy choices made by the legislators and presidents who won our hypothetical elections; these policy choices come after simulating the election by different sets of hypothetical citizens of 1,000 sets of policy-makers under each of a variety of electoral contexts according to the algorithmic rules discussed in Chapter 7. To simulate policy choices, we first define policy as the weighted average between the overall legislative median position and the position of the elected hypothetical executive. During this second weighting step, we try to account for variations in powers handed out to each branch in the PMP. We define a parameter that captures the extent to which PMPs favor the legislature vis-à-vis the executive – with a value of 0.5 indicating a parity of policy-making powers between the legislature and the president. We let this parameter vary from 0.25 to 0.75.[3] In doing so, we effectively capture potential policy outcomes under a variety of *institutionally* induced powers (and balance thereof), holding preferences constant within each simulated term.

Having thus produced policy proposals, we proceed by calculating the degree of winset congruence[4] and distribution-to-policy congruence between hypothetically elected policy-makers and their chosen policies. The results of these simulations, which illustrate the distribution of congruence values under a wide variety of plausible institutional and preference scenarios, are depicted in the top row of Figure 10.2.

The top left panel of Figure 10.2 shows the probability of winset-congruent policy proposals across a variety of electoral and policy-making powers contexts.[5] According to our simulation exercise, typical levels of winset congruence are close to 0.4, indicating that newly proposed policies, based on simulated policy moods, can be expected to satisfy both the executive and legislature (relative to the status quo) about 40 percent of the time. Contrast this with the observed levels of winset congruence, depicted in the bottom left panel of Figure 10.2: based on actually observed policy moods and policy-making powers, we would expect policy-makers to come up with winset-congruent policy proposals typically around 32 percent of the times. Considered on their own, these levels would seem discouragingly low from a more normative perspective, as they suggest that diverse systems of representation are generally incongruent in the sense that they make at least one of the two policy-makers worse-off than some alternative to which they could both agree.

---

[3] Although this may seem to wash away much of the variation of conditions under which executives and legislatures negotiate to generate policy outcomes, we believe that this level of abstraction is important to make substantive sense of the bewildering diversity of policy-making institutions. Indeed, the clustering exercise conducted in Chapter 8 was designed to help us reduce much of this complexity to a set of policy-making power combinations that could easily be arranged from most legislative-empowering to most executive-empowering – allowing us to classify observed scenarios along the dimension that our simulation parameter is meant to capture.

[4] By definition, winset congruence requires the use of a status-quo policy – that is, a prior location of policy is used to evaluate whether a newly selected policy is in the winset generated by new policy-maker preferences and the standing policy. In the simulation context, we arbitrarily initialize policy at zero, and then use each of the 1,000 subsequently chosen policies as the status quo for the next term in office.

[5] More specifically, we simulate elections and policy choices under each of 1,000 terms in office simulated using 48,600 different institutional arrangements. We consider twelve different district magnitudes between 1 and 120, four different thresholds between 0 and 0.5, seven different seat-allocation formulas, six different number of running parties, six different settings of the strategic behavior parameter, and five different values of the legislative vs. executive preponderance parameter. About 12,000 of these combinations are not plausible or meaningful (e.g., a D'Hondt allocation formula with district magnitudes equal to 1), so we exclude them from the simulation exercise. For each simulated term in office, we compute our measure of winset congruence, and average them over the 1,000 terms in office simulated for each institutional arrangement.

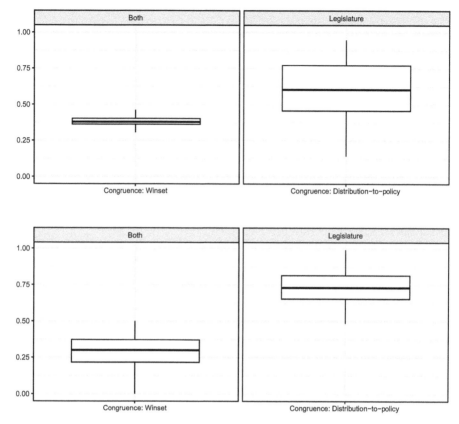

FIGURE 10.2. Winset and distribution-to-policy congruence among policy-makers. The boxplots depict the distribution of policy-maker to policy congruence, using the winset (left column) and distribution-to-policy (right columns) measures; panel titles refer to branches involved in measure (so "Both" indicates that executives and legislatures are involved in the definition of the measure). Top row: results under simulated conditions. Bottom row: results under observed conditions.

   In the context of possible values, however, the region seems to have fairly *typical* levels of winset congruence. And, although the normative point stands (viz. that winset congruence appears to be low in separation-of-powers systems), the normality of observed levels (vis-à-vis the simulation benchmark) offers a silver lining for the region. Latin America also shows a lot more variability than is evident in the simulation results. While Chile and Uruguay, for instance, display congruence close to 45 percent of the time, Venezuela and Colombia only do so about 15 percent of the time. Although this higher-than-expected variance could be the result of factors other than those associated with institutions and preferences that drive observed levels of winset congruence (such as international market forces, for instance), it is more likely a consequence of having fewer elections in the region than we consider in the simulation study.

In addition to this type of one-to-one congruence measure, it is important to keep in mind that legislatures are collegiate bodies with members whose preferences need not converge with those of the median legislator. Accordingly, we can think of *distributions* of policy moods, just as we did in the previous chapter when we considered citizens, lower, and upper houses. The degree to which economic policy orientations reflect the preferences of policy-makers should therefore take into account the potential heterogeneity of legislator economic policy moods. We rely on the measure designed in Chapter 9 to compute the degree of congruence between the distribution of legislators' moods and policy, and we reproduce its definition here as a reminder (*i* indexes individual legislators):

$$\frac{\sum_i (\text{Legislator's mood}_i - \text{Median legislator's mood})^2}{\sum_i (\text{Legislator's mood}_i - \text{Policy orientation})^2}$$

As before, this measure – which is not defined for executives, as they are unitary actors – also ranges from 0 to 1, with 1 indicating perfect congruence. The measure effectively tells us how much worse, on average, we do in predicting policy preferences of *individual* legislators when using enacted policies than when using the observed policy mood of the median legislator. If the policy orientation adopted reflects the preferences (mood) of the median legislator, our measure will show perfect congruence. However, the measure also captures dispersion, as it scores a more heterogeneous legislature as less congruent than a homogeneous one even if they both share the same median and the same policy locations.

The top right panel of Figure 10.2 shows the distribution of simulated many-to-one congruence measures between legislators and policy orientations. Although the median level is around 0.75, there is also a great deal of variation around that "typical" value. This is indicative of how important different electoral and policy-making rules are when it comes to reflecting the preferences of the entire legislature. Depending on what these conditions are, distribution-to-policy congruence measures can be as low as 0.2 or as high as 0.99 – almost perfect congruence. This important role played by institutions will be further supported by the results we present later in the chapter, as well as by the evidence we derive from the models in Chapter 11, where we consider conditions under which congruence between citizens and policies can be high. In our sample, mean values are almost exactly equal to the most commonly observed values in the simulation exercise, although variability around this level of congruence is much lower. In particular, we do not typically observe levels as low as the simulation would suggest are possible. Overall, Bolivia consistently scores low on this measure (with values hovering around 0.52), while Paraguay scores consistently high (with values around 0.82). With average scores of 0.72

and 0.75 (respectively), Guatemala and Nicaragua are close to the observed median. Typically observed distribution-to-policy congruences of 0.75 would suggest that, on average, 25 percent of the individual moods would be better reflected by the median legislator than by the enacted policy – or that, given majoritarian policy choice rules within legislatures, about 75 percent of legislators would be satisfied with the actual policy outcome when compared to what they could have achieved if policy was set by the legislature alone.

10.1.2 Measuring Policy-Makers to Policy Responsiveness

While the literature on responsiveness of policy-makers' preferences to changes in citizen preferences is well-established empirically and continues to generate new insights, the issue of responsiveness of policy orientations to changes in the moods of policy-makers has been largely theoretical in nature (e.g., Brady and Volden 2006, Krehbiel 1998). Lack of availability of data sources on policy-makers' preferences that are independent of the policies they choose make this a particularly difficult domain to study empirically. Moreover, most of the theoretical work has not considered policy-making as a repeated game (but see Dziuda and Loeper 2018 for a recent exception), and as a result intuitions about responsiveness often come in the form of comparative statics – or automatic changes in equilibrium outcomes as a function of changes in the model's parameters, like preferences of policy-makers. This conceptualization of responsiveness is closer in spirit to the use of the same term in the seats–votes curve literature we discussed in the previous chapter, and therefore is not informative with respect to the more dynamic approach we have adopted.

Fortunately, we can use many of the same ideas developed to study dynamic responsiveness of politician preferences to changes in citizen preferences to understand the extent to which policies change in ways that are consistent with the preferences of policy-makers. Accordingly, and based on our discussion in Chapter 9, we once again define responsiveness as the binary event in which policies move in the same direction as the preferences of pivotal actors (i.e., the median legislator and the president) in the time immediately prior. Thus, responsiveness at this stage is formally defined as

$$\delta_i = I(\text{sign}(\delta_{\text{policy-maker}, \, t-1}) \times \text{sign}(\delta_{\text{policy}, \, t}) > 0),$$

just as it was in the previous chapter.

To establish a point of reference, we use the same set of simulations employed to evaluate congruence between policy-makers and policies across different preference profiles and institutional settings, but this time we focus instead on recording our dichotomous measure of policy responsiveness. For each of the policies chosen under simulated preference and institutional contexts, we compute the proportion of times that hypothetical policies move in the same direction as the executive and the legislature. We then calculate the same

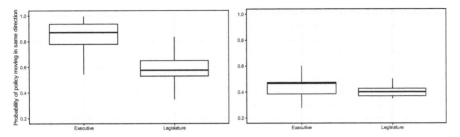

FIGURE 10.3. Responsiveness of policy to policy-makers. The boxplots show the distribution of responsiveness of policy moods to changes in policy-maker moods across different simulated (left panel) and observed (right panel) electoral and policy-making conditions, for legislators and executives.

measures based on moods and policy choices in the data. We compare both sets of results using the distribution of these proportions in Figure 10.3.

The difference between the extent to which policy is expected to track the changes in executive moods and changes in the moods of the median legislator is striking. Whereas simulated policy moves in the same direction as presidents' moods about 88 percent of the time, it only typically moves in the same direction as median legislator moods 57 percent of the time. The gap is also present in our own sample, although it is far less pronounced than the simulation suggests is possible. This gap is consistent with the idea that, even though presidents in the region are generally more powerful than legislatures, the role of the latter is not as ceremonial as is often believed in the policy literature (Stein, Tommasi, and Scartascini 2010). Actual levels of responsiveness, however, appear to be markedly lower than suggested by the simulation benchmark: overall, about 40 percent of policy changes occurred in the direction of the median legislator, while about 46 percent of them moved in the same direction of the president. The Dominican Republic and Brazil stand out among the most responsive countries in our sample (with same-direction changes happening 47.5 and 45.5 percent of the time, respectively), while Paraguay and Venezuela have the dubious honor of having the lowest levels of responsiveness throughout the period under study (at 30 and 29.2 percent, respectively). Responsiveness in the region is, therefore, relatively low – although lower in some cases than in others.

With these measures in hand, we can now evaluate whether PMPs identified in Chapter 8 affect the different measures of congruence we have defined and whether these same institutional arrangements have any impact on responsiveness with respect to the two branches of interest.

10.1.3 Do PMPs Affect Congruence?

As we proposed in Chapter 8, we expect the policy-making powers of legislators and presidents to structure variation in congruence. Recall that, after the classification exercise of Chapter 8, we ended up with a set of thirteen PMPs. These are labeled in ascending order – with PMP $= 1$ corresponding to the most legislature-empowering processes and PMP $= 13$ corresponding to institutional arrangements that grant the executive relatively more ample policy-making powers. The middling cases are instances of a relative balance in powers.

Our goal is to now evaluate how these different PMPs affect congruence – both in its median-to-policy (i.e., winset) form, and in its distribution-to-policy form for legislatures. Although the *expected* values for both types of congruence are measured over the same range of values (i.e., from 0 to 1), the two quantities are defined on different scales of measurement: the winset congruence variable is binary, while the distribution-to-policy congruence variable is continuous. Accordingly, we rely on a mixed-effects binomial logit model when modeling winset congruence, and a normal mixed-effects model when modeling distribution-to-policy congruence.

Despite these differences in stochastic components, both models use very similar linear predictors. Specifically, both models incorporate random inter-cepts by PMP that allow for flexibility in capturing the relationship between policy-making institutions and congruence levels while pooling that relation-ship toward a common level. As we discussed in Chapter 8, the frequency with which we observe the different PMPs in our sample varies substantially, so the partial pooling afforded by the random intercepts helps us estimate effects more precisely for PMPs that are used across fewer cases. As we did in the previous chapter, our model specifications are such that the partial pooling occurs toward a smooth relationship by including linear and quadratic terms for PMP in the sets of predictors (Ghitza and Gelman 2013). The sets of predictors also include controls for the preferences of the party of the president and the median party in the legislature, and a control for the distance between the president and the median legislator. The latter term controls for the fact that gridlock (and therefore lack of congruence) is more likely when presidents and the median legislator have very different opinions about the ideal role of the state in the economy. Table 10.1 presents the estimated values of these parameters, along with measures of model fit.

Overall, our models do a better job of capturing variation in winset-type congruence than of distribution-to-policy type congruence. The AUC-ROC is about 0.79 for the winset models – meaning that our model has a roughly 80 percent chance of correctly classifying a pair of randomly chosen congruent and noncongruent policies as such. In turn, the R^2 for the models of distribution-to-policy congruence (defined only for legislatures) hovers around 0.24, so that roughly a quarter of variation therein is accounted for by our model. Despite these differences in model fit, both models are informative regarding the relationship between PMPs and congruence, as revealed by Figure 10.4.

The left panel of Figure 10.4 shows the predicted levels of distribution-to-policy congruence for legislatures as a function of PMP, holding all other

TABLE 10.1. *Regression of policy congruence on PMPs. Multilevel linear regression of different congruence measures, with random intercepts by PMP, using different interpolation strategies for policy-maker moods.*

	Dependent variable: Congruence			
	Winset		Distribution to policy	
	Evolving	Constant	Evolving	Constant
Intercept	−0.09	−0.07	0.74*	0.80*
	(0.46)	(0.46)	(0.07)	(0.06)
Market friendliness of	−4.48*	−4.93*	0.17	0.21*
Executive party	(1.43)	(1.40)	(0.11)	(0.12)
Market friendliness of	1.84	2.51	0.18	−0.03
median LH party	(1.60)	(1.56)	(0.14)	(0.14)
Distance: Exec. to Median Leg.	−1.91*	−1.52*	−0.07*	−0.13*
	(0.32)	(0.27)	(0.01)	(0.02)
PMP	0.07	−0.04	0.05*	0.05*
	(0.17)	(0.16)	(0.02)	(0.02)
PMP^2	0.00	0.01	−0.00*	−0.00*
	(0.01)	(0.01)	(0.00)	(0.00)
Var. PMP (σ_2)	0.00	0.00	0.00	0.01
Var. residual (σ_1)	1.00	1.00	0.04	0.05
BIC	340.16	351.77	−15.80	29.75
Log likelihood	−149.89	−155.70	30.98	8.20
AUC-ROC	0.80	0.77	—	—
R^2	—	—	0.23	0.25
N	320	320	320	320

*$p < 0.1$.

predictors constant at their observed means. Our model suggests that this type of congruence – defined exclusively for legislatures – is lowest when PMPs favor the executive, as we anticipated in Chapter 8. In other words, when we consider the diversity of preferences in the legislature, policies adopted under PMPs that empower executives tend to be farther away from those preferred by the legislative assembly *as a whole*.

Perhaps more intriguingly, the model also suggests that this type of congruence is *not* highest when PMPs favor legislatures. In fact, distribution-to-policy congruence is predicted to be highest when PMPs strike a balance in the institutional policy-making resources available to both chambers – as is the case in Paraguay, the sole instance of two moderately strong branches, as we saw in Chapter 8. This is consistent with the idea that, when actual checks and balances features are implemented in separation-of-powers systems, broader policy coalitions (which per force incorporate the preferences of a wider variety of actors) are required to produce legislation – thus increasing the *distribution-*

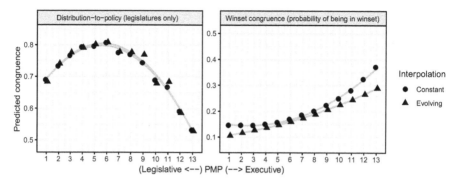

FIGURE 10.4. Predicted winset and distribution-to-policy congruence, by PMP.
Predicted levels of distribution-to-policy (left panel) and winset (right panel)
congruence, by mood interpolation strategy. Lowess smoother curves are added for
ease of interpretation.

to-policy measure of congruence to its highest levels (Persson, Roland, and
Tabellini 1997).

In turn, the opposite seems to be true about winset-type congruence, which
effectively measures how likely a new policy is to satisfy *both* branches relative
to the status quo. Our evidence suggests that the probability that a policy will
be in the winset of the status quo formed by the positions of the executive
and the median legislator generally increases as the PMP empowers executives
rather than legislators. The effect of empowering executives, which is similar
regardless of which assumption we make about the nature of moods between
elections, can take the probability of a policy being winset congruent from an
extremely low 10 percent to a more typical (according to our simulation exercise) 36 percent. In other words, our models suggest that, under more executive-
empowering PMPs, policies are much more likely to move to locations that
medians in *both* branches find more attractive than the status quo.

Why does congruence for both branches increase when PMPs favor the
executive? Although mechanisms are likely to be complex, a unitary executive
in a presidential system may be better equipped to quickly adjust to different
external conditions affecting the plausible location of policy (and, by extension,
of congruence). All policy issue areas, but particularly the economy, are
usually subject to national and international forces. In the region, for instance,
policy conditionality of international financial institutions created important
constraints on the degree to which policy could be state- or market-oriented in
countries that were forced to seek international assistance after the debt crisis of
the 1980s (Edwards 1995). As commodity prices rose in the international arena,
the need for such aid (and the constraints it came with) subsided, allowing
presidents to more freely move policy to a preferred location. This is consistent
with the upward trend in policy congruence for presidents. More recently, it is

also consistent with an explanation for the pink tide in economic policy after the election of state-oriented executives across the region (Murillo, Oliveros, and Vaishnav 2013).

Together, the two results paint a more nuanced picture of commonly held beliefs about the relative power of legislatures and executives in Latin America that is nevertheless in line with previous studies into these same matters (e.g., Johnson and Crisp 2003, Murillo 2009, Stokes 2001). While it is the case that executive-empowering PMPs result in better overall congruence, this increase in legislative efficiency seems to come at the expense of the preferences of non-median legislators. This seems to accurately capture systems like Argentina before the *Pacto de Olivos* reforms of 1994, Colombia prior to the 1991 Constitution, and Chile since its transition to democracy – all systems with executive-empowering PMPs but with low levels of distribution-to-policy congruence. As we will see in Chapter 11, these results combine with those of the previous chapter regarding citizen-to-policy-maker congruence in order to produce interesting trade-offs in the way in which citizen preferences are reflected in actual policy orientations.

10.2 DO PMPS AFFECT RESPONSIVENESS?

In the context of Linkage 2, responsiveness refers to the idea that the state-to-market orientation of policies should shift in reaction to changes in policy-makers' policy moods, moving in the same direction as their preferences. To evaluate this possibility and, specifically, systematic variation across PMPs, we use our dichotomous measure of dynamic responsiveness (equal to '1' when policy moves in the same direction as a *given* policy-maker at time $t - 1$) as the outcome in a random-effects binomial logit model. Most model features are shared with the models we defined for congruence earlier, except that the set of predictors now includes a fixed effect by branch. This is needed because the data format for this analysis is "long" – that is, the Argentine executive and legislature in 2000 furnish two different observations, and in general we have one observation per country-year-branch – to mirror the analysis of responsiveness in the previous chapter. As we did then, we restrict our analysis of responsiveness to observations of the first year in office of each policy-maker whenever we assume constant moods between elections (which explains the difference in the number of observations used by the models of responsiveness under different interpolation strategies). Finally, we again rely on the "bet-on-smoothness" approach to partial pooling, and include linear and squared terms for the PMP. Table 10.2 reports the maximum likelihood estimates of parameters in this model.

The models for responsiveness at this stage of the chain of representation do a relatively worse job at explaining their outcome than other models in the chapter, with AUC-ROC's around 0.56 – suggesting the models are only slightly

TABLE 10.2. *Multilevel model of responsiveness of policy to policy-maker mood change. Multilevel binomial regression of policy responsiveness to policy-maker moods as a function of PMP, by policy-maker mood interpolation strategy.*

	Outcome: Responsiveness	
	Evolving	Constant
Intercept	−0.29	−1.14[*]
	(0.24)	(0.53)
Market friendliness of	0.71	−2.77
executive party	(0.76)	(1.71)
Market friendliness of	−1.22	2.75
median LH party	(0.87)	(1.89)
PMP	−0.06	−0.01
	(0.09)	(0.20)
PMP^2	0.00	0.00
	(0.01)	(0.02)
Legislature	−0.15	0.33
	(0.16)	(0.37)
Var. PMP σ_2	0.01	0.00
Var. residual σ_1	1.00	1.00
BIC	889.29	212.52
Log likelihood	−422.03	−88.68
AUC-ROC	0.54	0.58
N	640	152

[*]$p < 0.1$.

better than predicting at random. This, however, may be the result of relatively low variation in policies to begin with, as we saw in Chapter 5.

Effects are also heavily dependent on whether we assume moods are constant for the duration of a term in office or are smoothly evolving over the course of that time. When apparent, the effect of PMPs appears to be exhausted by the smooth terms in the matrix of predictors $\mathbf{X}$, which explains why there is no additional variation across processes (i.e., $\hat{\sigma}_2 = 0$). The magnitude of these effects can be better appreciated in Figure 10.5, which shows the predicted probability that policies will move in the same direction as policy-makers, with separate lines for executives and legislators, while holding all variables at sample mean levels but allowing PMP to take on its thirteen possible values.

Recall that our expectations, outlined in Chapter 8, were that processes that privilege legislatures relative to executives would produce greater responsiveness of policy orientations to changes in legislators' preferences, and vice versa. The results depicted in Figure 10.5, however, show a different story.

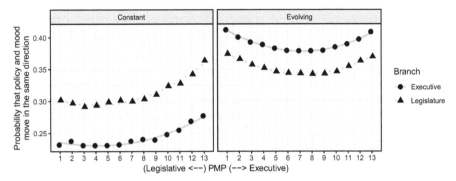

FIGURE 10.5. Predicted responsiveness of policies to policy-maker mood changes, as a function of PMP. The panels depict the predicted probability that policies will move in the same direction as policy-makers as a function of PMP. Solid triangles track predictions for legislatures, while solid circles track predictions for executives. The left panel shows results for a model using a constant mood interpolation strategy, while the right panel shows results under an evolving mood interpolation strategy.

When we assume moods remain constant throughout a term, the relationship between PMPs and responsiveness mirrors the relationship between PMPs and winset-congruence measures, with responsiveness highest under more executive-empowering PMPs. For executives, this is roughly as expected: when PMPs empower presidents, responsiveness of policy to presidents' mood changes is maximal. However, this is so *even for legislatures*, which are *also* more likely to see policies move in the direction of their own mood changes as PMPs become more executive-empowering. What is more, the result is not an artifact of a lack of an interaction between branch and PMP, as a more flexible model with an interaction (not shown) suggests the same patterns. And, even though the relationship appears to be more curvilinear when we assume moods evolve smoothly over time, policies are then predicted to be much more likely to follow changes in presidential moods (circles) rather than changes in legislative moods (triangles). In general, then, responsiveness to either the executive or to the legislature is generally at its highest when executives enjoy strong policy-making powers.

The models also show an interesting reversal in the branch-specific levels of responsiveness: while policy (when considered on a term-to-term, rather than a yearly, basis) can be expected to be much more responsive to changes in the direction of *legislative* moods when those moods are assumed to stay constant throughout a term in office, responsiveness is higher with respect to changes in the moods of *executives* when we focus on year-to-year policy shifts and allow moods of policy-makers to vary smoothly over time. Specifically, while policy responsiveness is expected to be almost 7.5 percentage points higher with respect to legislators than with respect to executives when we assume moods stay constant (regardless of PMP), policy is expected to be almost 4 percentage points higher with respect to executives when moods are assumed to evolve over the course of a term (again, regardless of PMP).

This would suggest that, while overall policy orientations do tend to track swings in median legislator preferences from one election to the next, presidents typically have a better chance of seeing year-to-year policies move in a direction they prefer. And, although levels of this more fine-grained, evolving responsiveness (generally hovering around a 37 percent chance of yearly policy moving in the direction of executive moods) are much lower than the typical 90 percent chance predicted in simulation, the gap between responsiveness to executives and responsiveness to legislatures that we found in those hypothetical scenarios is still present (and is statistically discernible) when we assume moods evolve smoothly.[6] Presidents, it would seem, have a better chance of affecting year-to-year policies, and, even when legislators' power to do the same is higher (i.e., when we consider terms as a whole and assume constant preferences throughout them), their ability to do so appears highest when PMPs favor executives.

10.3 CHAPTER SUMMARY

Overall, the evidence presented in this chapter suggests that policy-making powers are likely to affect the degree to which policy positions reflect the moods of policy-makers in charge of bringing them about (congruence), but that they are less predictive of the way in which policies *change* in response to changes in the moods of policy-makers (responsiveness).

When they are found to be predictive, PMPs seem to generate a trade-off between the ability to effectively move policy to a position that is more consistent with the preferences of both presidents and legislators, on the one hand, and the ability to adequately represent a variety of interests in the legislature, on the other. The first objective is more likely to be attained when PMPs clearly favor the executive. The latter objective is better achieved when powers are relatively matched across branches. Take, for example, Costa Rica – where neither branch is endowed with powers that would give it

---

[6] We mentioned in fn. 1 (Chapter 1) that some seemingly "anti-responsive" moves could actually improve congruence. Because of the nature of our definition of winset congruence, it makes little sense to gauge the correlation between responsiveness and winset congruence (as responsiveness is always defined in relation to *one* actor, whereas winset congruence is always in relation to *two* actors). Instead, we look exclusively at median-to-one congruence and responsiveness, which are defined with respect to legislatures. Here, we find that in about 3 out of 10 instances, policy orientation moves *against* the direction that the median legislator moves *and* makes congruence worse. Whereas this might be undesirable, many of these cases would actually improve congruence with the executive, which showcases how challenging the problem of potential anti-responsiveness is in a setting where we need to account for the preferences of two agents.

dominance during the PMP. Between 1994 and 1998, policy frequently reflected the interests of a congress that had formidable delegations on the center-left (Partido de Liberación Nacional) and the center-right (the Partido de Unidad Social Cristiana). In turn, and during the same period, Costa Rica's winset congruence was a low 0.25 – indicating the country's failure to satisfy both the executive (held by José M. Figueres, whose presidency moved farther right than the PLN would have preferred) and the legislature.

Either through PMPs that give executives an upper hand or through an ability to respond to annually evolving policy orientations, executives seem to hold more sway over the direction of policy than legislators – a fact that is consistent with the relative levels of responsiveness we find in simulation. These findings will help us better understand the relationship between the moods of citizens and the policy orientations adopted by policy-makers, and we turn to this analysis in the next chapter.

11

From Citizens to Policies

After considering each stage of the chain of representation separately, we now take stock of it by considering it in its entirety. In this chapter we evaluate the degree to which citizen preferences over the level of government involvement in the economy are actually reflected in the policies countries adopt (Stage 1 – Stage 3). To do so, we rely on the approach used to structure previous chapters. After a discussion of the different measures of congruence and responsiveness, we use multilevel models that mirror those used in previous chapters to evaluate how both these outcomes vary as a function of our two sets of institutions – electoral systems (Linkage I) and policy-making processes (Linkage II).

Our findings suggest that, overall, policy-making institutions play a much more important role in determining the congruence and responsiveness of policy orientations vis-à-vis the moods of citizens than electoral institutions. We also find evidence suggesting that, while *congruence* between policies and citizen preferences is higher in systems where policy-making powers either empower the legislature or encourage checks-and-balances (as we would expect, given how much more congruent with citizen moods legislators tend to be), *responsiveness* of policies to changes in the moods of citizens is higher where policy-making powers favor the executive. This is consistent with our findings at the end of Chapter 10, where evidence suggests that, even in instances in which policy is more responsive to changes in legislator moods, this responsiveness is highest when PMPs favor executives. Altogether, the results reinforce the notion that there is a trade-off between having policies that closely reflect the preferences of interested actors and the possibility of changing policies to reflect new interests in a way that is timely and efficient.

Before we present these results in more detail in the remainder of the chapter, a couple of notes are in order with respect to the data we use here. As we first discussed in Chapter 9, the data on which our measurement models are based do not always come in regular, yearly intervals. This is true even in the case of citizens, where AB and LB surveys with the relevant questions about the role of the state in the economy were not fielded in two of the twenty years under observation. Indicators for the different policies that we use as inputs in the same models, on the contrary, are available on a yearly basis. As a result, and to both properly align preferences and policies and maximize the data used in the models we estimate, we once again interpolate the citizen moods for which no observations were originally available. Contrary to policy-makers – who, as one option, can be thought of as having a stable mandate during their time in office – there are no reasons to expect citizens' moods (or, more specifically, the mood of the median citizen) to stay constant for any period of time. Accordingly, we assume that citizen moods evolve smoothly over periods for which no data are available, and use a cubic spline interpolation model to obtain yearly estimates of these quantities. Again, this procedure is only necessary for two years worth of data.

11.1 CITIZEN-TO-POLICY CONGRUENCE: TYPICAL LEVELS AND THEIR RELATIONSHIP TO THE CHAIN'S INSTITUTIONAL LINKAGES

The measurement model we introduced in Chapter 6 allows us to estimate a policy orientation score for every country-year in our sample. Having interpolated the few citizen mood observations that were missing from our measurement exercise, we are left with a complete set of policy orientation and citizen mood estimates for all the country-years in our sample. With these, we are then in a position to align each country-year observation of the policy orientation with the corresponding lagged citizen preference. Although this forces us to drop the first citizen mood observation from each country in our panel, it helps us assuage concerns of simultaneity or reverse causality, insofar as we can assume that citizens do not alter their moods as a result of future policy outcomes.

As was the case when considering citizen-to-politician and politician-to-policy congruence levels, we evaluate congruence using multiple metrics. If we rely on a spatial understanding of policy preferences, we can assume that citizens will prefer outcomes that are close to their own ideal (i.e., to their individual policy mood), in which case we would measure individual congruence as a function of the distance between policy orientations and individual policy moods. Instead, since we are interested in obtaining something like a *national* level of congruence, we consider the distance between policy orientation and the preference location that minimizes the *sum* of individual congruences: that of the median citizen. This idea, which is behind all of our one-to-one measures of congruence, can be operationalized by computing

$$\frac{1}{1 + |\text{Median citizen} - \text{Policy}|}, \tag{11.1}$$

where the comparability of the median citizen mood and the observed policy orientation is guaranteed by our measurement model. As before, this measure of congruence lies between o and 1, with 1 indicating perfect median citizen-to-policy congruence.[1]

This congruence measure shares some of the drawbacks of its counterparts in previous chapters. More specifically, it is just as liable to ignore heterogeneity of preferences. This weakness is particularly relevant when we consider the relationship between citizen moods and policy orientations, as democratic theory would suggest that policies should reflect *societal* preferences. Furthermore, there is nothing particularly desirable about the degree to which the median citizen's mood is represented by policies in place, thus perhaps rendering the measure less informative in terms of quality of representation in the eyes of those with more normative concerns.

To address these issues, an alternative way of conceiving of national congruence focuses on the *average* distance between the enacted policy and each individual citizen's preference. This change in focus allows us to account for the fact that, in general, it is easier for a single policy orientation measure to reflect the preferences of citizenry as a whole if the preferences of that citizenry are homogeneous. Accordingly, and relying on the form we have used to capture many-to-one congruence in previous chapters, we measure the degree of congruence between the *distribution* of citizen preferences and our estimated policy orientations by computing

$$\frac{\sum_i (\text{Citizen}_i - \text{Median citizen})^2}{\sum_i (\text{Citizen}_i - \text{Policy})^2}, \qquad (11.2)$$

which is also bound to lie in the unit interval.[2]

In our sample, average median-to-policy congruence is around 0.45, whereas average distribution-to-policy congruence is close to 0.34. Figure 11.1 shows, for each of our two congruence measures, the distribution of values in our sample. Recall from our discussion in Chapters 3 and 5 that, although citizen moods appear to be, for the most part, moving in relatively long cycles between middle-of-the-road and pro-market ends of the policy dimension since the mid-1990s, the policy orientations in the region have persistent trends over time, moving toward a more market-oriented economy in most countries since the mid-1980s. For some countries (e.g., Brazil, Ecuador, Honduras, Paraguay, and Peru) these trends result in increasing congruence over time – thus giving

---

[1] As before, and although it can be exactly equal to 1 whenever policies and median citizens are located exactly in the same place, the measure can only approach o in the limit as the distance between policy and median citizen approaches infinity.

[2] Just as we did in Chapter 9, we take $n = 1,500$ samples from the corresponding normal distribution of citizen moods to compute this measure of distribution-to-policy congruence. We are able to do so owing to the fact that our measurement model provides us with estimates of the mean and standard deviation of the assumed distribution of individual preferences.

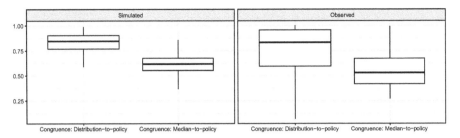

FIGURE 11.1. Observed and simulated congruence between policies and citizens. The boxplots on the left panel depict the distribution of congruence levels between policies and citizen moods across *simulated* cases in our sample. The boxplots on the right panel depict the same, for *observed* scenarios, differing with respect to actor preferences, electoral rules, and policy-making institutions.

the impression that policies are catching up with how market-oriented citizen preferences had been for some time.

The same trend, however, has resulted in lower levels of congruence over time in countries – such as Chile and the Dominican Republic – that have seen a shift in citizen preferences toward more state intervention. A notable exception to this pattern is Venezuela, where the decrease in congruence over time appears to be a function of the sharp pro-state turn taken by policy in the early 2000, as the Chávez regime reaped the benefits of the commodities boom to move policy closer to the executive's ideal, while citizen policy moods remained closer to the pro-market end of the preference spectrum.

What do these levels say about the state of policy congruence with respect to citizens in Latin America? To give us a sense of where these observed levels put the region relative to other possible systems, we once again rely on a simulation exercise like the ones conducted in Chapters 7, 9, and 10. Specifically, we define a host of different institutional arrangements (viz. over 60,000) and, for each one, simulate 1,000 elections and policy choices. We then compute the average levels of congruence between chosen policies and hypothetical citizen preferences, and average across the set of 1,000 elections and policy choices. The averages across institutional arrangements are presented in the left panel of Figure 11.1.

According to our simulations, typical levels of distribution-to-policy congruence are around 0.85, and generally range between 0.78 and 0.9. These levels are on par with those we found when conducting simulations to gauge establish benchmark congruence levels between citizens and legislators, but higher than those we found when simulating congruence between citizens and executives and between policy-makers and policies. In turn, typical values of median-to-policy congruence across simulations hover around 0.62, usually ranging from 0.55 to 0.68 – levels that are consistent with the range of values we found when establishing a benchmark of median-to-median congruence between citizens and policy-makers. These values provide a useful baseline to evaluate the quality of congruence in our own sample, the levels of which are summarized in the right panel of Figure 11.1.

Overall, although observed distribution-to-policy congruence values are much more skewed and display higher variance than expected under simulated conditions, the median value of about 0.87 is close to that derived from the simulation. And, as before, this level is consistent with observed distribution-to-median congruences between citizens and policy-makers – specially when we consider congruence between citizens and legislators in upper and lower houses (see Figure 9.2). As policies themselves are generally congruent with the distribution of legislators (see bottom right boxplot in Figure 10.2), the high levels of congruences between the distribution of citizens and policies is not too surprising.

In turn, citizen median-to-policy congruence appears indicative of representational issues, with typical values closer to 0.5 (on a scale that can range from 0 to 1) that are somewhat troubling from a normative perspective. This, however, is consistent with results in our previous chapters. First, recall that median-to-median congruences between citizens and policy-makers do tend to be lower than their distribution-aware counterparts.[3] More importantly, however, policies themselves are not highly congruent with representative policy-makers, as indicated by the generally low levels of winset congruence we discussed in Chapter 10. This combination of two normatively "bad" linkages in measures that only focus on point preferences and policies (rather than incorporating measures of heterogeneity of distributions) gives rise to a low average level of citizen median-to-policy congruence.

Despite this sobering result, and although congruence can indeed be unusually low in some countries (e.g., Argentina and Bolivia), it is important to highlight that levels do not appear alarming *compared to the simulation benchmark*. In other words, evidence would suggest there is no widespread "crisis of representation" – in the Andes or in other parts of the region (Mainwaring 2006) – that is not also typical under the myriad simulation contexts we explored. But does congruence vary systematically by combinations of electoral and policy-making institutions? We now turn to this issue.

11.1.1 Does Citizen-to-Policy Congruence Vary by Institutional Design?

To evaluate whether citizens' policy moods coincide with policy orientations in ways that depend systematically on the types of electoral and policy-making institutions in place, we once again rely on a set of multilevel models. To evaluate the congruence produced by the entire chain of responsiveness, we want to account for the way electoral and policy-making settings interact in order to translate citizen moods into policies. Accordingly, we define a model

---

[3] Furthermore, the two scales are not strictly comparable.

for both types of congruence that includes random intercepts by the electoral system group of each of the three branches as well as by PMP. Formally, the model is given by:

$$y_i \sim N(\mu_i, \tau^2)$$

$$\mu_i = \mathbf{x}_i\boldsymbol{\beta} + \eta^{(1)}_{\text{PMP}[i]} + \eta^{(2)}_{\text{Electoral group of executive}[i]} + \eta^{(3)}_{\text{LHGroup}[i]} + \eta^{(4)}_{\text{UHGroup}[i]}$$

with y_i standing in for either citizen median-to-policy congruence or citizen distribution-to-policy congruence, and the various $\eta^{(\cdot)}$ terms are normal random intercepts with estimable variance terms. As in the previous two chapters, the vector of predictors $\mathbf{x}_i$ includes linear and quadratic terms for the electoral groups of different actors and the PMPs in order to pool effects toward a smooth relationship with the congruence measures. In addition, and to account for the fact that some electoral system rules can have different effects depending on the PMP in place, we include interactions between electoral group and PMP. We also control for the positions of the median legislative party and the party of the executive, as we do in previous chapters. The maximum likelihood estimates of the model's parameters are presented in Table 11.1.

At the observation level, the random-intercept regression models reported in Table 11.1 capture about 16 and 9 percent of observed variation in median-to-policy and distribution-to-policy congruence measures, respectively. The results also suggest that there is little additional variation not captured by the smooth linear and quadratic terms for electoral system group and PMP, as indicated by the low estimated variance in many of the random intercept terms. In other words, for the most part we could have estimated completely pooled coefficients for the institutional predictors in the analysis – PMP and type of actor – and we would have achieved fairly similar results in terms of goodness of fit. The electoral system group under which executives are elected, however, shows a substantial amount of variation beyond the smooth terms – even with respect to the variance *within* groups.

A model with this many interactions is not always easy to interpret. Quantities of interest (e.g., marginal effects of interaction components) and their corresponding measures of uncertainty are generally functions of linear combinations of parameters reported in Table 11.1. Any single coefficient can mask ample heterogeneity in responsiveness across electoral groups and PMP. A better approach to evaluating the results of models like these is to generate plots of predicted outcomes. Figure 11.2 shows predicted levels of median citizen-to-policy congruence as a function of electoral system strength, by branch and PMP group. Recall that electoral rule groups are ordered from weakest (1) to strongest (6). In turn, PMPs are labeled from 1 to 7, in order from most legislature-favoring to most executive-favoring. Figure 11.2 shows that, in general, median citizen-to-policy congruence is higher when PMPs empower legislators (as indicated by the fact that predicted values are typically higher in upper than in lower panels). Figure 11.2 also indicates that the strength

TABLE 11.1. *Multilevel model of policy-to-citizen congruence. Random intercepts model of citizen-to-policy congruence levels.*

	Dependent variable: Congruence	
	Median citizen-to-policy	Citizen distribution-to-policy
Intercept	−0.71	−0.41
	(6.69)	(1.58)
Electoral system: group of lower	0.19	0.17
	(0.12)	(0.13)
Electoral system: group of upper	−0.06	−0.11*
	(0.04)	(0.05)
Electoral system: group of president	0.33	0.33
	(2.73)	(0.63)
Electoral system: group of lower^2	−0.03	−0.02
	(0.02)	(0.02)
Electoral system: group of president^2	−0.02	−0.03
	(0.27)	(0.06)
Electoral system: group of upper^2	0.01	0.02*
	(0.01)	(0.01)
PMP	0.10*	0.08*
	(0.03)	(0.05)
PMP^2	−0.01*	−0.01*
	(0.00)	(0.00)
PMP × electoral system group of lower	−0.01*	−0.00
	(0.01)	(0.01)
PMP × electoral system group of upper	0.00	0.01*
	(0.00)	(0.00)
PMP × electoral system group of president	−0.01	−0.00
	(0.01)	(0.01)
Market friendliness of executive party	0.26*	0.20
	(0.10)	(0.14)
Market friendliness of median LH party	−0.49*	−0.60*
	(0.14)	(0.19)
Variance PMP	0.00	0.00
Variance elected group of Senate	0.03	0.00
Variance elected group of lower	0.00	0.00
Variance elected group of executive	0.05	0.07
Variance residual	0.03	0.06
BIC	28.29	212.18
Log likelihood	39.62	−52.32
R^2	0.15	0.06
N	287	287

*$p < 0.1$.

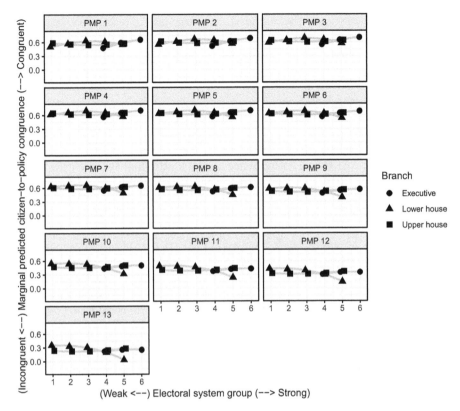

FIGURE 11.2. Estimated median citizen-to-policy congruence, by institutional arrangement. The panels depict median-to-policy congruence levels as a function of electoral system strength (going from weakest to strongest along the *x*-axis, using the classes derived in Chapter 7), by PMP (going from most legislative-favoring to most executive-favoring).

of rules for electing lower houses matter most in systems where PMPs favor the executive, with stronger rules decreasing median-to-policy congruence. In contrast, when PMPs favor legislatures, the effect of strength of rules to elect the president appear to make the most difference, with stronger rules resulting in higher levels of median-to-policy congruence.

These results complement those seen in Chapters 9 and 10. We showed there how congruence of citizen preferences and policy-maker preferences is generally lower for executives than it is for legislators. In turn, PMPs that favor executives typically result in policies that more effectively reflect the preferences of median policy-makers, but make it less likely that preferences of the legislature *as a whole* will be congruent with policy. When taken together, it is only natural that congruence between citizens and *policies* will also be lowest when PMPs favor the executive, as is the case in places like Argentina and Chile, which display some of the lowest congruence levels in the region (at 0.44 and 0.42, respectively). Thus, empowering congruent legislators during the PMP enhances citizen-to-policy congruence. And empowering presidents, unsurprisingly, leads to no improvement in congruence between citizen policy moods and policy orientations.

A similar pattern emerges when we take into consideration heterogeneity in citizen moods. Figure 11.3 shows the predicted levels of citizen distribution-to-policy congruence as a function of electoral system strength, by PMP and legislative chamber. As before, congruence of this kind is highest whenever PMPs encourage checks-and-balances by distributing policy-making powers across branches of government (i.e., PMPs 4–9) and is lowest when PMPs empower the president (i.e., PMPs 11–13). In general, we find a lot more variability across panels than within them, suggesting that both types of citizen-to-policy congruence are more sensitive to changes in PMPs than to electoral system rules. This highlights the importance of considering the chain of representation in its entirety, rather than reaching conclusions based on a single stage of the chain – in other words, democratic representation is a multistep process, and assessing how its quality is affected by political institutions requires considering the roles of both electoral rules *and* PMPs.

Thus, a system like that of Bolivia prior to the 2009 constitution (PMP 1, where presidents were elected under permissive rules, legislatures were elected under comparatively strong rules, and PMPs favored the latter) would be expected to have policies that were not close to those most preferred by citizens. This logic would also explain why Bolivia's congruence increased as a result of the constitutional changes on 2009, which altered the balance of power between branches (giving the executive a more prominent role), but left the electoral system largely intact.[4]

Furthermore, it appears as though clarity of responsibility for policy, which can be expected to be greatest when the PMP clearly favors one branch over the other, makes congruence between citizens and policies much more sensitive to differences in electoral system strength. The middle panels of Figures 11.2 and 11.3 tend to have fewer differences in congruence levels across electoral system groups. This is an important and somewhat surprising result – after all, we would expect contexts in which branches have to butt heads routinely in order to get policies enacted to be the ones in which the increased diversity of policy-maker preferences, as a function of electoral system permissiveness, would make it harder to relocate policy, and therefore harder to change how congruent policies are. This *is not* to say, however, that congruence is lower in these types of branch-balanced systems. In fact, congruence levels are predicted

---

[4] The one major electoral change in Bolivia – whereby a two-round system, rather than congressional appointments, would be used to elect the president when no candidate achieved a majority – arguably made the electoral system *weaker*.

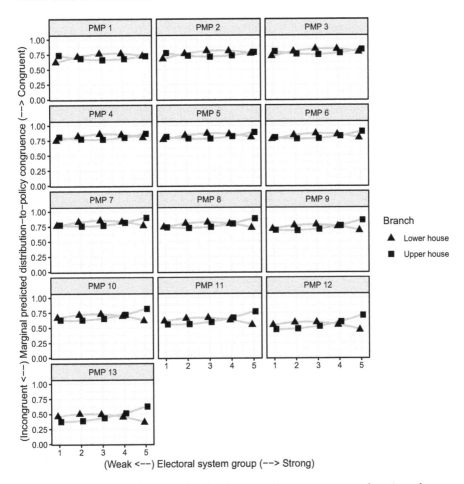

FIGURE 11.3. Estimated citizen distribution-to-policy congruence as function of electoral system strength, by PMP. The panels depict predicted distribution-to-policy congruence levels as a function of electoral system strength (going from most permissive to strongest), by PMP (going from most legislative-favoring to most executive-favoring) and branch (with lower houses depicted as triangles, and upper houses depicted as squares).

to be as high in some of these systems as they are in more legislative-favoring contexts. But it does suggest that, even though the most important differences are observed across PMPs, sometimes marginal increases in congruence could be induced by changes in the electoral rules used to elect representatives. Furthermore, as we will see in the next section, electoral systems will be far more important in determining the level of responsiveness of policies to changes in citizen moods.

Thus far, we have explored the degree to which policies and citizen preferences coincide, and have found systematic differences across sets of institutional combinations. Overall, the system predicted to be most conducive to citizen-to-policy congruence is a unicameral setting with strong electoral rules to elect the president, weak electoral rules to select the legislature, and ample policy-making powers for the legislative branch. An example of such a system is Venezuela in 1999, during the early days of the Chávez presidency, when congruence levels are among the highest in our sample (0.93 and 0.99 for median and distribution-based congruence measures, respectively). In contrast, the system predicted to be *least* conducive to promoting citizen-to-policy congruence is one with upper and lower houses selected via strong electoral institutions and with policy-making powers tilted in favor of the president. Chile is perhaps the closest case in our sample to having these conditions, with average congruence levels of 0.42 and 0.60 (for median-to-policy and distribution-to-policy measures, respectively) that are low, and close to the observed first quartiles of these variables in the data.

11.2 RESPONSIVENESS OF POLICY TO CHANGES IN CITIZEN MOODS

Responsiveness, as we have defined it throughout this book, is the extent to which two quantities – moods of citizens and of policy-makers, moods of policy-makers and policies – move in the same direction. Accordingly, we would say policies are responsive to changes in citizen moods if policies themselves shift in the direction of a more open economy as citizen moods become more market-oriented – and vice versa, of course. To measure responsiveness in this final look at the full chain of representation we therefore rely on the same dichotomous indicator of whether changes in policies occur in the same direction as changes in citizen preferences, or

$$\delta_i = I(\text{sign}(\delta_{\text{citizen},\,t-1}) \times \text{sign}(\delta_{\text{policy},\,t}) > 0),$$

as in the previous two chapters. After a brief discussion of how observed levels of responsiveness in the region compare to our simulation benchmark, we focus on evaluating whether these are, in turn, a function of the electoral and policy-making institutions in place.

In our simulation of 1,000 elections and policy choices under a variety of institutional constellations, we treat the relative frequency of instances in which policy moves in the same direction as citizen preferences as an approximation to the responsiveness under the corresponding conditions. In our simulations, policies typically respond to median citizen mood changes by moving in the same direction about 51 percent of the time. As can be seen in the left panel of Figure 11.4, the distribution around this median responsiveness probability is actually quite small. We can contrast these values generated by our simulations

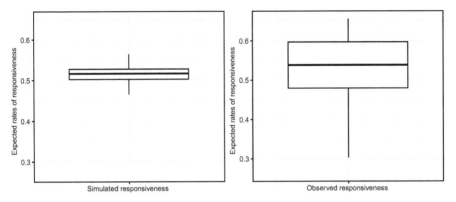

FIGURE 11.4. Simulated and observed citizen-to-policy responsiveness. The boxplots depict distributions of simulated (left panel) and observed (right panel) expected rates of responsiveness of policy to changes in citizen moods.

to the distribution of relative frequencies by country observed in our own data, depicted in the right panel of Figure 11.4.

Once again, the simulation benchmark allows us to be optimistic about the state of representation in Latin America: although there is clearly more variation than we would expect based on simulations, typical responsiveness levels appear to be higher than median responsiveness in the simulation exercise. Can this variation in responsiveness be attributed, at least in part, to institutional differences across countries in our sample? We evaluate evidence in favor of this proposition in the next and final section of this chapter.

11.2.1 Do Institutions Affect Responsiveness of Policy to Citizen Moods?

Relying on our dichotomous operational measure of responsiveness, we define a random-effects logistic regression model with a specification that resembles that of our congruence models. More specifically, although our citizen-to-policy responsiveness model includes the same set of random intercepts as our congruence models, our "bet on smoothness" becomes a "bet on linearity," as data sparseness requires us to drop the quadratic terms for all institutional variables.[5] We otherwise include all two-way interactions between policy-making institutions and electoral rules that we included previously, as well as all previously used party controls. The maximum likelihood estimates of the parameters of this final model appear in Table 11.2.

---

5 Technically, we run into issues of perfect separation when we estimate a fully-flexible model with quadratic terms. Although a Bayesian model with regularizing priors would help assuage these separation issues, we found the simpler specification presented in the text to perform similarly well in terms of AUC-ROC, taking only a fraction of time to estimate.

TABLE 11.2. *Mixed-effects model of citizen-to-policy responsiveness. Random effects logistic regression of responsiveness of policy to citizen mood changes.*

	Outcome: Policy responsiveness
Intercept	2.87
	(1.95)
Electoral system group of lower	−0.16
	(0.27)
Electoral system group of upper	−0.52
	(0.42)
Electoral system group of president	−0.10
	(0.16)
PMP	−0.16
	(0.23)
PMP × electoral system group of lower	0.05
	(0.04)
PMP × electoral system group of upper	0.02
	(0.05)
PMP × electoral system group of president	0.01
	(0.02)
Market friendliness of	0.12
executive party	(1.15)
Market friendliness of	0.18
median LH party	(1.44)
SD: PMP (intercept)	0.00
SD: Elected group of Senate (intercept)	0.00
SD: Elected group of lower (intercept)	0.00
SD: Elected group of executive (intercept)	0.00
BIC	444.02
Log likelihood	−182.77
AUC-ROC	0.60
N	272

$^{*}p < 0.1$.

With a AUC-ROC of 0.60, our model does a fair job of accounting for variation in policy orientations in the region.[6] In fact, with an AUC-ROC of 0.59, even a model that only uses institutional combinations is already substantially different from a dumb model that randomly predicts observations to be either responsive or not by flipping a coin. It is also evident that, once the model identifies a linear (conditional) association between the institutional

---

[6] As we discussed earlier, the AUC-ROC gives the expected proportion of times our model assigns a higher predicted probability to a randomly chosen instance of responsiveness than to a randomly chosen instance of nonresponsiveness.

variables and the probability of responsiveness, there is no additional variance to be captured by the random intercepts (thus resulting in estimated standard deviations equal to zero).

As before, teasing out insights from this model is difficult if we only focus on the point estimates of the model's parameters reported in Table 11.2. To better understand the model's implications, we therefore rely on a plot of predicted probabilities as a function of predictors of interest, holding all other predictors constant at their means. In Figure 11.5, each panel represents a PMP, and values along the x-axis correspond to electoral system groups used to elect executives, lower houses, and upper houses. Effects are therefore shown as we move from weakest to strongest electoral rules within panels, and from most legislature-centric to most executive-centric as we move from top to bottom across panels.

Our model suggests that, in the generation of responsiveness, there are important interactions between PMPs and electoral rule strength – much more so than in the generation of the different congruence measures. Overall, the probability that policies will move in the same direction as citizen preferences depends interactively on both the strength of rules under which legislatures (and particularly lower houses) are elected and on the types of PMPs in place. Whereas the probability of responsiveness is virtually unaffected by the rules under which legislatures are elected in settings with legislature-empowering PMPs, the effect of electoral rules used to choose legislatures is more marked in settings with executive-empowering PMPs: in the latter, the probability of observing responsiveness increases substantially with less permissive rules. In other words, powerful presidents move policy more easily when the legislature is likely composed of relatively few parties. A prime example of this is Uruguay, which (despite its relatively weak set of electoral rules) has largely remained a system with few parties (with an effective number of parties hovering around 3, Morgenstern and Vázquez-D'Elía 2007) and a high rate of legislative success for presidents (typically around 66 percent) (Programa de Estudios Parlamentariors 2018).[7] And, while expected responsiveness declines slightly as executive rules become more restrictive when PMPs favor the president, this negative relationship is much more pronounced when PMPs empower legislatures. This means that rules that try (and perhaps fail) to induce the greatest coordination behind the fewest presidential candidates lead to a lack of citizen-to-policy responsiveness, especially when presidents have relatively weak policy-making powers.

Overall, however, the largest effect on responsiveness is once again attributable to changes in the PMP, with more executive-empowering PMPs typically resulting in a higher probability that policy will move in the same direction as citizens. This happens, for instance, when presidents have impor-tant agenda-setting powers (such as the exclusive ability to propose legislation

---

7 Legislative success rate is defined as the percentage of bills initiated by the executive that utlimately become law.

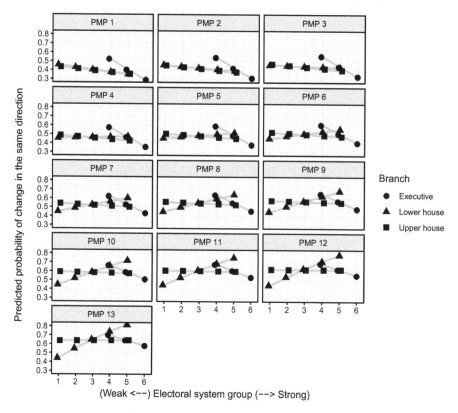

FIGURE II.5. Predicted policy responsiveness to citizen mood changes as function of electoral system strength, by PMP. Predicted probability that policy will move in the direction of median citizen mood changes as a function of electoral system strength, by PMP (going from most legislative-favoring to most executive-favoring) and branch (with predictions for presidents as circles, for lower houses as triangles, and upper houses as squares).

in certain issue areas, or the ability to request urgent consideration of some bills) and legislatures have very limited powers (such as inability to amend constitutions, increase budgetary spending, or override vetoes without the help of a qualified majority). Accordingly, the model implies that post-2003-reform Colombia would be one of the least responsive cases in our sample, and that Argentina (with its highly restrictive electoral rules and strongly executive-centric policy-making institutions) should be one of the most responsive countries in the region. In both cases the predictions turn out to be correct.

In general, in contexts in which the unitary executive has a lot of control over the PMP, and in which restrictive rules result in legislatures with few distinct preferences, it is not only very clear who is accountable for policy (namely, the president), it is also easiest to punish wayward agents (see Powell Jr. 2000 on "authorized representation" or voting for actors who control policy formation; see also Schwindt-Bayer and Tavits 2016).[8] In future work we would like to explore whether this is the follow-on story to Stokes's claims about mandate-switching presidents (Stokes 2001). Our findings suggest that, under specific institutional contexts, it is possible that presidents can be made to responsively pursue the preferences of citizens even when they, as presidents, would prefer to implement policy that takes the country in a different direction. As we suggested early on (fn. 1, Chapter 1) our responsiveness indicator must be interpreted carefully. Among all instances of policy-to-citizen anti-responsiveness, which make up about 45 percent of all movements in our data sets (i.e., 55 percent of all movements are "responsive," by our definition), the majority (about 56 percent) actually improve congruence. Consequently, only about one-fifth of all changes in policy orientations and citizen policy moods correspond to anti-responsive changes that worsen congruence.

11.3 CHAPTER SUMMARY

In this chapter, we considered the connection between citizens and policies, accounting for all the intermediate linkages that form the full chain of representation. In general, while we find that median and distribution-aware congruences are higher whenever PMPs empower legislatures, such PMPs make it harder for policy to accurately track the movements of citizen moods over time. In turn, while executive-empowering PMPs make it easy for policy to respond to changes in citizen moods (particularly when legislatures are elected under restrictive rules, and presidents are elected under permissive rules), this increased ability comes at the expense of accurately reflecting the preferences of citizens in terms of proximity.

The case of Nicaragua after Ortega's reelection in 2006 is a good example of this trade-off. With its institutionally weak executive and relatively stronger legislature, Nicaragua displayed high levels of congruence coming into 2006. At the time, policy (which remained largely stable throughout this period) was unable to track the ebbs and flows of citizen moods. After the institutional strengthening of the executive via the effective elimination of presidential term limits, overall levels of congruence dropped dramatically. This inability to keep abreast of citizen moods may have contributed to the disaffection that led to major social unrest in the period following our data's time span, after 2013.

---

[8] Powell Jr. and Whitten (1992) point out the importance of democratic institutional design in enhancing the clarity of responsibility, although they do not focus on variations within presidential regimes.

We also found, as we did in the previous chapter, that, even where congruence is low, responsiveness *can* remain high. In other words, citizens' moods can be reflected in the direction that policy is moving even when that policy remains somewhat distant from what most citizens would prefer.

We turn now to a final chapter where we summarize our original theoretical argument, the empirical findings that support that argument, and the empirical findings that would lead us to reformulate that argument before seeking to test it again on a different set of observations.

12

A Chain Is Only as Strong as Its Weakest Link

We began this book professing our curiosity about how the design of democratic institutions impacts the quality of representation. More specifically, we wanted to understand how elections and PMPs serve as instruments of democracy (Powell Jr. 2000), leading to more or less congruence between citizens and the policies that are adopted supposedly at their behest. We wanted to address these questions in separation of powers or presidential systems where the delegation relationship between citizens as principals and politicians as their agents is complex on two counts. First, voters choose multiple agents, and variations in electoral rules mean that one agent might like to be more congruent or responsive to one group of voters while another agent is focused on a different set of voters. Second, despite differences across agents in the extent to which they are representative, these agents must concur with one another, in theory, in order to make policy – although the design of the PMP might privilege one actor over another. In short, we found that electoral rules with very clear incentives about the need to coalesce behind some number of candidates, both those quite constraining and those quite permissive, promote congruence between the preferences of citizens and the legislators they choose. However, presidents, no matter how they are elected, were relatively less likely to share citizens' views regarding the balance to be struck between markets and states. This relative lack of congruence is compounded by the fact that it is powerful presidents (i.e., those with proactive powers) who are most able to obtain economic policies closer to their preferred points. What is more, even the chances of moving policy in a desired direction (if not closer to an ideal location) are improved under these executive-favoring PMP *for both presidents and legislators*. Thus, the challenge of obtaining good representation is twofold: citizens may select legislators who represent them, but those legislators can struggle to move policy without compromising. Put another way, citizens struggle to select presidents who actually share their preferences, but some of those presidents can end up being most capable of determining the location of policies.

In order to satisfy our curiosity, we assembled data from eighteen countries in Latin America for a nearly twenty-five-year period beginning in the early 1990s and ending in 2015. We went to great pains to locate citizens' moods (Stage 1 of the chain of representation), politicians' moods (Stage 2), and enacted policy orientations (Stage 3) on a *common space* – a *sine qua non* condition for any discussion of congruence. We chose to focus on some of the most important policies, in terms of impact on citizens' lives, a government must adopt, namely, the policies dictating the balance struck between state and market when governing the economy. Perhaps to the detriment of finding high-quality representation, these policies are also some of the policies most influenced by forces largely beyond the control of any government. We transparently detailed our efforts to capture each stage in the process of representation in a comparable fashion in Chapters 3–6.

The three stages of the chain of representation are linked together by institutions. Linkage I, covered in detail in Chapter 7, is made up of the electoral systems that elites face when deciding whether to declare themselves candidates and what policy promises to put on offer as they campaign. Electoral rules also shape the incentives that voters face when choosing among those entrants and their programs. The impact of electoral rules on proportionality and the need for coordination dictate how effective these institutions are in promoting congruence and responsiveness. Highly permissive or weak systems give citizens little pause for strategic thought, indicating to most voters across the spectrum that any candidate or party located near them is likely to be viable. Conversely, constraining or strong systems limit viability to a relatively small group of options, thereby indicating to voters that if they wish to avoid wasting their votes they should assess the viability of the options before them with great care.

In Chapter 8 we described Linkage II – the rules under which elected officials interact when attempting to implement policies – including the economic policies that operate somewhere between total state control and entirely free markets. We showed that in some cases these powers combine in ways that privilege the legislative branch, in others they empower the executive branch, and in still others they appear to create power parity across branches. It is all well and good to have an agent who is closely congruent with the preferences of citizens, but if that agent is marginalized by the powers allotted in the PMP, it should not be surprising to find that the policies ultimately adopted do not reflect the policy position preferred by the median voter.

In Chapters 9–11 we were finally able to examine how the institutional linkages in the chain affected the relationships between the stages. Our findings confirm that institutional linkages play a large role in promoting or hindering representation. Only a limited set of electoral systems were likely to lead to the selection of politicians whose moods were most congruent with the moods of citizens. Systems that did not send clear decisive signals regarding the amount of coordination required were associated with lower levels of congruence. In terms of responsiveness, strong electoral rules are consistently associated with politicians who are more likely to follow the lead of citizens – an effect that is true for both legislators and presidents, even if the latter (who are typically elected under stronger rules) tend to do so at lower rates than the former.

The ability to find a new policy that was preferred to the status quo by every pivotal player – the only or lower house, the upper house where they existed, and the president – increased with empowerment of the executive during the PMP. Not surprisingly, however, empowering presidents was not associated with congruence of policy to the *distribution* of legislators' moods. As one might expect, PMPs that empowered presidents led to increased responsiveness of policies to presidents' moods. If we assume that politicians' moods evolve over the course of a term, policy was responsive to legislators' moods only when the PMP favored that branch. And, even when we find a higher responsiveness of policy to changes in moods of legislators than to changes in moods of presidents (as we do when we focus on term-to-term variation, rather than annually evolving variation), this responsiveness is still higher under policy-making powers that empower presidents.

In the end, empowering politicians that have the least congruent preferences with citizens negatively affects the link between citizens' preferences and policies implemented. More specifically, congruence between the median citizen and policy is relatively low when the PMP favors presidents. While institutional contexts that strengthen presidents generated policies that were least congruent with citizen moods, they were also found to generate the most responsive policy changes. Perhaps it is simply a matter of noncongruent policies having more room to approach citizens' preferences, or perhaps it is the case that where politicians know that policies are furthest from citizens' preferences, they work hardest to move them in the citizens' directions. And it is important to remember that lack of responsiveness is not necessarily indicative of a representation failure – especially if a movement in opposite directions ultimately bring policies closer to the location most preferred by citizens.

In what follows, we summarize the takeaway points from each chapter, emphasizing some of the findings that we least expected, and illustrating how we were able to build to the findings summarized briefly earlier. At the end of this conclusion, we return to some of the broader lessons of our study and we reflect on a number of limitations.

12.1 STAGES IN THE CHAIN OF RESPONSIVENESS: MOODS AND POLICY ORIENTATIONS

Our first descriptive chapter presents an overview of the policy moods of citizens across space and throughout time. We start by describing the survey data on which our enterprise depends, paying particular attention to survey items publicly available in the AB and LB surveys that can be used as indicators of citizens' attitudes toward economic policies. When we talk about citizen policy moods, we in fact refer to what one might call the "policy mood of the median citizen"; however, the statistical model that we employ delivers a full probabilistic description of the moods of citizens within a country in any given year. We confirm that citizen policy moods display a cyclical behavior, alternating between center-left and center-right policies, that is, between more state intervention in and more market governance of the economy.

Since Stage 1 citizen policy preferences are the starting node in the chain of responsibility, we take special care to reflect on the validity of our indicator. This is difficult to ascertain; extant literature on Latin American behavior has furnished a number of scales on which to locate the preferences of citizens, but these are often built around self-placement on a left–right ideological scale or they combine party placements based on expert scores that are weighted by electoral shares. Neither of these strategies corresponds with the quantities of interest that we want to capture, namely, citizen positions on economic policy. Despite these differences, we find that our policy mood scores correlate positively with scales based on ideological placement. A–M scores, an alternative scaling method based on the same individual-level policy attitudes about economic policy that we inspect, also correlate very highly with our citizen mood scores.

Our descriptive inferences about the policy moods of Latin American politicians (Stage 2) could not be more different. In contrast with the strong regional trends in citizen policy moods, there is more cross-country variation in the policy moods of legislators. Also in contrast with the cycles in the moods of citizens, we find among politicians a mild but consistent turn away from markets as we move from the 1990s to the present day. As we explain in Chapter 4, the unavailability of data on the attitudes and preferences of senators and presidents forces us to give preeminence to the opinions of lower or only house members. We obtain information about the policy issue positions of Latin American deputies from seventy-nine surveys carried out by the PELA project between 1993 and 2013. The PELA surveys offer the advantage of providing consistent questions throughout time on a relatively large number of policy issues. Our measurements of legislators' policy moods are therefore based on a rich and broad data set. Our estimates of the policy moods of senators are basically the policy moods of deputies with a twist. Rather than weighting survey responses based on party seat shares of the responding deputies, we employ party seat shares in the upper house as the appropriate weights. Our estimates of the policy moods of presidents are based on an indirect "bridging" technique in which we combine legislators' assessments of their own and their president's left–right ideological scores to estimate the policy positions that the president would hold.

As was the case with citizen moods, we assessed the plausibility of our legislator policy moods by considering how they correlate with A–M scores and with measures of "voter-revealed rightism," which are indicators of the ideological balance of a legislature constructed by combining party vote shares with expert assessments of the left–right placement of parties. We find these correlations to be positive, but not inordinately high. Thus, the correlation between legislative policy moods and A–M scores hovers above 0.6, but the correlation drops to about 0.2 when we look at measures of voter-revealed rightism. A low correlation with ideological measures is hardly proof of lack of validity of our policy moods. Ideological labels like "left" and "right" or "liberal" and "conservative" usually capture more than just economic policy predispositions. There are a number of issues loosely tied to socio-cultural concerns that our policy mood measures do not capture. Our expectation is that weaving this kind of issues into a more complete description of "moods" – perhaps on two distinct dimensions – would improve their level of association with ideological self-placement measures. We leave validation of this implication to future work.

Chapter 5 contains our description of the pathways that implemented policy has followed in Latin America throughout time. We distinguish here between issue-specific policies – that is, privatization of government-owned assets, corporate tax rates, regulations regarding hiring in labor markets, the degree of openness to capital flows – and the general policy orientation of a country at any point in time. Policy orientations are latent constructs that, we submit, are informed by observed issue-specific policies, much as policy moods are underlying dimensions that give rise to opinions and attitudes about specific policy choices. To estimate policy orientations, we build on the pioneering work of Lora (2012), who scored a number of policy outputs on an annual basis throughout Latin America in an effort to build an index of structural reform. We update Lora's series, and include a few additional indicators to round out our collection of important economic policies. Our indicators provide information about fiscal, financial, trade, and labor policies, as well as about policies on privatization and international capital openness.

As noted by Lora himself, and by the literature that has followed in his footsteps, starting in the late 1980s the regional policy orientation was unmistakably pro-market, a consequence of the widespread adoption of policies dubbed the "Washington Consensus." This pro-market tilt continues well into the 2000s, but we do note that policy orientations plateau in countries like Chile, Colombia, or Costa Rica, and even see a pro-state turn in Argentina, Bolivia, or Brazil, among other countries portrayed as having been swept by a "pink tide" of left-oriented governments during the first decade of the new century. Unfortunately, we were unable to imagine a validation strategy for our policy-orientation measures. Other than "impressionistic" correspondences between our policy-orientation scales and our knowledge of the general governing orientations of Latin American incumbent politicians, we could not produce alternative indicators of policy orientation to at least gauge the plausibility of our own measures. Undoubtedly, the problem stems from the alacrity with which the policy community has embraced Lora's approach to measuring structural reform, which has led to several efforts to recombine the original indexes in different ways, but not necessarily to develop alternative indicators of policy output. Since we have now joined this bandwagon, we cannot also be fierce critics of this development. We can only acknowledge that we would have preferred to compare our scaling approach to policy against some alternative, as we did for our mood scores.

It may not have been obvious on the first read, but the measures presented in the three descriptive chapters that we have summarized in this section were deeply intertwined. As we explain in Chapter 6, our investigation into congruence and responsiveness is premised on our ability to place moods and policies on a comparable scale. In the absence of a common scale, claims about congruence or lack thereof ring hollow because we cannot ever be sure that the distances between the moods of citizens and policy-makers and between implemented policy and the moods of policy-makers represent anything other than measurement error. In the absence of a clear strategy to achieve common scaling, discrepant moods and orientations may or may not indicate a lack of congruence. For this reason, we developed a model that addresses this scaling challenge. Admittedly, as statistical models go, this is a relatively complex one, and one that, like even the most basic linear regression model, is based on a number of assumptions. We are careful to explain why the assumptions on which our model is based are appropriate and plausible, especially those assumptions that allow us to "bridge" moods and orientations by imposing constraints on the possible values that some parameters in our model can take. Furthermore, we take pains to explain how our model of "aggregate" behavior (the *percentage* of citizens or legislators that take a pro-market stance on any given issue) follows from microfoundations, that is, from relatively innocuous assumptions about how individuals make choices. Even then, the output of any given model is only as good as the data on which it is based and on the assumptions on which it depends, which is why we invite careful scrutiny of our decisions to ensure that we are not placing undue confidence in our results.

12.2 LINKS IN THE CHAIN OF RESPONSIVENESS: ELECTORAL SYSTEMS AND PMPS

In Chapter 7 we looked at three institutional rules that are part of every electoral system – district magnitude, seat allocation formula, and legal thresholds – in order to get an aggregate indication of each system's proportionality, or how its mechanical effects (and, by anticipation, its psychological effects) influence the translation of votes into seats. We referred to systems that encourage citizens to vote sincerely as weak or permissive. We referred to systems that encourage citizens to vote strategically as strong or restrictive.

By definition, separation of powers systems mean that citizens as principals get to choose at least two agents, sometimes three. As a result, when thinking about how electoral incentives induce more or less congruence between politicians and citizens and varying levels of responsiveness by politicians to the changing moods of citizens, we have to recognize that those incentives do not just vary across national settings, but also across agents within the same country. We used a clustering exercise to look for commonalities across our many elected branches and identified six different "nodes," which we ordered from permissive to constraining. Applying this categorization scheme to each lower or only house, upper house (where they existed), and executive, we found that voters in a given country rarely face equally permissive or equally constraining electoral incentives when choosing their multiple agents. As a result, it might not make sense to predict that voters would share the same level of congruence and responsiveness with all of the members of the policy-making bodies chosen to represent them at any given time. What is more, in virtually every one of our national cases, we observe instances of electoral reform that move at least one agent from a more permissive to a more constraining node or vice versa. By implication, then, we would not predict that voters in a given country would share an equal level of congruence and or equal amount of responsiveness with the members of the policy-making bodies chosen to represent them over time.

The amount of variation observed in electoral systems across agents and over time in Latin America during the roughly twenty-five years under study is really quite astounding. The existence of directly elected executives in presidential regimes means, of course, that we can readily observe several examples of very strong electoral systems calling for very high levels of coordination if a diverse set of voters is to avoid wasting its votes. However, even among legislative chambers we saw several examples with low average district magnitudes that similarly encourage voters to think long and hard about the viability of their most preferred candidates. At the other end of the spectrum, we saw very weak or permissive systems where the average district magnitude was high, the seat allocation formula favored small parties, and no legal thresholds prevented parties with minimal electoral presence from assuming office. Therefore, we had reason to expect that the levels of congruence and responsiveness we might observe would vary widely.

In Chapter 8 we identified three clusters of legislative chambers based on their ability to draft legislation that accurately reflects the preferences of the chamber's members and their authority to increase the deficit if they felt it was justified. The least powerful legislatures had neither of these two abilities. We also learned that in bicameral systems there is not a single upper chamber whose powers are widely divergent from those of the lower chamber. For presidents, we looked at both proactive powers – those used to change the policy status quo – and reactive powers – those used to protect the policy status quo – and again we identified three broad groupings. We found one group of presidents endowed with powers that seemingly would give them great control over the location of policy; we found a second group of presidents who had the ability to dominate the agenda, forcing their priorities to the fore; and we found a third group of presidents who lacked either of these abilities. Altogether, we recognized thirteen different types of PMPs that depend on the types of powers they provide to presidents, on the one hand, and lower and upper chambers (where they exist), on the other.

We found that the founders and framers of PMPs were typically stingy when it came to endowing politicians with the power to set policy where they wanted it. They never paired the most powerful presidents with the most powerful legislatures, perhaps fearing policy volatility or gridlock. Typically, they clearly advantaged one branch relative to the other. Contrary to what one might take from the existing literature, the region is not overwhelmingly characterized by constitutionally empowered presidents ready to run rough-shod over powerless legislators. To be sure, there are national PMPs where the executive appears relatively well armed, but there are plenty of instances where the converse is true as well. When institutional designs seem to strike relative parity between the branches, they do so with neither branch having a full array of possible powers.

12.3 CONGRUENCE AND RESPONSIVENESS: FROM CITIZENS TO POLITICIANS TO POLICY

In Chapter 9 we found that congruence and responsiveness were generally high, but they were at their highest, for legislators, when the incentive structure imposed by electoral laws was unequivocal. More specifically, the most permissive systems – those giving small incentive to vote strategically – and the most constraining systems – those that severely punished lack of coordination among voters – were both associated with the highest levels of congruence and responsiveness between citizens and members of congress. When electoral incentives suggested that some (but not all) among a diverse group of voters would need to coordinate around one candidate, and some (but not many) candidates would need to coalesce around a single platform, actors appear to err in assessing which candidates are in fact viable, waiting for someone else to compromise and failing to coordinate on viable candidates. We reasoned that the Latin American context often lacks information about candidates' positions (and their viability), as well as information about the ideological evolution of parties. Given the "noise" introduced into the democratic process, only the clearest signals sent by electoral institutions will reach candidates and voters, allowing for proper coordination. We found less congruence between the preferences of citizens and those of the presidents they chose, but both congruence and responsiveness seemed to increase with the strength of the electoral system. Again, it seems that rules with clear signals make it easiest for citizens to identify proximate politicians who wish to move policy in the direction traveled by citizens' moods. It is also possible that, over time, strong rules condition citizens' preferences, leading them to adopt more homogeneous, centrist positions that can be represented well with sufficient voting coordination.

In Chapter 10 we examined whether the design of PMPs had an effect on policy-makers' ability to have their moods reflected in the policies they adopted. We found that the distribution of politicians' preferences was best reflected in policy when the PMP empowered the legislative branch, and congruence with that distribution declined precipitously when presidents were at their most powerful. On the other hand, we found that "winset-congruence" – the ability to put in place a policy that all pivotal players found preferable to the status quo – was most likely when the PMP empowered presidents. It is perhaps in this sense that presidents dominate the policy-making arena across the region. However, we want to stress that the policies implemented by those strong presidents are winset congruent, which suggests that they also receive support from the median legislator. In other words, it is not as if strong presidents get to systematically ignore opposition to policy change in the lower chamber. Instead, what we find is that, if the winset of the status quo policy orientation was not empty, systems with strong presidents would move away from the inherited incongruent policy orientation more rapidly.

Responsiveness, we submitted, would be highest in favor of those actors empowered by a specific policy-making setting: in favor of presidents in executive-empowering systems, and in favor of legislators in legislature-empowering systems. This is not quite what we found. On the one hand, if we assume constant policy moods among policy-makers, we saw that policy was most responsive to executives in executive-empowering systems and least responsive to executives in systems that were legislature-empowering, which is along our original expectations. Paradoxically, we also found that policy was most responsive to legislators in systems that empowered the executive. When we focus on term-to-term responsiveness (i.e., if we assume policy moods are constant throughout terms), policy is more often responsive to legislators than to presidents. When we assume that policy moods evolve smoothly on a yearly basis, on the other hand, we find that policy was least responsive to either executives or legislatures in systems with balanced policy-making powers, which actually correspond to situations in which both the executive and the legislature are relatively weak. When we hold policy-making powers constant in these circumstances, policy orientations are more likely to be responsive to presidents than to legislators.

A natural avenue for future work would be to develop indicators of citizens' moods, politicians' moods, and policy orientations regarding an entirely different set of political issues – presumably on a liberal–conservative social dimension. Our suspicion is that the institutional design of PMPs might have a clearer, systematic impact on democratic congruence where the policies in question are reflective of domestic cultural cleavages.

In Chapter 11 we stepped back to examine the connection between citizen moods in Stage 1 of our chain of congruence and responsiveness with the policies that formed Stage 3 of that chain. A series of complex institutional links connects Stage 1 and Stage 3, and it is entirely possible that any number of decisions regarding institutional design could distort congruence along the way. We sought to account for both electoral incentives and policy-making powers. Congruence was generally lowest where presidents were at their most powerful. This makes sense given our earlier finding (see Chapter 9 about the distance between citizens' preferences and presidents' preferences). That said, policy was actually most responsive to citizens' moods where presidents were at their strongest. In other words, citizens' moods can be reflected in the direction that policy is moving, even when that policy remains somewhat distant from what most citizens would prefer. A pattern of citizens growing increasingly in favor of state intervention and presidents moving from strongly pro-market to more centrist locations would fit this description. Perhaps because of their collective nature, responsiveness was at its lowest point when the legislature dominated the policy-making process. Legislators are most likely to reflect the preferences of their constituents but apparently struggle to move policy toward the position they share with them.

12.4 A FINAL TAKEAWAY

Studying democratic congruence and responsiveness poses many challenges. We struggled with those challenges here, making several difficult decisions along the way about how best to maintain a tight connection between theoretical concepts and reasoning, on the one hand, and empirical indicators and models, on the other. Throughout the process, we endeavored to be as transparent as possible. We hope this transparency and our careful cataloging of our data and any transformations done to them will help other scholars to pick up where we have left off. In service of this goal, we have made available all data sets and thousands of lines of curated code in a web appendix accessible through GitHub.

We close by highlighting just a few of the strengths of our work. First, we have measures of citizens' preferences based on data other than their revealed preferences in elections (sourced from LB and AB). Without these data, looking at how electoral systems impact the congruence and responsiveness between citizens and politicians would be tautological. Likewise, we have individually expressed preferences of politicians based on questions about discrete economic policies. Regular, systematic surveys of sitting politicians are rare, and the data provided by the PELA project at the University of Salamanca provides a veritable treasure trove for these purposes. Their survey responses are much less subject to the exercise of agenda control or the enforcement of party discipline by leaders, making them more sincere indicators of individuals' preferences. In addition, distinct from their preferences over policy, we have an indicator of actually implemented policies (Lora 2012), not just those promised in campaign manifestos. Finally, and perhaps involving some heroic assumptions, we located indicators of all three stages of our chain on a single policy space. Without a shared policy space, any answers regarding the extent of congruence and responsiveness in political systems would have had to remain even more tentative.

For our institutional linkages – electoral systems and policy-making processes – we drew on and then augmented the best data sets available (Bormann and Golder 2013, Coppedge et al. 2017, Negretto 2014). Rather than attempting to weight individual institutions a priori in order to create indices or naively aggregating powers in an unprincipled manner, we used clustering algorithms to identify functionally similar electoral incentives and homologous policy-making processes. For both linkages, the results of these exercises were intuitive. We found electoral systems that ranged from weak or permissive to strong or constraining. We also learned that the region's democracies are characterized by policy-making processes that run the gamut – favoring the executive, favoring the legislature, or that strike a balance in powers between the two.

The wealth of data we were able to leverage were the input to our Bayesian measurement model, which allowed us to place citizens, policy-makers, *and* enacted policies on the same scale for the first time ever. Although previous works have given us partial pictures of the quality of representation in Latin America, our modeling strategy has allowed us to directly evaluate claims that hinge on having comparable measures of preferences and policies, over time and space. By defining a few anchoring questions and policy dimensions, we combined data of different types (discrete, ordinal, and continuous), from different sources (various surveys and economic indicators) and different country-years to produce a fully comparable, aggregate measure of moods toward a more or less market-oriented economy – a measure that can inform future research into areas of interest that go beyond the nature of representation in Latin America. As new data sources become available, our model can be easily expanded to incorporate them in order to update the measures on which we have based our analysis. Substantively, our results are complex, as complex as the institutional designs that characterize the separation of powers in Latin American democracies. Allowing for these complexities, we found plenty of evidence that congruence and responsiveness occur regularly, and that their presence or absence is in part a function of institutional linkages between citizens and politicians and between politicians and policy. That said, we also failed to uncover patterns supporting some of our expectations and managed to uncover patterns we frankly did not expect. Finally, we ought to recognize that, broad as our purview is, we only inspect the behavior of a subset of actors involved in the design of policy. This subset certainly includes the most important cogs in the policy-making process – deputies, senators, presidents – but we left aside the potential contributions of bureaucracies and courts, which have in the past played important roles in policy implementation in a number of Latin American countries. Again, we cannot do much other than marking the interaction between policy-makers and these additional actors as territory fertile for future theoretical analysis.

Appendix: Question Wording

This appendix contains the exact wording of all questions used in our analysis. As can be seen especially in the case of LB, question wordings are not perfectly consistent across waves. In comparing question wordings across data sources, we erred on the side of considering stimuli to tap into the same attitude or opinion, even if the statements that respondents were asked to consider were not exactly alike. Note also that the following statements appear in the exact form that they take in the respective surveys; recall that we recode all of these statements such that a high score corresponds to agreement with a pro-market position. All of the questions include the labels used by PELA, LB, and AB in the original surveys.

AMERICASBAROMETER

- `privatization.beneficial` El Estado [del país], en lugar del sector privado, debería ser el dueño de las empresas e industrias más importantes del país. ¿Hasta qué punto está de acuerdo o en desacuerdo con esta frase? (ros1)
- `state.reduce.inequality` El Estado argentino debe implementar políticas firmes para reducir la desigualdad de ingresos entre ricos y pobres. ¿Hasta qué punto está de acuerdo o en desacuerdo con esta frase? (ros4)
- `economy.best.in.private.sector` El Estado argentino, más que los individuos, debería ser el principal responsable de asegurar el bienestar de la gente. ¿Hasta qué punto está de acuerdo o en desacuerdo con esta frase? (ros2)
- `state.not.in.sanitation` El Estado, más que el sector privado, debería ser el principal responsable de proveer los servicios de salud. ¿Hasta qué punto está de acuerdo o en desacuerdo con esta frase? (ros6)

- `state.not.in.pensions` El Estado, más que el sector privado, debería ser el principal responsable de proveer las pensiones de jubilación ¿Hasta qué punto está de acuerdo o en desacuerdo con esta frase? (ros5)

- `state.not.in.job.creation` El Estado argentino, más que la empresa privada, debería ser el principal responsable de crear empleos. ¿Hasta qué punto está de acuerdo o en desacuerdo con esta frase? (ros3)

LATINBAROMETER

- `privatization.beneficial` The privatisation of state companies has been beneficial to the country (np14b-1998; p16st.a-2000; p15sta-2001; p22sta-2002; p26st-2003; p40stc-2005; p54sta-2007; q81st.d-2009); Private enterprise is beneficial for the country (np14f-1998); Private enterprise is indispensable for the development of the country (P40STE-2005; q81st.b-2009; q75st.a-2010; q69st.a-2011); The state should leave the economic activity to the private sector (p22stb-2002; np14a-1998); Privatization of state enterprises has been beneficial for the country (q69st.c-2011); The less that government intervenes in the economy the better is for country (p22essd-2002); Private enterprise is beneficial for the country (np14f-1998)

- `state.solves.problems` It is said that the State can solve our society's problems because it has the resources to do so. Would you say that the State can solve all the problems? (p15st-1996; p28st-2005; q52st-2007; q94st-2008; q70st-2009; q63st-2010); Some people think that State must solve all problems because it has the resources to do it, while other thinks that the market will solve all problems because it distribute the resources in an efficient way (p20n-2001; p12st-2003; q80st-2009); Do you think the State has the resources to solve the problems of our society, or you think the State do not have the resources to solve them (q62n-2010; q65st-2011)

- `state.reduce.inequality` The Government's responsibility should be to reduce the differences between the rich and the poor (p28e-1996)

- `economy.best.in.private.sector` The market economy is the most convenient for the country (np14d-1998; p16st.c-2000; p22st.c-2002); Only with a market economy can (country) become a developed country (p22nf-2003; p22std2004; p25sta-2005; q57st.e-2008; q81st.c-2009; q75st.b-2010; q69st.b-2011); The market economy is most suitable for the country (q81st. a-2009); A market economy is best for (country) (p54stc-2007)

- `state.not.in.price.control` The prices of products should be determined by free competition (np14c-1998; p16st.b-2000)

- `state.not.in.high.edu` Universities should mostly be in the hands of the State or private companies? (q93n.h-2008); Regardless of the educational system of (country), who do you think should pay for university education? (q3one.c-2011)

- `state.not.in.unemployment` The Government's responsibility should be to provide a decent standard of living for the unemployed (p28d-1996)

- `state.not.in.basic.needs` On a scale from 1 to 10, where 1 means that each person should take responsibility for his own welfare, and 10 means that the government should take responsibility for the welfare of people, where would you put yourself? (p19gb-2004)

- `state.not.in.sanitation` State must be in charge of Health (p15st.c-2001); Private sector should be totally in charge (1), have majority participation (2), have minority participation (3) or no participation(4) in healthcare (q56sta-2007; q93st.a-2008); The Government's responsibility should be to give health care to the sick (p28b-1996)

- `state.not.in.pensions` Pensions should mostly be in the hands of the State or mostly be in the hands of private companies? (p60g-1995;sp12g-1998; q93st.f-2008); The Government's responsibility should be to provide a decent standard of living for the elderly (p28c-1996); Private sector should be totally in charge (1), have majority participation (2), have minority participation (3) or no participation(4) in pensions (q56nc-2007)

- `state.not.in.job.creation` The Government's responsibility should be to give work to all those who want to work (p28a-1996)

- `state.not.in.primsec.edu` Regardless of the educational system of (country), who do you think should pay for primary and secondary education? (q3one.b-2011)

PARLIAMENTARY ELITES OF LATIN AMERICA

- `privatization.beneficial` ¿Cuál de los siguientes criterios resume mejor su actitud personal hacia el tema de las privatizaciones de los servicios públicos? (p43, p35, p34)

- `state.not.in.sanitation` ¿Dígame, qué grado de intervención mucho, bastante, poco o ninguno, debería asumir el Estado para dar cobertura general sanitaria? (p2906)

- `state.not.in.price.control` ¿Dígame, para control de precios, qué grado de intervención mucho, bastante, poco o ninguno, debería asumir el Estado? (p3501, p35ao1, p2901)

- `state.not.in.primsec.edu` ¿Dígame, para garantizar una educación primaria general y gratuita, qué grado de intervención mucho, bastante, poco o ninguno, debería asumir el Estado? (p3502, p35a02) ¿Dígame, para garantizar una educación secundaria general y gratuita, qué grado de intervención mucho, bastante, poco o ninguno, debería asumir el Estado? (p3505, p35a05) (p3502, p35a02, p2902)

- `state.not.in.housing` ¿Dígame, para proveer de vivienda al ciudadano, qué grado de intervención mucho, bastante, poco o ninguno, debería asumir el Estado? (p3503, p35a03, p2903)

- `state.not.in.job.creation` ¿Dígame, para dar trabajo a quienes quieran trabajar, qué grado de intervención mucho, bastante, poco o ninguno, debería asumir el Estado? (p3504, p35a04, p2904)

- `state.not.in.pensions` ¿Dígame, para dar cobertura de seguridad social, qué grado de intervención mucho, bastante, poco o ninguno, debería asumir el Estado? (p3506, p35a06, p2905)

- `state.not.in.high.edu` ¿Dígame, para garantizar una educación universitaria general y gratuita, qué grado de intervención mucho, bastante, poco o ninguno, debería asumir el Estado? (p3507, p35a07, p2907)

- `economy.best.in.private.sector` ¿Podría Ud. decirme si está más bien de acuerdo o más bien en desacuerdo con afirmar que en una sociedad tan compleja como la actual, El Estado debería intervenir lo menos posible en la sociedad y dejar a la iniciativa privada que atienda las necesidades de los ciudadanos? (p3404); ¿Podría decirme si está Ud. más a favor de una economía regulada por el Estado o por el mercado? (p34a, p28)

- `state.not.solves.problems` ¿Podría Ud. decirme si está más bien de acuerdo o más bien en desacuerdo con afirmar que en una sociedad tan compleja como la actual, el Estado es incapaz de solucionar de manera eficaz los problemas de los ciudadanos? (p3401, p34b)

- `state.not.reduce.inequality` ¿Podría Ud. decirme si está más bien de acuerdo o más bien en desacuerdo con afirmar que en una sociedad tan compleja como la actual, la intervención del Estado en la vida socioeconómica es la única manera posible de reducir las desigualdades sociales (p3402)

- `state.not.in.unemployment` ¿Dígame, para dar cobertura de seguro de desempleo, qué grado de intervención mucho, bastante, poco o ninguno, debería asumir el Estado? (p3508, p35a08, p2908)

- `state.not.in.basic.needs` ¿Dígame, para cubrir las necesidades básicas de todos los ciudadanos, qué grado de intervención mucho, bastante, poco o ninguno, debería asumir el Estado? (p3510, p35a10, p2910)

- `market.best` ¿Como Ud. conoce [sic], existe actualmente un debate entre las posiciones estatistas y neoliberales en diversos países del continente. Al respecto, ¿podría decirme si está Ud. más a favor de una economía regulada por el Estado o por el mercado?

- `state.limited.scope` ¿Podría Ud. decirme si está más bien de acuerdo o más bien en desacuerdo con la siguiente afirmación? El Estado debe concentrar su labor en una serie de campos concretos (sanidad, educación, justicia, etc.) y dejar el resto de actividades en manos de los particulares.

Bibliography

Achen, Christopher H. 1978. "Measuring Representation." *American Journal of Political Science* 22(3):475–510.

Achen, Christopher H. and Larry M. y Bartels. 2017. *Democracy for Realists: Why Elections Do Not Produce Responsive Government*. Princeton University Press.

Alemán, Eduardo and Thomas Schwartz. 2006. "Presidential Vetoes in Latin American Constitutions." *Journal of Theoretical Politics* 18(1):98–120.

Alemán, Eduardo and George Tsebelis. 2011. "Political Parties and Government Coalitions in the Americas." *Journal of Politics in Latin America* 3(1):3–28.

Amorim Neto, Octavio and Gary W. Cox. 1997. "Electoral Institutions, Cleavage Structures, and the Number of Parties." *American Journal of Political Science* 41(1): 149–174.

Andeweg, Rudy B. 2011. Approaching Perfect Policy Congruence: Measurement, Development, and Relevance for Political Representation. In *How Democracy Works: Political Representation and Policy Congruence in Modern Societies*. Amsterdam University Press, pp. 39–52.

Arnold, Christian, David Doyle, and Nina Wiesehomeier. 2017. "Presidents, Policy Compromise, and Legislative Success." *Journal of Politics* 79(2):380–395.

Austen-Smith, David and Jeffrey Banks. 1988. "Elections, Coalitions, and Legislative Outcomes." *American Political Science Review* 82(02):405–422.

Bafumi, Joseph, Andrew Gelman, David K. Park, and Noah Kaplan. 2005. "Practical Issues in Implementing and Understanding Bayesian Ideal Point Estimation." *Political Analysis* 13(2):171–187.

Bafumi, Joseph and Michael C. Herron. 2010. "Leapfrog Representation and Extremism: A Study of American Voters and Their Members in Congress." *American Political Science Review* 104(3):519–542.

Bailey, Michael A. 2007. "Comparable Preference Estimates across Time and Institutions for the Court, Congress, and Presidency." *American Journal of Political Science* 51(3):433–448.

Baker, Andy. 2009. *The Market and the Masses in Latin America: Policy Reform and Consumption in Liberalizing Economies*. Cambridge University Press.

Baker, Andy and Kenneth F. Greene. 2011. "The Latin American Left's Mandate. Free-Market Policies and Issue Voting in New Democracies." *World Politics* 63(1): 43–77.

Bauer, Paul C., Pablo Barberá, Kathrin Ackermann, and Aaron Venetz. 2017. "Is the Left-Right Scale a Valid Measure of Ideology? Individual-Level Variation in Associations with "Left" and "Right" and Left-Right Self-Placement." *Political Behavior* 39(3):553–583.

Benoit, Kenneth and Michael Laver. 2007. "Estimating Party Policy Positions: Comparing Expert Surveys and Hand-Coded Content Analysis." *Electoral Studies* 26(1): 90–107.

Besley, Timothy. 2007. *Principled Agents?: The Political Economy of Good Government.* Oxford University Press.

Bianco, William T. 1994. *Trust: Representatives and Constituents.* University of Michigan Press.

Blais, André and Marc André Bodet. 2006. "Does Proportional Representation Foster Closer Congruence between Citizens and Policy Makers?" *Comparative Political Studies* 39(10):1243–1262.

Booth, John A. and Mitchell A. Seligson. 2009. *The Legitimacy Puzzle in Latin America: Political Support and Democracy in Eight Nations.* Cambridge University Press.

Bormann, Nils-Christian and Matt Golder. 2013. "Democratic Electoral Systems around the World, 1946–2011." *Electoral Studies* 32(2):360–369.

Brady, David W. and Craig Volden. 2006. *Revolving Gridlock: Politics and Policy from Jimmy Carter to George W.* Westview Press.

Budge, Ian and Hans-Dieter Klingemann. 2001. Finally! Comparative Over-Time Mapping of Party Policy Movement. In *Mapping Policy Preferences. Estimates for Parties, Electors, and Governments 1945–1998,* eds. Ian Budge, Hans-Dieter Klingemann, Andrea Volkens, Judith Bara, and Eric Tanenbaum. Oxford University Press, chapter 2, pp. 19–50.

Carey, John M. 2003. Presidentialism and Representative Institutions. In *Constructing Democratic Governance in Latin America,* ed. Jorge I. Domínguez. Johns Hopkins University Press, pp. 11–42.

Carey, John M. and Simon Hix. 2011. "The Electoral Sweet Spot: Low-Magnitude Proportional Electoral Systems." *American Journal of Political Science* 55(2): 383–397.

Carey, John M. and Matthew S. Shugart. 1998. *Executive Decree Authority.* Cambridge University Press.

Cheibub, Jose Antonio, Argelina Figueiredo, and Fernando Limongi. 2009. "Political Parties and Governors as Determinants of Legislative Behavior in Brazil's Chamber of Deputies, 1988–2006." *Latin American Politics and Society* 51(1):1–30.

Chinn, Menzie D. and Hiro Ito. 2016. "The Chinn–Ito Index. A de Jure Measure of Financial Openness," http://web.pdx.edu/~ito/Chinn-Ito_website.htm.

Clark, William R. and Matt Golder. 2006. "Rehabilitating Duverger's Theory: Testing the Mechanical and Strategic Modifying Effects of Electoral Laws." *Comparative Political Studies* 39(6):679–708.

Coppedge, Michael. 1998. The Evolution of Latin American Party Systems. In *Politics, Society, and Democracy: Latin America,* eds. Scott Mainwaring and Arturo Valenzuela. Westview Press, pp. 171–206.

Coppedge, Michael, John Gerring, Staffan I. Lindberg, et al. 2017. "V-Dem Dataset v7.0." Varieties of Democracy (V-Dem) Project.

Cox, Gary W. 1987. "Electoral Equilibrium under Alternative Voting Institutions." *American Journal of Political Science* 31(1):82–108.

1990. "Centripetal and Centrifugal Incentives in Electoral Systems." *American Journal of Political Science* 34(4):903–935.

1997. *Making Votes Count: Strategic Coordination in the World's Electoral Systems*, vol. 7. Cambridge University Press.

Cox, Gary W. and Scott Morgenstern. 2001. "Latin America's Reactive Assemblies and Proactive Presidents." *Comparative Politics* 33(2):171–189.

Crisp, Brian. 2000. *Democratic Institutional Design: The Powers and Incentives of Venezuelan Politicians and Interest Groups*. Stanford University Press.

Crisp, Brian F., Scott W. Desposato, and Kristin Kanthak. 2009. "Legislative Pivots, Presidential Powers, and Policy Stability." *The Journal of Law, Economics, & Organization* 27(2):426–452.

Dahl, Robert. 1989. *Democracy and Its Critics*. Yale University Press.

Downs, Anthony. 1957. *An Economic Theory of Democracy*. Harper and Row.

Duverger, Maurice. 1959. *Political Parties: Their Organization and Activity in the Modern State*. Methuen.

Dziuda, Wioletta and Antoine Loeper. 2018. "Dynamic Pivotal Politics." *American Political Science Review* 112(3):580–601.

Edwards, Sebastian. 1995. *Crisis and Reform in Latin America: From Despair to Hope*. Oxford University Press.

Erikson, Robert S., Michael B. MacKuen, and James A. Stimson. 2002. *The Macro Polity*. Cambridge Studies in Political Psychology and Public Opinion. Cambridge University Press.

Escaith, Hubert and Igor Paunovic. 2004. "Reformas Estructurales en América Latina y el Caribe en el Período 1970–2000: Índices y Notas Metodológicas." Documento electrónico LC/W.10.

Fearon, James. 1999. Electoral accountability and the Control of Politicians: Selecting Good Types versus Sanctioning Poor Performance. In *Democracy, Accountability, and Representation*, eds. Adam Przeworski, Susan C. Stokes, and Bernard Manin. Cambridge University Press, chapter 2, pp. 55–97.

Ferland, Benjamin. 2016. "Revisiting the Ideological Congruence Controversy." *European Journal of Political Research* 55(2):358–373.

Fernández, Andrés, Michael W. Klein, Alessandro Rebucci, Martin Schindler, and Martín Uribe. 2015. "Capital Control Measures: A New Dataset." IMF Working Paper 15/80.

Fiorina, Morris. 1974. *Representatives, Roll Calls, and Constituencies*. Lexington Books.

García Montero, Mercedes. 2009. *Presidentes y parlamentos: ¿quién controla la actividad legislativa en América Latina?* Centro De Investigaciones Sociológicas, CIS.

Gelman, Andrew and Jennifer Hill. 2007. *Data Analysis Using Regression and Multilevel/Hierarchical Models*. Cambridge University Press.

Gelman, Andrew and Gary King. 1990. "Estimating Incumbency Advantage without Bias." *American Journal of Political Science* 34:1142–1164.

Ghitza, Yair and Andrew Gelman. 2013. "Deep Interactions with MRP: Election Turnout and Voting Patterns among Small Electoral Subgroups." *American Journal of Political Science* 57(3):762–776.

Golder, Matt and Jacek Stramski. 2010. "Ideological Congruence and Electoral Institutions." *American Journal of Political Science* 54(1):90–106.

Grofman, Bernard. 2004. "Downs and Two-Party Convergence." *Annual Review of Political Science* 7(1):25–46.

Hinich, Melvin J. and Michael C. Munger. 1992. "A Spatial Theory of Ideology." *Journal of Theoretical Politics* 4(1):31–52.

Honaker, James, Gary King, and Matthew Blackwell. 2011. "Amelia II: A Program for Missing Data." *Journal of Statistical Software* 45(7):1–47, www.jstatsoft.org/v45/i07/.

Huber, John D. and G. Bingham Powell Jr. 1994. "Congruence between Citizens and Policymakers in Two Visions of Liberal Democracy." *World Politics* 46(03): 291–326.

Huber, John D. and Matthew Gabel. 2000. "Putting Parties in Their Place: Inferring Party Left-Right Ideological Positions from Manifestos Data." *American Journal of Political Science* 44(1):94–103.

Inter-Parliamentary Union. 2017. "PARLINE Database on National Parliaments," http://archive.ipu.org/parline-e/parlinesearch.asp.

Jackman, Simon. 2009. *Bayesian Analysis for the Social Sciences.* Wiley.

Jessee, Stephen A. 2009. "Spatial Voting in the 2004 Presidential Election." *American Political Science Review* 103(1):59–81.

   2010. "Partisan Bias, Political Information and Spatial Voting in the 2008 Presidential Election." *Journal of Politics* 72(2):327–340.

   2012. *Ideology and Spatial Voting in American Elections.* Cambridge University Press.

Johnson, Valen E. and James H. Albert. 1999. *Modeling Ordinal Data.* Springer.

Johnson, Gregg B. and Brian F. Crisp. 2003. "Mandates, Powers, and Policies." *American Journal of Political Science* 47(1):128–142.

Kang, Shin-Goo and G. Bingham Powell Jr. 2010. "Representation and Policy Responsiveness: The Median Voter, Election Rules, and Redistributive Welfare Spending." *Journal of Politics* 72(4):1014–1028.

Kim, HeeMin and Richard Fording. 1998. "Voter Ideology in Western Democracies, 1946–1989." *European Journal of Political Research* 33:73–98.

Kim, HeeMin, G. Bingham Powell Jr., and Richard C. Fording. 2010. "Electoral Systems, Party Systems, and Ideological Representation: An Analysis of Distortion in Western Democracies." *Comparative Politics* 42(2):167–185.

King, Gary, Christopher J. L. Murray, Joshua A. Salomon, and Ajay Tandon. 2003. "Enhancing the Validity and Cross-Cultural Comparability of Measurement in Survey Research." *American Political Science Review* 97(04):567–583.

Kingdon, John W. 1973. *Congressmen's Voting Decisions.* Harper and Row.

Kitschelt, Herbert, Kirk A. Hawkins, Juan P. Luna, Guillermo Rosas, and Elizabeth J. Zechmeister. 2010. *Latin American Party Systems.* Cambridge University Press.

Krehbiel, Keith. 1998. *Pivotal Politics: A Theory of U.S. Lawmaking.* University of Chicago Press.

Laakso, Markku and Rein Taagepera. 1979. "'Effective' Number of Parties: A Measure with Application to West Europe." *Comparative Political Studies* 12(1):3–27.

Leys, Colin. 1959. "Models, Theories and the Theory of Political Parties." *Political Studies* 7:127–146.

Lijphart, Arend. 1984. *Democracies: Patterns of Majoritarian and Consensus Government in Twenty-One Countries*. Yale University Press.

2012. *Patterns of Democracy: Government Forms and Performance in Thirty-Six Countries*. Yale University Press.

Linzer, Drew A. 2012. "The Relationship between Seats and Votes in Multiparty Systems." *Political Analysis* 20(3):400–416.

Lora, Eduardo. 2012. "Structural Reforms in Latin America: What Has Been Reformed and How to Measure It." IDB Working Paper 346.

Lupu, Noam, Lucia Selios, and Zach Warner. 2017. "A New Measure of Congruence: The Earth Mover's Distance." *Political Analysis* 25(1):95–113.

Mainwaring, Scott. 2006. "The Crisis of Representation in the Andes." *Journal of Democracy* 17(3):13–27.

Mainwaring, Scott and Matthew S. Shugart. 1997. *Presidentialism and Democracy in Latin America*. Cambridge University Press.

Manin, Bernard, Adam Przeworski, and Susan Stokes. 1999. "Elections and Representation." In *Democracy, Accountability, and Representation*. Cambridge University Press, pp. 29–54.

Mansbridge, Jane. 2003. "Rethinking Representation." *American Political Science Review* 97:515–528.

2009. "A 'Selection Model' of Political Representation." *The Journal of Political Philosophy* 17(4):369–398.

Martin, Andrew D. and Kevin M. Quinn. 2002. "Dynamic Ideal Point Estimation via Markov Chain Monte Carlo for the U.S. Supreme Court, 1953–1999." *Political Analysis* 10(2):134–153.

Mayhew, David R. 1974. *The Electoral Connection*. Yale University Press.

McDonald, Michael D. and Ian Budge. 2005. *Elections, Parties, Democracy: Conferring the Median Mandate*. Oxford University Press.

McDonald, Michael D., Silvia M. Mendes, and Ian Budge. 2004. "What Are Elections For? Conferring the Median Mandate." *British Journal of Political Science* 34:1–26.

McGann, Anthony J. 2013. "Estimating the Political Center from Aggregate Data: An Item Response Theory Alternative to the Stimson Dyad Ratios Algorithm." *Political Analysis* 22(1):115–129.

McGhee, Eric. 2014. "Measuring Partisan Bias in Single-Member District Electoral Systems." *Legislative Studies Quarterly* 39(1):55–85.

Miller, Warren E. and Donald E. Stokes. 1963. "Constituency Influence in Congress." *American Political Science Review* 51:45–56.

Morgenstern, Scott and Benito Nacif, eds. 2002. *Legislative Politics in Latin America*. Cambridge Studies in Comparative Politics. Cambridge University Press.

Morgenstern, Scott and Javier Vázquez-D'Elía. 2007. "Electoral Laws, Parties, and Party Systems in Latin America." *Annual Review of Political Science* 10:143–168.

Morley, Samuel A., Roberto Machado, and Stefano Pettinato. 1999. "Indexes of Structural Reform in Latin America." Documento electrónico LC/L.1166.

Murillo, Maria V., Virginia Oliveros, and Milan Vaishnav. 2013. Economic Constraints and Presidential Agency. In *The Resurgence of the Latin American Left*. Johns Hopkins University Press, pp. 52–70.

Murillo, Maria Victoria. 2009. *Political Competition, Partisanship, and Policy Making in Latin American Public Utilities.* Cambridge University Press.

Negretto, Gabriel. 2014. *Making Constitutions: Presidents, Parties, and Institutional Choice in Latin America.* Cambridge University Press.

Pachón, Monica and Matthew S. Shugart. 2010. "Electoral Reform and the Mirror Image of Inter-Party Competition: The Adoption of Party Lists in Colombia." *Electoral Studies* 29(4):648–660.

Palanza, Valeria. 2018. *Checking Presidential Power: Executive Decrees and the Legislative Process in New Democracies.* Cambridge University Press.

Pemstein, Daniel, Kyle L. Marquardt, Eitan Tzelgov, et al. 2017. "The V-Dem Measurement Model: Latent Variable Analysis for Cross-National and Cross-Temporal Expert-Coded Data." Working paper 21.

Pérez-Liñán, Aníbal. 2007. *Presidential Impeachment and the New Political Instability in Latin America.* Cambridge University Press.

Persson, Torsten, Gérard Roland, and Guido Tabellini. 1997. "Separation of Powers and Political Accountability." *The Quarterly Journal of Economics* 112(4):1163–1202.

Persson, Torsten and Guido Tabellini. 2005. *The Economic Effects of Constitutions.* MIT Press.

Poole, Keith T. 1998. "Recovering a Basic Space from a Set of Issue Scales." *American Journal of Political Science* 42(3):954–993.

Poole, Keith T., Jeffrey B. Lewis, Howard Rosenthal, James Lo, and Royce Carroll. 2016. "Recovering a Basic Space from Issue Scales in R." *Journal of Statistical Software* 69(7):1–21.

Powell Jr., G. Bingham. 2000. *Elections as Instruments of Democracy: Majoritarian and Proportional Visions.* Yale University Press.

   2004. "The Chain of Responsiveness." *Journal of Democracy* 15(4):91–105.

   2013. "Representation in Context: Election Laws and Ideological Congruence between Citizens and Governments." *Perspectives on Politics* 11(01):9–21.

Powell Jr., G. Bingham and Georg S. Vanberg. 2000. "Election Laws, Disproportionality and Median Correspondence: Implications for Two Visions of Democracy." *British Journal of Political Science* 30(03):383–411.

Powell Jr., G. Bingham and Guy D. Whitten. 1992. "A Cross-National Analysis of Economic Voting – Taking Account of the Political Context." *American Journal of Political Science* 37(02):391–414.

Programa de Estudios Parlamentariors. 2018. "Tasa de Eficacia Legislativa," https://parlamentosite.wordpress.com/2018/02/17/tasa-de-eficacia-del-pe/.

Reilly, Ben, Andrew Ellis, and Andrew Reynolds. 2005. *Electoral System Design: The New International IDEA Handbook.* International Institute for Democracy and Electoral Assistance.

Remmer, Karen. 2012. "The Rise of Leftist-Populist Governance in Latin America: The Roots of Electoral Change." *Comparative Political Studies* 45(8):947–972.

Rosas, Guillermo. 2005. "The Ideological Organization of Latin American Legislative Parties: An Empirical Analysis of Elite Preferences." *Comparative Political Studies* 38(7):824–849.

Saiegh, Sebastián. 2009. "Recovering a Basic Space from Elite Surveys: Evidence from Latin America." *Legislative Studies Quarterly* 34(1):117–145.

   2011. *Ruling by Statute: How Uncertainty and Vote Buying Shape Lawmaking.* Cambridge University Press.

2015. "Using Joint Scaling Methods to Study Ideology and Representation: Evidence from Latin America." *Political Analysis* 23:363–384.

Sartori, Giovanni. 1968. Political Development and Political Engineering. In *Public Policy*. Cambridge University Press.

Schwindt-Bayer, Leslie A. and Margit Tavits. 2016. *Clarity of Responsibility, Accountability, and Corruption.* Cambridge University Press.

Shugart, Matthew S. and John M. Carey. 1992. *Presidents and Assemblies: Constitutional Design and Electoral Dynamics.* Cambridge University Press.

Soroka, Stuart N. and Christopher Wlezien. 2010. *Degrees of Democracy: Politics, Public Opinion, and Policy.* Cambridge University Press.

2015. "The Majoritarian and Proportional Visions and Demorcratic Responsiveness." *Electoral Studies* 40:539–547.

Stein, Ernesto, Mariano Tommasi, and Carlos Scartascini, eds. 2010. *How Democracy Works: Political Institutions, Actors and Arenas in Latin American Policymaking.* Inter-American Development Bank.

Stevenson, Randolph T. 2000. "The Economy and Policy Mood: A Fundamental Dynamic of Democratic Politics?" *American Journal of Political Science* 45(3): 620–633.

Stimson, James A. 1991. *Public Opinion in America.* Westview Press.

1999. Party Government and Responsiveness. In *Democracy, Accountability, and Representation.* Cambridge University Press, pp. 197–221.

Stimson, James A., Michael B. Mackuen, and Robert S. Erikson. 1995. "Dynamic Representation." *American Political Science Review* 89(3):543–565.

Stokes, Susan C. 2001. *Mandates and Democracy: Neoliberalism by Surprise in Latin America.* Cambridge University Press.

Taagepera, Rein and Matthew S. Shugart. 1989. *Seats and Votes: The Effects and Determinants of Electoral Systems.* Yale University Press.

Tsebelis, George. 2002. *Veto Players: How Political Institutions Work.* Princeton University Press.

Van Buuren, Stef and Karin Groothuis-Oudshoorn. 2011. "mice: Multivariate Imputation by Chained Equations in R." *Journal of Statistical Software* 45(3):1–67, www.jstatsoft.org/v45/i03/.

Warwick, Paul V. and Maria Zakharova. 2013. "Measuring the Median: The Risks of Inferring Beliefs from Votes." *British Journal of Political Science* 43(1):157–175.

Wiesehomeier, Nina and David Doyle. 2013. "Discontent and the Left Turn in Latin America." *Political Science Research and Methods* 1(2):201–222.

Williamson, John. 1990. What Washington Means by Policy Reform. In *Latin American Adjustment: How Much Has Happened?*, ed. John Williamson. Institute for International Economics, pp. 5–20.

Zechmeister, Elizabeth J. 2006. "What's Left and Who's Right? A q-Method Study of Individual and Contextual Influences on the Meaning of Ideological Labels." *Political Behavior* 28(2):151–173.

Zechmeister, Elizabeth J. and Margarita Corral. 2010. "The Varying Economic Meaning of 'Left' and 'Right' in Latin America." *AmericasBarometer Insights Series* 38:1–10.

Zeileis, Achim and Gabor Grothendieck. 2005. "zoo: S3 Infrastructure for Regular and Irregular Time Series." *Journal of Statistical Software* 14(6):1–27, www.jstatsoft.org/v14/i06/.

Author Index

Achen, Christopher H., 7, 20, 175, 182
Ackermann, Kathrin, 48
Albert, James H., 96
Alcántara, Manuel, 53
Aldrich, John H., 45
Alemán, Eduardo, 18, 73
Altman, David, 151, 239
Amorim Neto, Octavio, 138
Arnold, Christian, 60, 72
Austen-Smith, David, 121

Bafumi, Joseph, 101, 112
Bailey, Michael A., 112
Baker, Andy, 33, 36, 42, 43, 46, 50, 69, 70
Banks, Jeffrey, 121
Barberá, Pablo, 48
Bartels, Larry M. Y, 28
Bauer, Paul C., 48, 49
Benoit, Kenneth, 49
Bernhard, Michael, 151, 239
Besley, Timothy, 28
Bianco, William T., 19
Blackwell, Matthew, 39
Bodet, Marc André, 22, 122, 123, 175
Booth, John A., 30
Bormann, Nils-Christian, 239
Brady, David W., 202
Budge, Ian, 21, 60, 122

Carey, John M., 18, 27, 58, 193
Carroll, Royce, 46
Cheibub, Jose Antonio, 73
Chinn, Menzie D., 79, 80

Clark, William R., 138
Coppedge, Michael, 73, 151, 239
Corral, Margarita, 46
Cox, Gary W., 7, 8, 12, 20–22, 120, 121, 135, 138
Crisp, Brian F., 29, 58, 72, 198

Desposato, Scott W., 198
Downs, Anthony, 4, 8, 121, 122, 175
Downs,Anthony, 121
Doyle, David, 33, 60
Duverger, Maurice, 8, 121
Dziuda, Wioletta, 202

Edwards, Sebastian, 206
Ellis, Andrew, 127
Erikson, Robert S., 93, 173
Escaith, Hubert, 78, 108

Fearon, James, 7, 19
Ferland, Benjamin, 122
Fernández, Andrés, 78
Figueiredo, Argelina, 73
Fiorina, Morris, 20
Fish, Steven M., 151, 239
Fording, Richard C., 46, 50, 122

Gabel, Matthew, 103
García Montero, Mercedes, 164
Gelman, Andrew, 179, 182, 204
Gerring, John, 151, 239
Ghitza, Yair, 182, 204
Glynn, Adam, 151, 239

Golder, Matt, 7, 42, 138, 176, 239
Greene, Kenneth F., 33, 43, 46, 69
Grofman, Bernard, 18, 21
Groothuis-Oudshoorn, Karin, 55
Grothendieck, Gabor, 46

Hawkins, Kirk A., 46
Herron, Michael C., 112
Hicken, Allen, 151, 239
Hill, Jennifer, 182
Hinich, Melvin J., 105
Hix, Simon, 193
Honaker, James, 39
Huber, John D., 18, 20, 103

Ito, Hiro, 80

Jackman, Simon, 99, 103
Jessee, Stephen A., 112
Johnson, Gregg B., 29, 72
Johnson, Valen E., 96, 101, 107

Kang, Shin-Goo, 21
Kanthak, Kristin, 198
Kaplan, Noah, 101
Kim, HeeMin, 46, 50, 122
King, Gary, 39, 45, 179
Kingdon, John W., 19
Kitschelt, Herbert, 46
Klein, Michael W., 78
Klingemann, Hans-Dieter, 60
Knutsen, Carl Henrik, 151, 239
Krehbiel, Keith, 72, 202
Krusell, Joshua, 151, 239

Lührmann, Anna, 151, 239
Laakso, Markku, 138
Laver, Michael, 49
Lewis, Jeffrey B., 45, 46
Leys, Colin, 12
Lijphart, Arend, 126, 131
Limongi, Fernando, 73
Lindberg, Staffan I., 151, 239
Linzer, Drew A., 179
Lo, James, 46
Loeper, Antoine, 202
Lora, Eduardo, 25, 78–80, 85, 86, 88–90, 108, 233
Luna, Juan P., 46
Lupu, Noam, 175

Machado, Roberto, 78, 80
MacKuen, Michael B., 93

Mainwaring, Scott, 18, 149, 159, 162, 165, 216
Manin, Bernard, 172, 179
Mansbridge, Jane, 19, 20
Marquardt, Kyle L., 151, 239
Martin, Andrew D., 112
Mayhew, David R., 20
McDonald, Michael D., 21, 122
McGann, Anthony J., 49, 94, 95, 97–100, 107, 109
McGhee, Eric, 179
McKelvey, Richard D., 45
McMann, Kelly, 151, 239
Mechkova, Valeriya, 151, 239
Mendes, Silvia M., 21
Miller, Warren E., 19
Morgenstern, Scott, 18, 73, 149, 165, 225
Morley, Samuel A., 78, 80, 108
Munger, Michael C., 105
Murillo, Maria Victoria, 207
Murray, Christopher J. L., 45

Nacif, Benito, 18, 149, 165
Negretto, Gabriel, 151, 156, 158, 239

Olin, Moa, 151, 239
Oliveros, Virginia, 207

Pachón, Mónica, 128
Palanza, Valeria, 18, 21
Park, David K., 101
Paunovic, Igor, 78, 108
Paxton, Pamela, 151, 239
Pemstein, Daniel, 151, 239
Pernes, Josefine, 29, 151, 239
Persson, Torsten, 206
Pettinato, Stefano, 78
Poole, Keith T., 45, 46
Powell Jr., G. Bingham, 1, 6, 18, 20, 21, 27, 42, 122, 123, 172, 179, 187, 227, 229
Przeworski, Adam, 172, 179

Quinn, Kevin M., 112

Rebucci, Alessandro, 78
Reilly, Ben, 127
Remmer, Karen, 33
Reynolds, Andrew, 127
Roland, Gérard, 206
Rosas, Guillermo, 46, 73
Rosenthal, Howard, 46

Saiegh, Sebastián, 18, 21, 45, 112
Salomon, Joshua A., 45
Sanhueza Petrarca, Constanza, 151, 239
Sartori, Giovanni, 12
Saxer, Laura, 151, 239
Scartascini, Carlos, 203
Schindler, Martin, 78
Schwartz, Thomas, 18
Schwindt-Bayer, Leslie A., 227
Seim, Brigitte, 151, 239
Seligson, Mitchell A., 30
Selios, Lucia, 175
Shugart, Matthew S., 18, 27, 123, 128, 135, 149, 159, 162, 165
Sigman, Rachel, 151, 239
Skaaning, Svend-Erik, 151, 239
Soroka, Stuart N., 21, 179
Staton, Jeffrey, 151, 239
Stein, Ernesto, 203
Stepanova, Natalia, 151, 239
Stevenson, Randolph T., 50, 93
Stimson, James A., 92–95, 100, 172, 173, 179
Stokes, Donald E., 19
Stokes, Susan C., 29, 60, 72, 172, 179, 190, 227
Stramski, Jacek, 7, 42, 176

Taagepera, Rein, 123, 135, 138
Tabellini, Guido, 206

Tandon, Ajay, 45
Tausanovitch, Chris, 45
Tavits, Margit, 227
Teorell, Jan, 151, 239
Tommasi, Mariano, 203
Tsebelis, George, 5, 197

Uribe, Martín, 78

Vaishnav, Milan, 207
van Buuren, Stef, 55
Vanberg, Georg S., 18, 122
Venetz, Aaron, 48
Volden, Craig, 202
von Römer, Johannes, 151, 239

Warner, Zach, 175
Warwick, Paul V., 50, 72
Whitten, Guy D., 227
Wiesehomeier, Nina, 33, 60
Williamson, John, 78
Wilson, Steven, 151, 239
Wlezien, Christopher, 21, 179

Zakharova, Maria, 50
Zechmeister, Elizabeth J., 46, 49
Zeileis, Achim, 46

Subject Index

AB, *see* AmericasBarometer (AB)
accountability, 94, 172, 193
Aldrich–McKelvey scores, 45, 47, 49, 69, 73, 232
Alianza PAIS, 89
AmericasBarometer (AB), 9, 23, 34, 35, 53, 238
anti-market trend, 64
anti-responsive movements, 191, 210
anticipatory form, representation, 20
Argentina, 37, 62, 67
  aggregate information from mass surveys, 40, 41
authorized representation, 172

Bánzer, Hugo, 71
Bachelet, Michelle, 71
bank reserve requirements, 80
bicameral systems, 5, 7, 53, 57, 124, 131, 148, 151, 156, 164
block vote systems, 126
Bolivarian constitution, 57
Bolivia, 220
budget outcome, 158
budget veto, *see also* veto, 158
bureaucratic capacity, 79

Caldera, Rafael, 173
campaign promises, 1
candidate viability, 120
capital openness, 79, 80, 83–85, 88, 98
CART, *see* Classification and Regression Tree
centrifugal incentives, 121

centrist candidate, 8, 96, 101
Chávez, Hugo, 71, 72, 173, 215
chain of representation, 3, 6, 8, 18, 19
  congruence, 20
  connections, unmade, 27
  electoral systems, 234
  institutional linkages, 11, 25
  policy-making processes, 234
  preferences and policies, 23
  stages, 231
Chamber of Deputies, 58
chamber, characteristics of, 164
Chile, 215
citizen policy preferences, 19, 33, 42, 212, 232
  country-by-country breakdown, 35
  data coverage, 34
  indices and policy moods, 45
  in Latin America, 33
citizen-to-executive
  congruence, 186
citizen-to-policy
  congruence, 213, 216, 220, 222
  responsiveness, 223, 224
citizen-to-politicians, 3, 181
  congruence, 4, 9, 120, 213
  economic moods connection, 5
  responsiveness, 4, 120
citizens' moods, 1, 54, 173, 174, 185, 213, 214, 237
  chain of representation, 230
  heterogeneity, 181, 187
  responsiveness, 222
  see also citizen policy preferences; policy moods

Classification and Regression Tree (CART),
    26, 137–139
coalition, 196
Colombia, 88
Comparative Manifesto Project, 60
congressional authorization, 149
congruence, 3, 15, 88, 94, 174, 177, 179, 185,
    187, 236
  citizen-to-executive, 178, 186
  citizen-to-legislators, 68, 178
  citizen-to-policy, 213, 216, 220, 222
  citizen-to-politicians, 4, 213
  defined, 174
  distribution-based measures, 176
  distribution-to-distribution, 4, 182, 187
  distribution-to-median, 186, 216
  distribution-to-policy, 199, 204, 214, 216
  electoral system strength, 185
  legislator-to-citizen, 6
  many-to-many, 20, 21, 119, 121, 122
  many-to-one, 5, 20, 119, 147, 186, 201, 214
  measurement, 174
  median-to-median, 122, 182, 184, 216
  median-to-policy, 214, 215, 219
  median-to-president , 184
  one-to-one, 20, 21, 119, 121, 122, 147,
    196, 201
  policy-to-politician, 7
  politician-to-citizen, 7, 21
  politician-to-policy, 4, 213
  predictors of, 148
  president-to-citizen, 6
  simulation-based benchmark, 176
  winset, 198
  see also responsiveness
consensual visions of democracy, 176
conservation-of-disproportionality dynamics,
    123, 187
constant or evolving moods, 172
constitutionally allocated powers, 5, 27, 147
constraining system, 122
copartisans, 59
  candidates, 64
  legislators, 58
corporate tax, 79
cross-border capital, 79
  mobility, 24

D'Hondt seat allocation formula, 125, 129,
    132, 138, 139, 177, 185
de Kirchner, Cristina Fernández, 67
decree authority, 27, 159

decree content, 158
decree outcome, 158
democratic representation, 19
democratically elected representatives, 42
deputies, 52, 53
deregulation, 85
  labor and financial markets, 78
directly elected presidents, 29
disproportionality, 136, 139
distribution-to-distribution, 176
  congruence, 4
  measures, 177
distribution-to-median
  congruence, 186, 216
  measures, 177
distribution-to-policy
  congruence, 199, 204, 216
district magnitude, 12, 25, 124, 126, 129,
    132–134, 234
Dominican Republic, 37, 58, 65, 215

Economic Commission for Latin America and
    the Caribbean, 78
economic liberal-conservative attitudinal
    divide, 93
economic liberalism, 93
economic performance, 123
economic policies, 107, 153
  Latin America, reform in, 36
  preferences, 48
  stimuli, 54
economic-distributive divide, 61, 72
effective threshold, 126
El Salvador, 62
electoral formulas, 184
electoral incentives, 12
electoral rules, 1, 3, 5, 6, 9, 11, 119, 121, 230
  time-serial variation, 133
electoral strength
  levels of, 172
electoral sweet spot, 123
electoral systems, 2, 12, 28, 30, 119, 126, 135,
    137, 148, 180, 217
  citizen-to-politician congruence and
    responsiveness, 120
  coding, 136
  complexity, 140
  components, 124, 129, 133
  congruence and responsiveness, 120
  district magnitude, 124
  electoral incentives, 141
  executives, 133

families, components into, 127
family, 129, 133
legal thresholds, 126
lower or only houses, 129, 130
seat allocation formula, 125
simulation-based taxonomy, 133
six-way classification scheme, 141
strength, 8, 12, 124, 181, 217, 220
upper houses, 131, 132
electoral thresholds, 124
electoral viability, 120
elite coordination failures, 135
exchange arrangements and exchange
    restrictions, 80
executives, 133, 148, 194, 195

Fernández de Kirchner, Cristina, 84, 88
financial regulations, 78, 79, 81, 83, 84, 88
free markets, 9, 14, 21, 230
    change, 4
    forces, 6
fused ballot, 58

Gaviria, César, 88
going public, 164
government performance, 14
gyroscopic representation, 20

Hare, 138, 177
hiring flexibility, 79, 82

import-substitution industrialization, 78
incongruent policy orientation, 237
institutional incentives, 125
institutional linkages, 2, 11, 25
institutional variation, 167
Inter-American Development Bank (IADB),
    10, 78
interbranch relations, 9, 14, 18
interest rate liberalization, 82
international financial institutions, 206
international financial liberalization, 78

job termination cost, 79
Justicialista, 67

Kirchner, Néstor, 67

labor markets
    policy, 85
labor reforms, 78
LatinBarometer (LB), 9, 23, 34, 53, 238

Law of Conservation of Disproportionality,
    135
LB, *see* LatinBarometer (LB)
legal thresholds, 12, 126, 132, 137, 138, 234
legislative heterogeneity, 67
legislative party positions, 72
legislative policy mood, 64
legislative powers of presidents, 163
legislator-to-citizen congruence, 6
legislators, 53
    median, 72, 73
    policy-making processes, 151
legislature-empowering processes, 194, 204
legitimacy of democracy, 14
liberalization, 78, 84
limited nomination, 132, 138, 177
liquidity shocks to banking system, 80
list plurality, 126
lower or only houses, 153
    policy-making processes, 153

Madison's logic, 148
majoritarian systems, 12, 185
majority, 133, 138
    formulas, 177
    rules, 175
malapportionment, 58, 122
mandate, 172
    model, 173
    switching, 14
manifesto pronunciations, 1
many-to-many
    congruence, 20, 21, 119, 121, 122
    proximity, 8
    representation, 3
    responsiveness, 20, 21
many-to-one
    congruence, 5, 20, 119, 147, 148, 176, 186,
        201, 214
    representation, 3, 8
    responsiveness, 20, 147
market economy, 39
market freedom, 78
market friendliness, 182
market moods, 182
    measurement, 171
market-oriented economy, 3, 10, 11, 23, 48,
    78, 173
mean district magnitude, 138
median legislator, 62, 65, 72, 73, 202
median policy-maker, 22, 122
median voters, 28, 72

median-to-median, 175
  congruence, 122, 178, 216
  measures, 177
  representation, 4
median-to-policy
  congruence, 214, 215, 219
Menem, Carlos, 67
Mexican senates, 59
Mexico, 62
minimum wage, 79
mixed-member electoral systems, 12, 128–130
moderate candidates, 120
Morales, Evo, 71
Movimiento Al Socialismo, 88
multimember districts, 125
multiple nontransferable vote (MNTV) system,
  126, 128, 131

nationwide district, 125
neoliberal policies, 64
Nicaragua, 153, 227
nonelected bureaucracies, 77

one-round system, 127
one-to-one, 175
  congruence, 20, 21, 119, 121, 122, 147,
    196, 201
  correspondence, 175
  representation, 3
  responsiveness, 20, 21, 147

Paraguay, 153
Parliamentary Elites of Latin America (PELA),
  9, 52, 53, 57
  surveys, 54, 232
    in Mexico, 60, 61
parliamentary systems, 18
partial promulgation, 158
Partido dos Trabalhadores, 67
partisan politics, 64
party system flux, 123
party-level vote-shares, 136
party-specific medians, 74
Pastrana, Andrés, 88
permissive systems, 122
personal tax, 79
Peru, 57
pink tide, 33, 43, 64, 78, 233
plurality, 132, 133, 138, 175, 177
plurality/majority systems, 127, 138
PMP, *see* policy-making processes
polarization, 94

policy making processes, 217
policy moods, 4, 11, 33, 34, 42, 43, 45, 48, 50,
  52, 54, 57, 62, 64, 65, 67, 68, 72, 74,
  91, 92, 99–102, 110–113, 115, 127,
  197, 215
  Argentina, 67
  citizens, 39
  Chile's president, 64
  congruence and responsiveness, 196
  country-specific, 42
  deputies, 92, 99
  elected representatives, 44
  legislators, 52, 54, 60, 91, 232
  lower and upper houses, 58
  median legislator, 65
  Mexican Senate, 60
  Paraguay's president, 64
  policy-makers, 91, 193
  politicians, 53, 127
  presidents, 52, 60, 64, 70, 92
  senators, 52, 57, 70, 92
  see also citizens' moods
  upper houses, 57, 58
policy orientations, 10, 22, 60, 78, 79, 85, 86,
  89, 91, 108–110, 115, 193, 233
  country-specific, 85
policy outputs, 78
policy responsiveness, 226
policy switches, 60
policy volatility, 167
policy-makers and policy, 194, 196, 202, 203
policy-makers' preferences, 52, 53, 77, 195
  adaptation, 173
  rational anticipation, 173
policy-making powers, 13, 19, 27, 80, 147,
  148, 150, 198, 209, 210
policy-making processes, 3, 4, 7, 9, 10, 13, 27,
  30, 145, 147, 149, 150, 162, 164–166,
  194, 198, 203, 204, 206, 209, 211,
  225, 229
  chain of responsiveness, 234
  effect of, 208
  electoral groups, 217
  legislators, 151
  lower or only houses, 153
  presidents, 156
  proactive and reactive powers, 161
  proactive powers, 159
  reactive powers, 161
  responsiveness, 207
  separation-of-power systems, 148, 164
  upper houses, 156

policy-to-politician
  congruence, 7
  correspondence, 9
political crises, 14, 29
political parties
  left-right spectrum,, 46
politician-to-citizen
  congruence, 7, 21
  responsiveness, 7, 21
politician-to-policy
  congruence, 4, 9, 213
  responsiveness, 4, 7
politicians' moods, 4, 10, 230
politicians' preferences, 20
post-election coalition formation, 120
powers of politicians, 147
president-to-citizen congruence, 6
presidential policy moods, 60, 70, 72
presidential power, 2, 5, 26, 27
presidential races, 127
presidential types, 165
presidential vetoes, 153
presidents, 52, 55, 70, 159, 184, 229
  anti-responsive, 190
  constitutionally allocated proactive powers,
    161
  decree authority, 159
  legislative powers, 163
  moods, 203
  policy-making powers, 158
  policy-making processes, 156
  reactive powers, 162
  recalcitrant, 156
private enterprise, 45
privatization, 9, 79, 83, 84, 88, 98
  state-owned companies, 78
privatized assets, 79
pro-market citizenry, 51
pro-market economic policy, 34
pro-market percentage, 61
pro-market policies, 81, 107
  mood, 43
  positions, 37, 38
  proclivities, 97
  propensity, 95
pro-market responses, 38, 39, 43, 55, 96, 100
  percentages, 48
pro-state policies
  orientations, 110
  moods, 65
proactive and reactive powers
  policy-making processes, 161

proactive powers, 13, 26, 27, 159, 161
proportional representation (PR), 12, 124,
    127, 128, 138
proportionality, 138
public goods provision, 14
public mood, 92, 93
public policies, 78, 82, 91
  measurement, 77

quality of representation, 9

reactive powers, 13, 26, 159
  policy-making processes, 161
reference model, 123
referendum, 158, 159
regulation of labor markets, 111
relative permissiveness, 133
representation, 94
  democratic institutions, 229
  dynamic, 172
  gyroscopic form, 20
  many-to-many, 3
  many-to-one, 3, 8
  median-to-median, 4
  one-to-one, 3
  promissory form, 20
representative assembly, 121
representative democracies, 2, 3, 6, 33
representativeness, 174, 193
reserve requirement, 79, 81, 90
reserved area, 158
responsiveness, 3, 15, 88, 91, 94, 174, 196,
    203, 228, 236, 237
  citizen-to-policy, 223, 224
  citizen-to-politician, 4
  citizens moods, 222
  conceptualization, 202
  defined, 3, 174
  determinants of, 3
  dynamic, 188
  electoral institutions, function of, 188
  many-to-many, 20, 21
  many-to-one, 20, 147
  measurement, 179
  one-to-one, 20, 21, 147
  operationalization, 196
  policy to policy-makers, 203
  politician-to-citizen, 7, 21
  politician-to-policy, 4, 7
  predictors of, 148
  simulation-based benchmark, 180
  see also congruence

restrictive systems, 120, 121, 131, 184
revealed rightism, 68, 69
right-wing president, 61, 64
rightist, 101
Rodríguez Echeverría, Miguel Ángel, 71
Rousseff, Dilma , 65

Sainte-Laguë seat allocation formula, 125,
    129, 134, 138, 177
Samper, Ernesto, 88
sanction model, 20
seat allocation formulas, 8, 12, 124, 125, 129,
    132, 234
    plurality/majority systems, 126
    see also D'Hondt seat allocation formula
seat shares, 136
seats-votes curve, 179
senates, 52, 53, 57, 58, 69, 132
separation-of-powers systems, 3, 4, 18, 72,
    196, 197, 200
simulated responsiveness, 180
simulating elections, 135
single nontransferable vote (SNTV) system,
    126, 128
single-member district decided by plurality
    (SMDP) system, 8, 125, 127, 128,
    131–133, 136
social security tax, 79
socialism in Latin America, 43
socioeconomic inequality, 9
state extraction capabilities, 79
state intervention, 78
state or private ownership, 78
state regulation, 33
state-market
    balance, 4
    continuum, 5, 7–9, 13, 15, 29, 94, 121, 150
    dimension, 10
    disposition, 95–97
    divide, 93
    location, 22
    policy orientations, 78, 207
state-of-the-union speeches, 60
state-owned companies, 9
state-run economies, 29
strategic coordination, 5, 58, 136
    voters, 120
strategic voting, 135

structural adjustment, 78
structural reform index, 10, 15, 25, 86, 88
super-plurality, 126, 133, 138, 184

tax policy, 79
tax reforms, 78
Tequila crisis, 42
threshold of exclusion, 126
threshold of inclusion, 126
trade dispersion, 82
trade liberalization, 83
trade policy, 78, 79, 82–84
two-party system, 121
two-round (TR) systems, 126, 127, 133

unemployment benefits, 102
unicameral systems, 7, 52, 53, 57, 58, 149,
    156, 195
upper houses, 131
    policy-making processes, 156
urgency bills, 158, 159
Uribe, Álvaro, 88
Uribista party, 70
Uruguayan chambers, 70

value-added tax rate, 79
Venezuela, 57, 64
    voters, 58
veto override, 165
veto players, 5, 147, 194
veto-proof coalition, 73
voter-revealed positions, 46
voter-revealed rightism, 47–49, 233
voters, 7, 11, 28, 120, 135, 230
    ability, 119
    distinct configurations of, 148
    median, 72
    moods, 177
    strategic coordination, 120
    Venezuelan, 58

Washington Consensus, 11, 78
winset, 197, 198
    congruence, 198, 199, 206, 210, 237
    distribution-to-policy congruence, 200
work flexibility, 79, 82

Zelaya, Manuel, 71

Lightning Source UK Ltd.
Milton Keynes UK
UKHW012303110320
360208UK00001B/15